14

International
Library of the
Philosophy of
Education

**Education,
values and mind**

International
Library of the
Philosophy of
Education

Education, values and mind

Essays for R.S. Peters

Edited by

David E. Cooper

Routledge & Kegan Paul

London, Boston and Henley

First published in 1986
by Routledge & Kegan Paul plc
14 Leicester Square, London WC2H 7PH, England
9 Park Street, Boston, Mass. 02108, USA, and
Broadway House, Newtown Road,
Henley on Thames, Oxon RG9 1EN, England

Set in Baskerville 10 on 11 pt
by Columns of Reading
and printed in Great Britain
by T.J. Press (Padstow) Ltd
Padstow, Cornwall.

Library of Congress Cataloging in Publication Data

Main entry under title:

Education, values and mind.
(International library of the philosophy of
education)
Bibliography: p.
Includes index.
1. Education—Philosophy—Addresses, essays,
lectures. 2. Peters, R.S. (Richard Stanley),
1919- —Addresses, essays, lectures. I. Peters,
R.S. (Richard Stanley), 1919- . II. Cooper,
David Edward. III. Series.
LB1025.2.E369 1986 370'.1 85-8076

British Library CIP data available
ISBN 0-7100-9905-3

Contents

v

Contents

Introduction

David E. Cooper

Early in 1972, while I was teaching in the United States, I received news of my appointment as a lecturer in the philosophy of education at the University of London Institute of Education. Since, at the time, my interest in this subject was incipient rather than seasoned, I quickly consulted some American colleagues on how I might best 'mug up' on it. The most knowledgeable of them advised me to read four books before all others. These four books turned out to have one thing in common: each was written or edited by the same man—Richard Peters. Here was my first inkling of the remarkable influence that a single person had come to exercise in his subject—and within only ten years of his own full entry into it. I did read the four books, and was delighted to find my incipient feeling confirmed that here was an area of philosophy, however neglected, in which good and intriguing work could be done.

Full awareness of Richard Peters's impact only emerged after I had begun teaching at the Institute where, of course, he was now my Professor. It emerged, for example, that the whole content and structure of the philosophy courses taught had largely been moulded by him—a content and structure which had quickly percolated, through his energy and prestige, into Colleges not only in this country, but throughout the Commonwealth. It emerged, indeed, that he had played a crucial role in determining the shape that education of teachers, whether at PGCE or B Ed levels, was taking—in particular, the integration of the 'foundation' subjects, philosophy, sociology, and psychology. It quickly became clear, as well, to what degree the burgeoning literature in the philosophy of education bore Richard Peters's stamp. Books and articles that did not, in some way, continue the enterprise he had begun, were usually reactions against it. Either way, it was a fair bet that his would be the name with most entries in the index.

The atmosphere at the Institute, when I arrived, was a remarkable one. Peters's colleagues, without in any sense being clones of their Professor, shared a sense of the relevant questions to ask and, to a lesser but significant degree, of the proper approach towards answering them. The place fairly buzzed with PhD students, flown in from all corners of the earth to study either under or in the orbit of Richard Peters. The weekly seminars he conducted were genuinely communal events, with students and staff alike united by a sense, not only of the importance of what they were doing, but of its radically novel character. Optimism, indeed pride, suffused this communal atmosphere.

At the time I searched, in vain, for a parallel to the influence that a single person, in so short a time, had exercised upon a branch of philosophy. I am still unable to come up with a convincing one. J.L. Austin, it is said, had a riveting effect upon many philosophers in Oxford during the 1950s, generating a sense of communal effort directed at reasonably well-defined goals. But Austin never had, nor intended to have, the kind of impact upon organisation and curriculum that Peters has. Nor, of course, did the Austinian approach elbow out all other philosophical approaches. Indeed, within a very few years of his death, voices from across the Atlantic, notably that of W.V. Quine, were sounding much louder than those of Austin's followers.

Richard Stanley Peters succeeded Louis Arnaud Reid in the Chair of Philosophy of Education at the University of London in 1962. Born in 1919, he attended school at Clifton College in Bristol, from where he proceeded to Oxford, where he read Classics, and then to Birkbeck College, London, to gain a PhD in philosophy. During the war, he served with the Friends' Ambulance Unit and the Friends' Relief Service, after which his professional career began as a schoolmaster at Sidcot School in Somerset. In 1946, however, he returned to Birkbeck, this time as a part-time lecturer. He remained at Birkbeck, becoming Lecturer and Reader in turn, until taking up the Philosophy of Education Chair. He held this Chair until ill-health forced him to retire in 1983, whereupon the University honoured him by making him Emeritus Professor. During his tenure of the Chair, he held many Visiting Professorships—at Harvard, the University of British Columbia, the Australian National University, and the University of Auckland. In addition he was Dean of the Faculty of Education at London for several years. Despite all this business, he managed to produce an enormous volume of books, articles, and public lectures during these years, as the bibliography on p. 215 amply demonstrates. The man's energy was truly enviable. I remember him telling me, in 1973, that he was sitting on forty-four committees (a number only surpassed, surely, by the sixty plus that Paul Hirst tells me he is now on).

It is not my aim in this introduction to chart Richard Peters's thoughts on education nor to chronicle his influence upon his subject. His closest collaborator for many years, Paul Hirst, provides a much better informed account, in his contribution to this volume, than I could have done. Another close collaborator, Robert Dearden, also supplies a good sketch of the development of Richard Peters's thinking in the first part of his contribution. Let me simply stress, here, that Peters's thinking *did* develop over twenty years. He is rightly angered by the tendency, equally marked among acolytes and critics, to focus exclusively upon the claims made in an early work like *Ethics and Education*, as if his ideas on education had mummified by 1966. A good deal of criticism has been levelled against these claims; but often enough it is Richard Peters who has been the sharpest critic. Certainly the charge, levelled from several directions, that education à la Peters is too refined a thing is one that is fully met in his later writings with their emphasis upon education as the means for 'coping with the "human condition" '.

The papers by Hirst, Dearden and Ray Elliott are the only ones in the volume which are exclusively *about* Richard Peters's ideas. Some of the others, like Alan Montefiore's and Mary Warnock's, focus critically upon particular, distinctive theses of his; but others, such as those by Michael Bonnett, Anthony O'Hear, and John and Pat White, prefer to take initial cues from Peters's writings in order to develop independent discussions. Whatever the degree of Peters's presence in the articles, however, each testifies to the unparalleled stimulus he has given to philosophical discussion about education. Not, incidentally, that each contribution is explicitly and directly concerned with education. David Hamlyn, for instance, writes on motivation as a topic of philosophical interest in its own right. There is nothing inappropriate in the fact that education has, so to speak, a low profile in such a paper. For one thing, we should not forget that Richard Peters did not spring into being, bionically equipped, in 1962. He had written a good deal on matters, like motivation, prior to his engagement with the philosophy of education; and it is right, in a volume of this sort, that these earlier concerns are recognised. Second, and more important, one of Peters's great gifts to his subject has been to show the relevance to educational discussion of matters, like the emotions or motivation, which had received scant attention from earlier philosophers of education. If some of the papers in this volume are not themselves essays in educational philosophy, there are none which do not lend themselves to integration with it. It goes without saying that this volume would not honour a man who has so persistently emphasised the importance, indeed moral value, of criticism, unless the contributions were themselves critical. Some of the authors, such as Ray Elliott and Michael Bonnett, write from a philosophical or educational perspective that is emphatically different from Richard Peters's own. But no reader, I hope, will expect to find the papers collected here passively mirroring Peters's general outlook, let alone regurgitating more particular theses with which his name is associated.

I would like to take the opportunity this introduction affords me of making a few remarks on 'the state of the art', for it seems to me that this state is not as healthy as it deserves to be, given the efforts made on its behalf by Richard Peters. Several years ago, at a banquet marking the tenth anniversary of the Philosophy of Education Society of Great Britain—which was founded by Peters, and whose Journal was edited by him—he made a slightly sad speech, ruing the narrowness and orthodoxy of much of the literature being produced. I recall him saying that he could scarcely bear reading yet another article or dissertation with a title like 'Two senses of "teaching" ' or 'The concept of the curriculum'. To an extent, of course, he was ruing the almost inevitable effect of his own uniquely powerful influence; for innovators must typically pay the penalty of epigones. I doubt that his judgment on today's literature, nine years on, would be very different. For one thing, depressingly, most books on the philosophy of education are *introductions* to the subject, few of which do more than re-introduce the same material in similar ways. Despite a professional competence displayed, much of the literature, it seems to me, bears the stamp of the production-line. One must not, of course, exaggerate the degree of orthodoxy and the recycling of tired topics that the literature exhibits. Last year I heard a 'radical philosopher' demanding that philosophers of education give up their obsession with analysing notions such as teaching and education and turn, instead, to live and relevant subjects such as equality. He was unaware, presumably, that three members of the audience he was addressing had recently written books on just that topic.

It would, I think, be hard to deny that the fire which inspired Richard Peters, his colleagues and students at the Institute during the 1960s and early 1970s—the same fire that attracted swarms of newcomers to the subject—has died down. Partly this is because all fires, unless artificially fanned, die down. One can only retain the sense of doing something new for so long. But there are other reasons. Philosophers of education, like others, need good enemies—confused ideologies and doctrines on which to feed. In the 1960s 'Progressivism' provided several such good enemies, the 'de-schoolers' and their less extreme relatives. To combat the pretensions of such doctrines was an important stimulus to the earlier writings of Peters, Hirst, and Dearden. The good enemy of the early 1970s was furnished by those sociologists of knowledge associated with the book *Knowledge and Control*, with its philosophically crude onslaught on notions like reason and objectivity. Today there is no good enemy. There is, to be sure, an enemy: that mindless technological vocationalism that dominates government educational policy. But philosophically, and otherwise, the policy is a bad enemy; for it is as devoid of stimulating ideas, even confused ones, as the kind of education it seeks to promote. It is incapable, therefore, of generating the critical philosophical reaction that earlier ideologies were able to do.

It would also be hard to deny that one of Richard Peters's great ambitions has remained only incompletely realised: that of drawing into the philosophy of education, full- or part-time, professionally trained philosophers. Very few of those who teach and write on the subject have first and higher degrees in philosophy, and the number of 'pure' philosophers engaged in philosophy of education remains modest. Even now, it is as rare to find articles on education in major philosophy journals as it is to find ones in education journals by 'pure' philosophers of stature. The reason for this continuing relative isolation of philosophy of education can no longer be—after the work of Peters, Hirst, and others— that it is an 'unrespectable' subject. The explanation goes deeper. Peters and his early collaborators had come to educational theory with that broadly identifiable conception of philosophy which had increasingly dominated British philosophy during the two decades after the Second World War. According to this dominant view, philosophy was first and foremost 'conceptual analysis', to be conducted primarily by close attention to the uses of words. This is a view of philosophy that lends itself well to educational philosophising, for education is more than handsomely furnished with its stock of unclear and confused concepts. For better or worse, this conception of philosophy is no longer dominant. As P.F. Strawson put it, philosophy has 'gone West', and the most influential figures over the last twenty years have been Americans, such as Quine and Donald Davidson, whose more formal and ontological interests do not so easily lend themselves to application to educational questions. One knows what philosophy of science, and even ethics, inspired by Davidson's account of truth and meaning look like, but not what a philosophy of education similarly inspired might be. The result is that younger philosophers, caught up in these newer enthusiasms, cannot find a ready outlet for them in educational philosophy.

There are, however, currents flowing in the opposite direction. First, and perhaps as a reaction against the concentration on logic and semantics just mentioned, there is the rapidly growing interest in 'applied philosophy', in philosophically informed discussion of such particular issues as famine-relief or transplant surgery. Witness the recent founding, by two of my colleagues at the University of Surrey, of an already flourishing Society and Journal of Applied Philosophy. It is to be hoped, indeed expected, that philosophy of education will benefit from this current of interest. A second very recent development has been the turn towards Continental philosophers, from Hegel to Foucault, of a kind previously neglected in this country. Richard Peters himself displayed relatively little interest in contemporary French and German philosophy, and in hindsight this may be a matter for regret; for there are few signs that philosophers of education are willing to profit from this Continental turn. Nevertheless, there are some signs. Recent issues of the *Journal of the Philosophy of Education* have contained articles on Nietzsche, Heidegger, and Sartre; and readers of this book may be as surprised as I was by the number of references made in it to these writers. Some, of course, might challenge my assumption that there is something to 'profit' from in this turn; but it is my view that mining in these foreign fields could do much to refuel that fire which, if I am right, has been dying down. Many feel that the limit of what can be achieved by way of 'conceptual analysis' of educational terms has already been reached. If so, the attempt must surely be made to tap previously untried sources for new thoughts and perspectives on education. By the nature of their interests, it is likely to be Continental philosophers like those mentioned, rather than Quine or Davidson, who provide such sources.

I do not know to what extent Richard Peters would concur in my assessment of, and fears and hopes for, the intellectual aspects of 'the state of the art'. I am more sure that he would join me in decrying its disturbing institutional aspects. For philosophy of education, like philosophy more generally, and like civilising thought at large, is under threat. Let me mention a few of these disturbing aspects. To judge from the attitude taken by Her Majesty's Inspectors in their recent report *The New Teacher in School*, it will not be long before philosophy of education, as well as other 'foundation' subjects, enjoys a less-favoured position on the curriculum for teacher education—a curriculum which, like that in the schools, threatens to become increasingly and crudely pragmatic. It is already the case that teachers wishing to study philosophy of education at Higher Degree level find it harder to obtain grants than students of almost any other educational subject, and that funds for research in this area are almost unavailable. A very different, but significant, sign of the times is that the Chair which Richard Peters made into the most important of its kind in the world remains unfilled since his retirement, and that no urgency in filling it is being displayed. The profession has not only lost a leader but, for some years, the position from which he led. Chairs in more vocationally and technically relevant areas of educational studies are, of course, filled without delay. As a final witness to the times, I might mention that the 'pure' philosophy department whose members have been more engaged with philosophy of education than those of any other such department in the country will have been closed for financial reasons by the time this volume is published. I refer to the department of philosophy at the University of Surrey.

If the threatening atmosphere in which philosophy of education lives is to improve, it will only be as the result of larger climatic change. If the ideology of microchips with everything wins out against the values of civilised and civilising reflection, that atmosphere may become truly deadly. For in large part that ideology is an educational one, a modern-dress, space-age version of that 'bread-winning' pedagogy against which Nietzsche tried to battle. I can think of few better ways to stiffen one's spirit against such an ideology than to read and reflect upon the work of the man to whom this volume is dedicated. Those who do so will not want to confuse education's true concern, the moral and intellectual condition of man, with the financial and industrial state of a nation.

Note

I would like to be able to say that the idea for this volume was my own. In fact, though, it was proposed to me by Dr Ved P. Varma, a consultant psychologist and psychotherapist. I am grateful to him not only for the proposal and suggestions on how it might be executed, but for the generous way in which he decided to entrust the editorship to someone he felt to be better acquainted with the relevant areas of thought.

Richard Peters's contribution to the philosophy of education

Paul H. Hirst

When Richard Peters began his outstanding work in philosophy of education the subject barely existed in Britain as a distinct academic and professional area. No philosopher of any distinction had begun to make effective use of contemporary philosophical methods or their exciting achievements for the development of educational ideas and principles. The work being taught in colleges and universities was out of touch with all that was happening in the parent discipline and had become little more than a historical study of the contribution to educational thought of a selection of philosophers, from Plato to Dewey. It was also largely dissociated from contemporary educational policy and practice, there being little by way of any systematic critique of current developments in curricula, teaching methods or the organisation of the school system. But with hindsight one can see that the scene was set for someone with the necessary philosophical expertise, the necessary insight into and understanding of education, and the necessary commitment to the enterprise, to give new life to the subject and to re-characterise philosophy of education as a major intellectual enterprise of practical significance. On the one hand philosophers such as Ryle and Hare were giving very strong leads as to the educational issues raised by their own work. On the other hand the controversy surrounding new educational practices in primary and comprehensive secondary schools was itself throwing up philosophical questions that manifestly required systematic attention. In this situation Richard Peters proved to be the right man in the right place at the right time. He was a first-class philosopher with both the range and depth of philosophical experience required for the task. He was knowledgeable about, and intensely concerned about, the development of education in schools. But he revealed too the personal qualities that made him able to respond to the challenge and devote himself unstintingly to the task in hand. He thereby not only redefined British philosophy of education but set its programme for some twenty years and has been its dominating creative thinker throughout that period.

Philosophy of education and philosophical analysis

In his most detailed statement about the philosophy of education, written relatively early in his involvement in this work,[1] Peters insisted that the subject should be seen as fundamentally philosophical in character concerned to do that job which trained philosophers can do, bringing to bear on the issue of education their distinctive skills and the distinctive achievements of philosophy. This paper repeatedly indicates the pressing need for philosophical work to be done both to help sort out current educational debates and to critically reassess current educational practices. To this end he thought it important to underline the distinction then gaining acknowledgment between the task of the philosopher in relation to educational issues and the task of formulating, discovering and passing on practical educational principles.

> It is important to realise that the philosopher, *qua* philosopher, cannot formulate such principles . . . any more than he can formulate principles of medicine or politics. Such principles are logical hybrids. . . . This does not mean, of course, that there is no place for principles of education in educational research or in the training of teachers. Quite the reverse. . . . All it means is that the formulation, discussion and passing on of such principles cannot be the peculiar function of the philosopher of education.[2]

He distinguished too the development of philosophy of education from a concern with the history of educational ideas and its use in illuminating contemporary educational ideas. Again it is to be noted that he was not decrying a proper attention to such ideas. It is just that such a concern for educational principles, even when they have been propounded by distinguished philosophers, is no substitute for engaging systematically in seeking to answer the strictly philosophical questions that educational issues raise. A careful reading of this paper, as well as even a superficial reading of much of his own philosophical work shows that Peters was seeking to demarcate the philosophy of education from the pursuit of education principles, contemporary or historical, and not at all wishing, as has been suggested, to separate contemporary philosophy of education from historical work of the same character.[3]

When it comes to a positive account of the nature of philosophy, Professor Peters has confined himself to certain general indicative statements, recognising that philosophy, like other theoretical pursuits, develops in character with the introduction of new

9

methods and areas of enquiry. He has on the whole preferred to engage in major philosophical work and let his method speak for itself rather than devote time to self-consciously analysing the nature of this pursuit. His clearest statement of his position occurs in his first article 'The Philosophy of Education' and in the Introduction to his major work *Ethics and Education*.[4] There he outlined the 'second-order' concern of philosophy with forms of thought and argument expressed in Socrates' questions, 'What do you mean?' and 'How do you know?', and Kant's questions about what is presupposed by our forms of thought and awareness.[5] This means that the philosopher is engaged in

> the disciplined demarcation of concepts, the patient explication of the grounds of knowledge and of the presuppositions of different forms of discourse. Philosophers make explicit the conceptual schemes which (competing) beliefs and standards presuppose; they examine their consistency and search for criteria for their justification. This does not imply that philosophers can only produce an abstract rationale of what is in existence, like a high-level projection of the plan of a house. For enquiry at this level can develop with some degree of autonomy. Presuppositions can be drastically criticized and revised; grounds for belief can be challenged and new ones suggested; conceptual schemes can be shown to be radically inconsistent or inapplicable; new categorizations can be constructed. The philosopher is not entirely the prisoner of the presuppositions of his age.[6]

Peters then goes on to distinguish between those brands of philosophy which are concerned with the analysis and justification of answers to theoretical questions about what is the case, why and when, and that branch concerned with practical questions, questions about what ought to be the case and with reasons for action. Educational issues he sees as necessarily raising both types of questions before they can be settled and the philosopher's task in this area as therefore being to apply to educational concerns analyses of concepts and theories of justification that have been developed in other branches of philosophy—especially in ethics, social philosophy, epistemology and philosophical psychology. He suggested four main areas of work.

 (i) The analysis of concepts specific to education, an area which can be seen as falling under philosophical psychology and social philosophy.
 (ii) The application of ethics and social philosophy to assump-

tions about the desirable content and procedures of education.

(iii) Examination of the conceptual schemes and assumptions used by educational psychologists about educational processes.

(iv) Examination of the philosophical character of the content and organisation of the curriculum and related questions about learning.[7]

In this outline, and indeed throughout his philosophical work, it is clear not only that Peters values the developments of the post-war 'revolution in philosophy' but that he sees the continuity of recent work with the historic roots of philosophy. There is a characteristic refusal to be dogmatic about the nature of philosophical arguments and, in particular, about the nature of current forms of philosophical analysis. His approach, though contemporary in its emphasis, has always been eclectic and open-ended, drawing on a variety of traditions for both philosophical techniques and doctrines. What is more, in his return from time to time to a number of topics of central concern to him, especially the analysis of the concept of education and the justification of the content of education, Peters can be seen to be willing to change his mind not only about the validity of particular arguments but also about the validity of certain kinds of argument. This refusal to be doctrinaire about the nature of philosophy is no doubt in part the result of his very considerable studies in classical philosophy, the history of modern philosophy—especially social philosophy and the British empiricists—and the history of psychology. It is no doubt also in part the result of the many different contemporary influences on him during his formative years, influences ranging from the work of Moore, Ryle and Wittgenstein to the personal impact of study and collaboration with Popper, A.C. Mace, Oakeshott, Hamlyn and Phillips Griffiths.

The central features of Peters's philosophical position were thus being formed when new and distinctive types of philosophical analysis were being developed—and hotly disputed. Not surprisingly, therefore, he came to attach considerable importance to the mapping of conceptual relations through the examination of linguistic usage and his application of analytical techniques to educational concepts is rightly seen as one of his most important contributions to philosophy of education. But he constantly reiterated his own uncertainties about the character of this technique and the precise significance of its results. He repeatedly insists that conceptual analysis alone in its endless exploration of distinctions is 'scholastic' or a major philosophical sin that is avoided only when analysis is linked with some other issue such as the justification of beliefs.[7] This being his approach, it is surely not only unsympathetic, but seriously misleading to critically assess his analytical work as if it were undertaken independently of its value for educational issues. And it is equally misleading to seek to assess his procedures in terms of strict adherence to forms of analysis to which he was in no way committed.[8] There is, for instance, no reason whatever to suppose that Peters saw himself as providing ordinary language analysis on the assumption that ordinary language in general provides any unassailable final court of appeal in seeking to understand education, its processes or institutions.[9] Indeed, there is much evidence to the contrary in his concern for the understanding available to educationists in psychology and sociology and the importance of philosophers working in constant association with such specialists in the development of educational theory. Further, he considered it necessary for there to be, and himself sought to provide, arguments setting out the place of the conceptual schemes of commonsense within psychological research.[10] What he sought to do in education was to examine the language educationists use, whether everyday or technical, so as to explore the concepts underlying this for their coherence and applicability, and thus their significance in educational argument.

There is perhaps much more justification for seeing Peters as at times committed to the belief that an adequate analysis will reveal the 'essential' meaning of a statement and he seems to believe that by examining our use of a term like 'education' we could eventually sort out what all those coherently employing it must mean, no matter what their social or other context might be. And if there is such a universal unit of meaning it is because it picks out something of fundamental significance in human experience. This charge of 'essentialism' is, I suggest, both true and false. It reflects uncertainty in Peters's mind at times as to what exactly analysis can achieve. But a careful and sympathetic reading of his work suggests a coherent position that is not as readily dismissed as certain critics consider. It seems to me quite false to argue that for Peters analysis is in any way tied to an essentialist theory of *meaning*, if by that is meant either that analysis is searching out Russell-type fundamental linguistic atoms of meaning or even that there are 'central uses' to terms that can be shown to be necessary to all coherent discourse. He has, I suggest, espoused no particular theory of meaning either explicitly or implicitly. He has certainly sought to map conceptual usage often hunting for necessary and sufficient conditions to set out the relations between concepts. But in no way has he insisted that that pursuit is in any sense definitive of the analytical procedure. In his recurring concern to disentangle 'the' concept of education it is manifestly the case that it is the complexity of the elements within contemporary educational thinking that interests him rather than any *a priori* linguistic necessities. Nowhere does he suggest that this is the way our concepts must be. His sternest critics have had to recognise that throughout his writings from his earliest work on motivation[11] to his major writings on education,[12] he has stressed the dependence of concepts on the social context in which they arise and operate and the philosophical insensitivity of those seeking to find a single formula for the uses of words like 'justice', 'knowledge' or 'education'. In one place he quite specifically raises the question of whether in his analysis of 'education' he has set his foot on the path to 'essentialism'. To this he replies, 'Frankly I do not much mind if I have. What would be objectionable would be to suppose that certain characteristics could be regarded as essential irrespective of context and the questions under discussion.'[13] In another he asserts roundly that 'the point of examining ordinary usage is not to spot some linguistic essence but to take one route to explore distinctions which may prove important in the context of a thesis.'[14] This, I take it, confirms the view that he is in no doctrinaire sense pursuing essentialist analysis but rather seeking to sort out the fundamental features of concepts from within the contexts in which they operate.

This charge of essentialism has, I suggest, arisen because in attempting to sort out what goes under the label of terms like 'education' in contemporary discussion, he has endeavoured to see the relationship of such concepts to the more fundamental, even categorial notions we employ in making sense of human life. It is the relationship of the notion of 'education' to our concepts of a person, value, knowledge, reason that has interested him. What is more, he has sought to map not merely the concepts that particular groups employ, but to articulate, indeed construct, a coherent set of relations that these uses indicate. But such a mapping he considers of itself justifies nothing, it simply sets out the framework of a coherent point of view. All that is claimed, within such a framework, and indeed all that might be claimed for that framework he considers to need an appropriate form of justification. It is a characteristic feature of his work that he sees very sharply the need for the justification of both the philosophical beliefs he holds and the educational principles they might support. But the value of such an analysis of educational concepts therefore must depend in significant measure on the characteristics of this wider general philosophical position within which it is located and the justification of that position. In much of his writing on education Peters sets out this wider context with clarity and where he stands on many of the most fundamental matters in ethical theory, in social philosophy and in philosophy of mind is not in doubt. But his very concern to locate his educational work in such fundamental philosophical considerations when only limited defence of that could be given across such a vast canvas has only served to make the accusation of 'essentialism' seem more justified. He has seemed to be not only setting out the ultimate underpinnings of the philosophical position he considers most defensible, but to be asserting those underpinnings as if in their very assertion can be seen their *a priori* necessity.

And this impression has been accentuated further by his use in two areas of Kantian-style transcendental arguments for the justification of certain fundamental philosophical beliefs. His conviction that any adequate philosophical work must seek to get at the most fundamental elements of our thinking and seek for some ultimate justification for these led him to explore the use of this type of argument for the justification of a range of fundamental moral principles (e.g. the consideration of interests and liberty) and the justification of the value of a distinctive range of human activities (e.g. science or agriculture as against Bingo) as part of 'the good life'.[15] By using such arguments it seems only too clear that Peters is claiming a universal, ultimate necessity for certain values irrespective of all social contexts and the demonstration of this simply by asserting certain conceptual relations to be the case in all coherent thought. Arguments of this type have long been the subject of controversy and their limitations have to be carefully watched. Whatever significance Kant may have considered them to have, it was central even to his position that they revealed at most the limits or boundaries of human experience and thought and not anything of an ultimate, ontological character. But in so far as he was even seeking to show that any one set of categories or principles must necessarily apply universally in all experience and thought he was surely going beyond anything that could possibly be demonstrated from within any given categorial scheme. The most that can be shown are the limits there are to the schemes we have. As Körner has clearly argued, 'the defect of all transcendental arguments is their failure to provide a uniqueness-proof, i.e. the demonstration that the categorial framework is universal.'[16] An argument that could establish any such *a priori* uniqueness would itself have to extend beyond the framework and thereby would demonstrate that the framework was not universally necessary. But if transcendental arguments cannot establish unique categorial necessities it is still perfectly possible for arguments of this type at least in principle to articulate the boundaries of the categories of experience and thought as we now have them.[17] And that, I suggest, is what Peters can be seen to offer. It is, however, another question whether any of the transcendental arguments that Peters, or others, have produced are indeed themselves valid. It may be, for instance, that what have been claimed to be fundamental principles of moral reasoning in so far as that makes coherent sense have not been shown to have that status. In his paper on these arguments[18] Professor Charles Taylor stresses the very considerable difficulty there is in articulating the boundary conditions of experience and thought when in moral life we focus on what is observed and thought within these and are unconcerned with what it is to perceive or think as such. Our attempts to formulate these conditions so that they can be seen to be self-evidently valid can seriously distort them and the very attempt can be infected by particular philosophical doctrines we may subscribe to. He concludes that such arguments

> articulate a grasp of the point of our activity which we cannot but have, and their formulations aspire to self-evidence; and yet they must articulate what is most difficult for us to articulate, and hence are open to endless debate. A valid transcendental argument is indubitable; but it is hard to know when you have one, at least one with an interesting conclusion. But then that seems true of most arguments in philosophy.[19]

It is also the case that the enterprise may be distorted by what are in fact socially or ideologically relative infections so that an argument elucidates nothing more than the conceptual boundaries of a particular and limited point of view. Whether or not that is the case in Peters's uses of this form of argument is again another question. What I am concerned with here is rather that this undertaking is in principle not only philosophically acceptable, but an attempt to deal with certain of the most difficult questions that philosophy and philosophy of education have to face. This highlights too another characteristic feature of Peters's work, his recognition that if a philosopher of education is to contribute effectively to educational debate, he must be prepared at times to come off the philosophical fence on what are important, if extremely controversial, matters.

Yet if Peters could never be properly described as an essentialist it is however true to say that in practice his elucidation of educational concepts has paid only very limited attention to the social contexts in which they operate and the implicit value judgments that they encapsulate. He has sought always to get beyond that context to the wider fundamental framework in which we can make sense of education and justify what we do. In so doing he has certainly sought to set out that framework at least committed to progressively articulating a position that would be the most coherent and comprehensive, and the most defensible against the sceptic. This is to be at least committed to the search, in debate with all others, for a position that is effectively universal. It is to reject acceptance of any ready form of ultimate categorial relativism or pluralism even if it is also to reject any universal necessary certitudes.[20] If such an enterprise is ever to be successful, it seems that philosophers must work hand in hand with psychologists, sociologists, scientists, historians and others. No other way can they help in the development of an adequate account of human nature or society. And the philosopher of education must be in on the same multidimensional pursuit. Abraham Edel has shown well the weakness in analysis as practised in recent philosophy of education, when it jumps too quickly through empirical, valuational and socio-historical considerations, claiming fundamental status for distinctions and doctrines that have no such standing.[21] These other elements, he argues, must play a full part in the analysis itself if we are ever to get clear about the concepts we use, our use of them and their presuppositions. If these elements play their part surreptitiously, they determine unnoticed the shape of the resulting analysis. How this can happen he illustrates not only from Ryle's analysis of 'know-how' and 'know-that' but also from Peters's progressive analysis of 'education'. That this weakness exists in his early work on 'education' Peters himself recognises in a recent paper[22] and he goes on to make the general criticism that 'conceptual analysis has tended to be too self-contained an exercise. Criteria for a concept are sought in the usage of the term without enough attention being paid to the historical or social background and view of human nature which it presupposes.' He then advocates the need for philosophers to integrate their work with that of other disciplines, to widen the notion of analysis beyond verbal usage to the examination of technical as well as common-sense approaches, and to introduce more stress on social values and human nature. Indeed it seems to me that Edel expresses very well the position Peters takes, if not in quite the words he might use:

> Analysis is any way which God or angel or man or beast can
> devise to make clearer the conceptual instruments one is using

and the processes of using them in specific materials, and to dig out the presuppositions in the questions asked, and the problem, and purposes involved so as to be able to refine and improve them in the light of the stage reached by mankind in its total development of life and society.[23]

In the light of this weakness in past work it is understandable that Peters has been accused of building into his work on education and his underpinning accounts of human nature and society very particular beliefs and values, that do not have the fundamental status he attaches to them. His advocacy of rational autonomy and of liberal values and procedures has seemed to many much too easy, these elements being assumed throughout in analyses when they ought more properly to have been unearthed and called in question.[24] As a consequence, his work has been criticised as inherently conservative. There is certainly some substance in this charge though, as has been suggested already, Peters's work can be read more cautiously as articulating a position which he recognises needs more defence than he has given. His periodic admissions of the weakness or absence of the defence have gone unnoticed.[25] What has not helped either have been rather indiscriminate accusations that Peters has believed his analytical work to be second-order, formal in character, not concerned with issues of substance, including substantive values and also value-free, when in fact it is none of these things.[26] In claiming that philosophy of education is second-order or formal, Peters has made it quite clear that it is the asking of questions about meaning, the grounds of justification and presuppositions that he has in mind. That such questions have no bearing on matters of substance, or that they have no significance for the development of 'first-order' forms of thought and experience, he has explicitly denied.[27] To distinguish these philosophical concerns from others is not to deny a relationship with, significance for, or dependence upon, these other concerns. That he considers philosophy could justify certain moral values or principles of reason by exploring the presuppositions of reason is witnessed by his interest in transcendental arguments. What he has maintained, however, is that lower-level principles involved in the application of these fundamental principles in particular contexts cannot be justified on philosophical grounds alone. The suggestion that he has sought to defend philosophical work as value-free by making improper use of 'the naturalistic fallacy' seems to me simply mistaken. Nor could Peters be held to believe other than that philosophical analysis is committed to reason and objectivity and that in that sense it is certainly not

17

value-free. It seems to me Brenda Cohen is quite right in her paper 'Return to the Cave: New Directions for Philosophy of Education'[28] when she concludes that philosophy of education as developed by Peters in the analytic tradition is committed to a significant body of liberal values. To see Peters's work as an attempt to articulate and defend in its most fundamental philosophical terms an approach to education committed to such values is, I suggest, to focus on its central features and to begin to see the real significance of what he achieved.

The concept of education

At the heart of Richard Peters's work in philosophy of education has been his recurrent concern to map the central features by which we distinguish the activities of education from other human pursuits. His inaugural lecture at the University of London Institute of Education, 'Education as Initiation',[29] and the first part of his subsequent major book 'Ethics and Education'[30] were devoted to this issue in an attempt to get a grip on what is basically at stake in the upbringing of children and the work of schools and colleges. His outline of what education is about was characteristically forthright, throwing out a string of challenges to which most serious writers on the subject continue to respond. Central to his account in these publications are three complex criteria that he sees us as using to demarcate education.[31] First, education is concerned with the development of desirable states of mind in the transmission of what is worthwhile to those who themselves come to care about these valuable things. No restriction is set on what is transmitted other than that it is judged to be worthwhile in itself and not merely to be useful or a means to some other end. Secondly, education is concerned with the acquisition of a body of knowledge and understanding that gives some form of cognitive perspective to the person's activities, so transforming their outlook. Thirdly, the processes of education involve at least some understanding of what is being learnt and what is required in the learning, together with some minimal voluntary participation in the process. To this general, but in fact very controversial, characterisation of the concept of education Peters then explicitly adds two major philosophical doctrines to form a distinctive positive view of what he considers education in these terms to be fundamentally about. One doctrine concerns the nature of mind and its development, the other concerns the determination of just what activities and pursuits are worthwhile within education.

His account of the nature of mind is perhaps best briefly

summarised in the following extracts from *Ethics and Education.*

A child is born with a consciousness not as yet differentiated into beliefs, purposes and feelings. . . . His 'mind' is ruled perhaps by bizarre and formless wishes in which there is no picking out of objects, still less of 'sense-data', in a framework of space and time, no notion of permanence or of continuity, no embryonic grasp of causal connection or means-ends relationship. . . . The differentiation of modes of consciousness proceeds pari passu with the development of this (previously absent) mental structure. For they are all related to types of objects and relations in a public world. . . . The point is that consciousness, which is the hall-mark of mind, is related in its different modes to objects. The individual wants *something*, is afraid of or angry with *somebody* or *something*, believes or knows that *certain things are the case.* The objects of consciousness are first and foremost objects in a public world that are marked out and differentiated by a public language into which the individual is initiated . . . the individual represents a particular and unrepeatable viewpoint on this public world. Furthermore he adds his contribution to the public world. The development of a structure of categories and concepts for picking out objects in a space-time framework and for noting causal connections and means-ends relations is only a stage in the development of mind. Further differentiation develops as the mastery of the basic skills opens the gates to a vast inheritance accumulated by those versed in more specific modes of thought and awareness such as science, history, mathematics, religious and aesthetic awareness, together with moral, prudential and technical forms of thought and action. Such different actions are alien to the mind of a child or pre-literate man—indeed perhaps to that of a pre-seventeenth century man. . . . The process of initiation into such modes of thought and awareness is the process of education.[32]

On this view, learning, seen as an initiation into a shared, public, socially formulated and selected world, is constitutive of the development of mind. And in Peters's other writings it is quite clear that it is in relation to this primarily cognitive development that we can best understand the development of an individual's other capacities such as those of character, feeling and executive skills.[33] Such an account is rooted in Kantian or Hegelian philosophy, though it shows also the particular influence of Michael Oakeshott and Karl Popper.

Peters's determination of what activities are most worthwhile

19

is a more complex matter. His argument rests in part on a sharp distinction between those pursuits which are valued for extrinsic, utilitarian reasons and those which are valued because of their own intrinsic features, the latter being of more fundamental importance as the basis from which instrumental value is derived. This leads him to exploring the claim that activities of this kind are valued because of their capacities to maintain interest and provide distinctive pleasures. They are thus distinguished by such features as their richness and variety of content, their fecundity, their demand on our skills, knowledge and resources, their mutual compatibility both within the life of the individual and in social terms. On these grounds, theoretical pursuits in particular come out well, especially in their capacity for adding their qualities to so many otherwise necessarily somewhat limited pursuits in life. But such arguments, though important, still leave unanswered the basic question: Is the capacity to maintain our interest or provide distinctive pleasures all the justification there can be for theoretical pursuits? Are these features all that we can point to in deciding what pursuits are worthwhile, in answering the question 'Why do this rather than that?' Peters makes two further moves. First he argues that theoretical and cognitive pursuits are valuable in that they are necessary to any serious attempt to answer this question as to what is most worthwhile. They provide our understanding of what we are choosing between and reasons for the choice we make. But even that is a limited argument as it seems to justify these pursuits in instrumental or extrinsic terms, as merely useful in the answering of the question. It does not justify even theoretical pursuits in themselves and that is what is being sought. Peters then finally argues that certain theoretical pursuits are such that they are not merely useful to *answering* the question, but are in fact presupposed in the very *asking* of the question.

> For how can a serious practical question be asked unless a man also wants to acquaint himself as well as he can of the situation out of which the question arises and of the facts of various kinds which provide the framework for possible answers? The various theoretical inquiries are explorations of these different facets of his experience. To ask the question 'Why do this rather than that?' seriously is therefore, however embryonically, to be committed to those inquiries which are defined by their serious concern with those aspects of reality which give context to the question he is asking.[34]

It is thus in a form of 'transcendental deduction' that Peters ultimately rests his case for the value of the worthwhile activities he considers at the heart of education—those activities being the pursuits of knowledge and understanding necessarily presupposed in the question 'Why do this rather than that?' Putting together this view of worthwhile activities, his view of the development of mind and the need to satisfy the three criteria for a concept of education he thus presented and in significant measure sought to defend a positive view of education as consisting of 'initiating others into activities, modes of conduct, and thought which have standards written into them by reference to which it is possible to act, think and feel with varying degrees of skill, relevance and taste.'[35]

Of the three elements in this mapping of the basic features of education, two have been the subject of extended critical debate: the criteria for the concept and the determination of the worthwhile activities with which education should be concerned. The three criteria were immediately attacked as demarcating a specific concept of education that is by no means universally shared even in our society. Further, it was maintained that by presenting these particular features as part of an agreed concept he was improperly trying to establish simply by conceptual analysis a defence of an education devoted largely, if not exclusively, to cognitive development. This impression seems to have been accentuated by his presenting, alongside an analysis of the concept that accentuated the cognitive elements in education, a more positive account of education with so extended and developed a defence of cognitive pursuits. These two distinct parts of Peters's enterprise tended to become confused in superficial reading. The use of a transcendental argument to justify cognitive pursuits only served to compound the confusion when such arguments seem in part to parallel closely the claiming of necessary relations within a conceptual analysis.

Peters's response to these general criticisms of his criteria was to defend his approach but to modify certain of his claims. In 1970, following slight shifts in terminology in the intervening years, he published a paper 'Education and the Educated Man' expressly examining the three criteria and the general significance of his analysis. He now distinguished sharply between the concept of 'education' and that of 'an educated man'. The former he saw as a very general notion concerned with the upbringing of children wherever it might take place. His previous analysis he now expressed as concerned with the characteristics of an educated person as that emerged in the nineteenth century. This distinction enabled him to answer some of the criticisms of his original account of what is meant by 'education', seeing them as relating to

21

an older more general concept whose continuing use he had failed to recognise. To this he added a detailed re-examination of the importance within the criteria of both the cognitive demand and the link with intrinsically, non-instrumental, worthwhile activities. He argued robustly that both these elements have a place in our ideal of an educated man, neither being able adequately to subsume what the other is articulating. In the process he particularly stressed that the worthwhile activities that concern the educated man are by no means only the disinterested pursuit of knowledge, nor even the strictly non-instrumental.

> Our concept of an educated person is of someone who is capable of delighting in a variety of pursuits and projects for their own sake and whose pursuit of them and general conduct of life is transformed by some degree of all round understanding and sensitivity. Pursuing the practical is not necessarily a disquali-fication for being educated; for the practical need not be pursued under a purely instrumental aspect. This does not mean, of course, that an educated man is oblivious of the instrumental value of pursuits—e.g. of science. It means only that he does not view them purely under this aspect.[36]

He also readily acknowledged that his original concept, now seen more clearly as that of a particular educational ideal, did encapsulate certain values that some might reject. He stressed that philosophical analysis cannot provide a justification for these values, concluding his paper with a series of questions that need answering if this ideal of an educated person is to be adequately defended.

In his response to his critics Peters's reworking of his criteria helped much in elucidating further the important strands in current educational discussion to which he had originally drawn attention. It served too, to introduce directly into the philosophical debate attention to the social context and historical shifts that have radically influenced our educational ideas. But the view that there are basically just two concepts seemed to many not to go far enough in recognising the complexities that any analysis doing justice to the wider social context of education really must take on board. What is more, his concept of an educated man, general though it might be in some respects, began to look much too specific to express any current agreed ideal, let alone one whose justification should be the focus of our critical concern. The distinction between the two concepts also served to deflect attention from the distinction between what was now described as the notion of 'an educated man' and the limited elements within that notion which he considered justified by a transcendental argument. Increasingly the part became identified with the whole and that in spite of the final section of 'Education and the Educated Man'.[37] Somewhat misguided earlier criticisms of the particularity of the original concept that fastened on the limited range of personal development it emphasised continued to be voiced. Meanwhile criticisms that the concept encapsulated an unacceptable set of moral and social values became more insistent.[38]

Alongside criticism of his analysis of the concept of education, Peters also had to face strong criticism over his justification of the theoretical pursuits of understanding and knowledge in a transcendental argument and his seeming restriction of what is justifiable education to these pursuits. On some of the problems of transcendental arguments in general I have already commented and Peters's use of such an argument in this context has certainly proved difficult to assess. In the debate that has ensued, marked particularly by Peters's detailed reformulation of the argument in his paper 'The Justification of Education',[39] a number of serious weaknesses have emerged within the enterprise. At best the argument would seem to justify theoretical pursuits in so far as they are concerned with the pursuit of reasons for doing things. Only in these terms is the pursuit of reasons for doing things intelligible. This can be interpreted as justifying particular rational pursuits because they constitute ways of asking and answering questions of distinctive kinds which have their own internal criteria and are thus valuable in themselves. But if so, these pursuits are being regarded simply as self-contained enterprises valued for their internal characteristics rather than their significance in human life. They are viewed in a perfectly valid, but nevertheless limited and, even trivialising, way as glorified 'rational games'. For many teachers and researchers one fears that that is often exactly what they do indeed become when surely the real value of these pursuits properly conducted must lie in their much wider significance in human life. As Peters has himself argued they are properly seen not as 'hived-off' pursuits. That, therefore, cannot be what Peters is really seeking to justify. It is, therefore, certainly more appropriate to see his argument as justifying these pursuits in some way as fundamental to the determination of the rational life and therefore central to education. In that case, however, other difficulties arise, and that at a number of levels. At the first level it is not clear what elements in the pursuit of such theoretical activities as, say, mathematics, science and history are in fact constitutive of questions that are fundamental to the rational life. What matters in the rational life at this basic level for all of us is peculiar to us as particular individuals in particular social circumstances. Therefore what is being justified for whom is obscure. The argument is operating at so general and dissociated a level that its application is uncertain. Seen this way, however, the argument does draw attention to a general principle of very considerable significance: that education should be concerned with those areas of under-standing and knowledge that are necessary to the questions of the rational life. But if this is the force of the argument, difficulties arise at another level. If theoretical pursuits are justified as constitutive of questions in the rational life, their justification now rests on the place of such questions within the rational life. What makes up the rational life for any of us is however immensely diverse in its character and the asking and answering of questions is only a part of that. What else then, besides theoretical pursuits, must be seen to be of value and what is in competition with these theoretical elements for a place within education? Further, the significance of these theoretical pursuits for the rational life is not in fact restricted to their place in the asking and answering of questions. They provide concepts, beliefs, attitudes, values, skills, which are of far-reaching import and it is clear that Peters sees his argument as encompassing in some way this wide-ranging determination of life by theoretical pursuits. Yet the argument itself is cast in terms of the activity of questioning and it is not at all clear that it in any way justifies the pursuit of theoretical activities for these wider purposes. And there is yet a further level of difficulty with the argument. If the justification of these theoretical elements rests ultimately in their significance within the develop-ment of the rational life, then the argument cannot rest where Peters left it with a consideration of questioning in a transcendental argument, but must ultimately go on to consider the vastly wider justification of the rational life. In saying that, however, I am not suggesting that the justification for theoretical pursuits in life or in education is simply utilitarian, that they are useful means to our achieving our goals. Just as Peters quite rightly insisted that these pursuits are constitutive of the questions which they are necessary to answering, so their place in the rational life can be seen as certain of the elements that in complex ways constitute that form of life. But the ways in which they do this are difficult to disentangle and it is not clear that from that clarification alone can stem an acceptable transcendental argument for their place in life in general, let alone in education.

Marshalling the difficulties with the very particular transcen-dental argument that Peters originally used in seeking to justify certain worthwhile activities, does scant justice to his own extended comments on the rational life and the significance of education for that. Indeed, if one ceases to be concerned with the details of this particular argument and turns to his own reflections on the search for justification, he can himself be seen to sketch the central features of a form of justification for the pursuit of knowledge and understanding within a justification of the rational life. The following extracts from his paper 'The Justification of Education' reveal his approach to this as early as 1973.

> Human beings, like animals, have from the very start of their lives expectations of their environment, some of which are falsified. With the development of language these expectations come to be formulated and special words are used for the assessment of the content of these expectations and how they are to be regarded in respect of their epistemological status. Words like 'true' and 'false' are used, for instance, to appraise the contents, . . . knowledge is similarly distinguished from opinion. Our language, which is riddled with such appraisals, bears witness to the claims of reason on our sensibility. The same point can be made about human conduct. For human beings do not just veer towards goals like moths towards a light; they are not just programmed by an instinctive equipment. They conceive of ends, deliberate about them and about the means to them. . . . Man is a creature who lives under the demands of reason . . . human life is only intelligible on the assumption that the demands of reason are admitted and woven into the fabric of human life. . . . This is not to say, of course, that there are not other features of life which are valuable—love for others, for instance. It is not even to say that other such concerns may not be more valuable. It is only to say that at least some attempt must be made to satisfy the admitted demands that reason makes upon human life. If, for instance, someone is loved under descriptions which are manifestly false, this is a fault. . . . The point about activities such as science, philosophy, and history is that they need not, like games, be isolated and confined to set times and places. A person who has pursued them syste-matically can develop conceptual schemes and forms of appraisal which transform everything else that he does.[40]

By 1977 Peters was himself becoming concerned about other features in his original approach to both the concept of education and the justification of its content. In a paper significantly entitled 'Ambiguities in Liberal Education' he showed the inadequacies for sorting out the content of education of any distinction between knowledge seen as harnessed to vocational or utilitarian ends and knowledge viewed as 'for its own sake'. Both practical and theoretical activities can be pursued 'for their own sakes' or for other purposes, both can bring about a transformation of the general framework of our attitudes and beliefs, and it is not obvious that practical knowledge and enquiries are of any less value than theoretical knowledge and enquiries. The distinction may be useful in the advancement of knowledge but in education it will only serve to mask 'the need to develop beliefs and attitudes which will help a person to make sense of and take up some stance toward the various situations and predicaments that he will inevitably encounter as a human being'.[41] In this paper for the first time he also brought directly into an explicit discussion of the nature of education questions about the development of a rationally autonomous person. Up to this time he had, alongside his work on the concept of education and the justification of education, been writing on both the social aspects and significance of education and on the nature of moral education. In 'Freedom and the Development of the Free Man'[42] he brought these social and moral concerns together in a major treatment of the nature of rational autonomy and the forms of learning that its achievement entails. The wider significance of this parallel and quite separate strand in Peters's work is commented on further below, but here it is its importance in the development of his overall approach to education that is of note. By 1977 these interests were converging in a way that demanded a reformulation of the concept of education and its justification. The result was his 1979 paper 'Democratic Values and Educational Aims'.[43]

Peters begins this paper with the suggestion that 'education' is an essentially contested concept, that it is used evaluatively and with a lack of precision in its application. This he rejects in so far as it might imply that we can each simply stipulate our own criteria for the concept. 'At least it denotes some kind of *learning* – and not any sort of learning either.'[44] Retaining the distinction between the very general concept of education and that of 'an educated man', he roundly re-asserts that this second concept is concerned with developing the 'whole man', not just training for a particular job or a role, pivotal though these might be in a person's education. Not that education is consistent with any form of becoming a person, nor that it can transform the whole personality. What it does is develop a person's awareness by enlarging, deepening and extending it. 'Its impact is cognitive, but it also transforms and regulates people's attitudes, emotions, events and actions because all these presuppose awareness and are impregnated with beliefs.'[45] The processes of learning that this development involves imply 'mastering something or coming up to some standard as a result of experience'.[46] To this re-assertion of elements in the original criterion he now adds that if this understanding is not to be 'inert' it must have application to people's lives, it being related to 'the human condition' as all must face that. Men face a natural world and are part of nature themselves. They inhabit an interpersonal world of human affection and hate, friendship and loneliness. They are part of an economic, social and political world of poverty and affluence, consensus and dissent. Education is thus concerned with learning how to live in these spheres, but the specific ways in which a person's beliefs, attitudes, desires and emotional reactions are developed will depend on the values and emphasis of the particular society and time in which he lives. This outline of the areas of cognitive development within the criteria for 'an educated man' replaces Peters's previous notion of all-round understanding and knowledge, a demand which he now regards as too narrow and certainly contestable. From this point on, any further detailing of the concept must relate to particular social conditions and values.

In this reconstructed form the general demarcation of the non-contestable elements of the concept of an educated man are now consciously kept as separate as possible from any particular account of the nature of mind or any justification of the detailed elements that education should include. The processes of education are now simply seen as forms of experiential learning and the cognitive demands are tied to learning how to live in the face of the fundamental characteristics of 'the human condition'. Certainly the idea of learning is basic to much of our concern for education and can generally be taken as an agreed element in a shared concept. It can then be asserted as an incontestable element for that group and debate about education be conducted on that basis. If the meaning of the learning is at all specific, however, nothing more can be claimed for its status, unless it can be shown that the concerns of education cannot be coherently elucidated in any other way. That may be the case, indeed I think it is, but Peters has not in this brief paper made this clear. If, therefore, we take Peters's claim that learning is incontestably part of the concept of education as making other than a general descriptive point, if we take it as asserting something universal or necessary, then we must see it within a wider account of the nature of the human person and of personal development. Whatever Peters's intention in the paper, there is every reason to believe that he does still hold to such an account, that provides strong argument for understanding education in this way. But such an account itself needs arguing. Without that, learning is certainly not an incontestable element in the concept in any particularly forceful sense. With it, there begins to be real point to demarcating the concept in this way.

The notion that education is necessarily concerned with capacities for living is altogether more plausible as a universal claim. Indeed it is surprising that it has been missing in philosophical considerations of education until very recently. Perhaps that is because of the platitudinous, almost empty character of the notion until one unpacks in some way what 'living' entails. Peters clearly considers that a number of fundamental areas of living common to man can be set out and his very general description of these is surely defensible. To do this certainly begins to locate education positively in terms of the nature and range of human concerns. As Peters rightly says, however, what one cannot do without raising all the contestability issues again is go on to outline any particular way of living within these concerns that goes beyond setting out the features the individual will encounter. But maybe that entails much more than we have yet spelt out. What is more controversial, it seems to me, is for Peters to continue to insist that the concept be restricted so firmly to the cognitive aspects of living and those other aspects that are transformed through cognitive development. This is surely once more to include a demand that is only acceptable as fundamental if a particular account of the nature of the person and of human development is accepted. The concept as Peters now sees it may be incontestable in these elements on any coherent grasp of the nature of man, but that does need rather more explicitly showing. The valuational element now seems to enter the concept through the fact that if one is to develop capacities for living, that must be not only in a given context, but necessarily in terms of a specific way of living that is considered worthwhile. This however is now seen as the introduction of essentially contestable elements.

> Insofar, therefore, as education is concerned with learning how to live, (the person's) beliefs, attitudes, desires and emotional reactions in these spheres will have to be developed and disciplined in various ways. But in what ways? In trying to answer this question we have surely arrived at the contestable aspect of this more specific concept of education. For filling in the respects in which a person's awareness should be enlarged, deepened, sensitized, disciplined, and so forth, depends first on the values with which a society confronts these various aspects of the human condition and second on the emphases selected by its educators.[47]

In keeping with this analysis, when it comes to setting out his own more positive view of an educated man, Peters now first outlines the basic values distinctive to the type of democratic society in which we live. His formulation of this is essentially that elaborated in 'Ethics and Education'.[48]

> Democracy . . . is a way of life in which high value is placed on the development of reason and principles such as freedom, truth-telling, impartiality and respect for persons, which the use of reason in social life presupposes. This development of reason would be unintelligible if value were not also accorded to the overarching ideal of truth. In spite, however, of this firm commitment to specific values in a democracy, it will be noted that they are predominantly of a procedural sort. By that I mean that they make demands on how social, political and personal life ought to be conducted. They do not provide a blue print for an ideal society or indicate what sort of life is most worth living.[49]

When it comes to the individual's personal good, he sees this as stemming from respect for persons. It involves the individual's self-fulfilment in a range of activities for the enlargement of life and in the roles and occupations we are part of as social beings. Doing this in face of the options open to us demands that man's capacities for choice be developed

> so that ideally he will achieve some degree of autonomy and commit himself authentically to tasks that he genuinely feels he ought to perform or activities that he genuinely wants to pursue, as distinct from devoting himself to externally imposed duties and secondhand interests that are merely socially expected.[50]

In all this he stresses the value of truth as an ideal and the use of reason in social life and personal autonomy. He adds too a concern for those other ways in which men have sought to make sense of and give sense to the human condition especially in aesthetic and religious terms. Though these are not necessary to or distinctive of the democratic way of life as such, they are perspectives on life that have enriched and given insights into the human condition and have their place within a democratic framework. Finally he proceeds to generate a series of more specific aims for education in the areas of interpersonal morality, knowledge and understanding of the human condition in its three aspects, the self-fulfilment of the individual and, more questioningly, preparation for work.[51] The details of these aims are presented with richly illuminating comments of the kind that one comes to expect in Peters's work.

29

But what of this quite new approach to the construction of a positive concept of education and what of its justification? The values on which this positive concept rests are those which Peters has always espoused. The attempt to apply them to our own context is new, is surely to be wholly welcomed and its details considered with care. In particular the way in which social and personal good are seen as inter-related is manifestly of importance. What is not so clear now is the precise form of Peters's justification for education in these terms. He quite explicitly did not set out to give this in this particular paper, though some indications are there. The values of truth and knowledge he asserts as fundamental and not merely a matter of their relevance to discerning the contours of the human condition and solving practical and social problems. 'Truth just matters irrespective of its pay off.'[52] The other democratic values, such as those of freedom and respect for persons would also seem to retain this status from his earlier writing. In that case the social and personal life that embodies these derives its justification from them and from that we can go on to justify a form of education. But how then are these fundamental values to be established? Are they still to be seen as resting on the transcendental arguments in *Ethics and Education*?[53] Those arguments may not obviously suffer to the same extent from the narrowness and detachment from context which is so damaging to the argument for worthwhile activities, but it is far from clear that they can in the end escape the same form of criticism. And even if these arguments hold, what now is the defence of those other 'worthwhile' activities in life that fall outside these particular 'democratic' values? Maybe what is still needed is a yet more thorough following through of the line of argument Peters himself introduced in 'The Justification of Education'[54] on which I commented earlier. To make a coherent and wide-ranging enough case for the rational life as that must be, it is surely necessary to bring together a mapping of the wide-ranging elements that make up the nature of the human person, including elements that are usually neglected, an account of the nature of the interpersonal and social conditions that man encounters and an analysis of the place of cognition and reason within this whole. What positive concept of education and what justification exactly would come out of that it is hard to be sure. Something still wider than Peters is now suggesting, I surmise. Such a request is overwhelming but it seems increasingly clear that anything short of this is a doomed enterprise. Peters's repeated attempts to characterise education in its most fundamental terms and to give any adequate justification for a positive form of it, has led him into questions from which most philosophers shy away. Progressively his work has carved a way through a great complex of considerations if only to encounter further previously unsuspected difficulties. As in most philosophical work, the task remains uncompleted, but the mapping of the major issues and kinds of arguments in this territory has been masterly. Some of his critics have suggested that this task could not be profitably undertaken, the search for fundamentals being altogether mistaken. To judge so is simply to give up what are ultimately the most important issues in philosophy of education and it is to fail to appreciate the very profound illumination Peters has brought to these questions.

The moral life and moral education

Though any single paper discussing Peters's contribution to philosophy of education must necessarily omit even references to, let alone consideration of, many areas of his work, to leave without comment his writings on moral education would be to radically distort all sense of his achievement. One of his first published papers was on 'Nature and Convention in Morality'[55] and before he ever arrived at the London Institute of Education he had written on 'Freud's Theory of Moral Development in Relation to that of Piaget'.[56] His strong interest in philosophical psychology resulted in studies on motivation, the nature of emotions, character, habit and the relationship between reason and passion.[57] Underlying this was the steady working out of a concept of the person as a rational autonomous being. His early interest in social philosophy with work on authority, responsibility, freedom and democracy[58] was rooted in a well-focused ethical theory. These two areas of interest when brought together in their bearing on education resulted in a succession of papers developing a sophisticated account of the moral life and moral education, most of which are collected in his volume *Moral Development and Moral Education.*[59]

Basic to this account is a notion of rational universalistic morality as this has emerged from the clash of codes of living and competing views of the world as a result of social change and economic expansion. Reflecting about which view of the world was true, which code was correct, men came to accept higher-order principles of a procedural sort for determining such questions.[60] By these means matters of morals came to be distinguished from matters of custom or law, codes could be criticised and revised, and men gradually became able to stand on their own feet as autonomous moral beings.[61] Principles of truth-telling, freedom, fairness and consideration of interests have thus emerged as giving us general criteria for determining moral issues. They prescribe what sort of considerations count as reasons, providing a framework for working out the arrangements for our lives together. Applying these to what we by nature are and our conditions of life, these result in basic rules about such matters as property, contracts, and care of the young, without which social life would be impossible and about which a fair degree of consensus is achievable. But beyond these there is room for vast disagreement and alternative patterns of life, without considering that the whole of the fabric of society is unstable. Stability and consensus at a basic level are quite compatible with change and experiment at other levels. There is no secure resting place in social or personal life and principles have to be interpreted in concrete traditions. But principles do rule out certain courses of action and sensitise us to the normally relevant features of situations.[62]

In these terms Peters sees principled morality as rooted in a form of public reasoning, similar in major respects to other forms of reasoning, if distinct in its concern for human behaviour. This form involves seeing actions under classifications that connect what is done and is to be done with the past and the future by means of generalisations and rules. These generalisations in conjunction with particular circumstances constitute reasons for acting and the moral life is conducted both personally and socially in these terms. But the individual does not reason in this way simply by nature. Reason in any of its forms is a developing public tradition constructed and maintained in appropriate language and institutional forms. The individual comes to reason by being initiated into this tradition, sharing in its discourse and patterns of thought, engaging in it as a self-critical enterprise with its own standards of achievement.[63]

But the moral life is a matter of feeling and passion, of action and behaviour, not simply of reason, which of itself seems inert. Peters's characterisation of the relation between these dimensions is perhaps most systematically presented in his paper 'Reason and Passion'. In this he depicts three levels of life only the last of which is that of moral reason. The first is the level at which young infants live all the time and may be called

> a-rational in that it has not reached the level at which
> experience is structured by categories of thought associated with
> reason. . . . This low-grade type of experience is dominated by
> wishes and aversions . . . it lacks a sense of reality, it does not
> follow the causal principle. . . . Classification is based on an

affectively loaded similarity without regard to identity. There are missing those passions that help the individual to stick to any activity he is engaged in.[64]

At the next level of life, reasons do now get a grip, but they are very limited. Beliefs are 'infected with particularity'. There is little attempt to make them consistent, to test them by counter-examples. They are likely to be based on authority or to suit the individual. The viewpoint is certainly partial and arbitrary. And this particularly infects the sphere of the will for the urgency of the present asserts itself. Life at this level tends to be 'sense-bound', swayed by pleasures and pains of the moment and emotions are roused only by particular people and situations.[65] The third level is that at which conduct is connected with the use of reason and is intelligible only if we postulate the development of certain distinctive passions such as the concern for truth, consistency, sincerity and the like.

> These are internalisations of principles which give structure and point to theoretical enquiries; but they are also involved in practical activities and judgments in so far as these are conducted in a rational manner. . . . To describe the transformation of 'natural' passions such as fear, anger and sexual desire would be, more or less, to attempt an Aristotelian analysis of the virtues; but more emphasis would have to be placed on the passionate side of reason than in Aristotle's account. . . . He was not sufficiently aware that the use of reason is a passionate business.[66]

This picture of the moral life is further filled out by Peters's account of the place in it of the ideal of personal autonomy. All that has been said thus far presupposes that man is in fact a chooser, that he can entertain different goals, weigh alternatives in the light of evidence, decide what to do and translate that into action. But the fundamental principle of freedom that is part of rational morality implies that choice is an ideal in that form of life. This means that the person himself both decides what to do and accepts or makes the rules he will live by. But in so far as this 'authenticity' is an element in rational morality, the person's decisions will also be subject to the other principles of rational reflection and criticism that are entailed such as fairness and the respect for persons. He will be subject too to the facts about the limitations on his knowledge, his time and the constraints of his context. He will, therefore, not always reflect before each act, but he will rationally consider the rules of his life and be disposed to think for himself in new situations. These two elements of authenticity and rational reflection which are usually taken to constitute what is meant by autonomy, Peters thus sees as the hallmarks of the personal moral life.[67]

Finally one must note those five facets of the moral life he distinguishes, facets related to man's nature and circumstances, into all of which a concern for rational principles must be built. First there are those many good, desirable or worthwhile pursuits, from the arts, sciences and technologies to games and pastimes that provide not only occupations but vocations and ideals in life. Secondly there are our social roles and the 'duties' that arise from these positions as for example husband, citizen or member of a profession. Thirdly, there are those 'duties' that fall to us as members of society in general in terms of our personal and institutionalised relationships. Fourthly, there are those wide-ranging goals that mark out our lives in terms of virtues and vices. Finally, those very general character traits often associated with 'the will' that mark out the manner in which we pursue our purposes, for example, integrity, determination and consistency.[68]

From this comprehensive delineation of the rational moral life, Peters has sought to spell out the necessary features of moral education. Not surprisingly his concern for 'principled morality' led him to see much of value in Kohlberg's account of moral development. Elaborating on Piaget's claim that there is an invariant order of stages through which development takes place, Kohlberg spelt these out as stages in how behavioural rules are seen, not in their content.

> Children start by seeing rules as dependent upon power and external compulsion; they then see them as instrumental to rewards and the satisfaction of their needs; then as ways of obtaining social approval and esteem; then as upholding some ideal order; and finally as articulations of social principles necessary to living together with others—especially justice.[69]

It is claimed that this sequence of development is logically necessary, each stage presupposing the earlier stages. The transition from stage to stage is seen not as a form of maturation but as a result of social participation in a context in which one is provoked or stimulated to a higher level of conceptualisation and thinking. The earlier stages prove inadequate for making sense of one's situation. All this implies that there are some universal structural dimensions in the social world as there are in the physical world, arising from the existence of a self in a world composed of other selves who are both like the self and different from it.[70] Peters has not only found Kohlberg's philosophical claims about the development of moral thinking broadly accept-able, he has agreed too with Kohlberg's view that the emotional aspects of the moral life can only develop on the basis of cognitive changes. There is much here that fits with Peters's notion of 'levels of life'. But Peters has been critical of Kohlberg's account on a number of significant scores. The precise logical connections between moral thinking at the different stages has not been spelt out, nor their relationship to structural features in the social world. Kohlberg has denied the importance of explicit teaching in providing the cognitive stimulation necessary for development to occur. But direct instruction is not the only form that teaching can take and a more detailed analysis of the necessary features of 'stimulation' and the role of agents in achieving these is necessary to developing any adequate programme of moral education.[71]

Peters's main criticism of Kohlberg, however, has been con-cerned to bring out the major elements that are omitted from this picture but which must necessarily feature in any account that adequately considers the development of the moral life as a whole. Kohlberg, for example, with his stress on the form of moral reasoning, demotes heavily the importance of the content of morality. In one sense, there is a very significant content at the highest level with its concern for rational principles of justice, human welfare, respect for persons and society and, presumably, truth-telling, which Kohlberg seems not to mention. But such principles have to be applied in particular circumstances and without a content of lower-order rules they have no application. A given society must therefore have a substantive morality which structures the moral life of the individual as well as the formal principles. What is more, moral rules of this kind are necessary not only for practical living by those at the lower stages of development, they are logically necessary for the process of development. Without them children would never come to understand the significance of rules for themselves or have a content of rules for later critical consideration.[72]

Peters argues that there is another serious question of 'content' later in development as Kohlberg sees this. For his view of rational principles never seriously embraces the principle of the 'considera-tion of others' interests' and the demands that this makes on any developmental sequence. Drawing on the work of Martin Hoffman and others, Peters seeks to complement Kohlberg's account to provide for the development of altruistic beliefs and related motivation.[73]

Finally there is Peters's insistence against Kohlberg that the whole dimension of character-traits, virtues and vices is central to the moral life and must be catered for developmentally. Kohlberg considers these elements very secondary in principled morality because of their linkage to specific kinds of behaviour. He thus makes a sharp distinction between principles that operate primarily cognitively and the more habitual behaviour associated with virtues and vices. But if, as Peters suggests, character-traits should be seen rather as the internalised operation of principles as much as more specific rules, then they will be seen as having a major place in the moral life. True, some character-traits may be too specific to be adequate at the higher levels of moral development. Those of a more general character may come later in that sequence. Some, like those concerned with 'the will' may be of higher order and not related to particular principles. But the place of these elements in Peters's 'five facets' of the moral life gives clear indication of the significance he sees them to have. Reinstating character-traits against Kohlberg's emphasis is to restore an Aristotelian strand to both our understanding of morality and its development. It is to restore habit as a supplement to reason and habituation as a supplement to cognitive development.[74]

To this enrichment of Kohlberg's work, with all its attendant educational implications, Peters also adds further considerations provoked by his study of the Freudian theory of moral development. Though these are not worked out in great detail, he sees here not a rival account of development but another contribution to understanding matters on which Kohlberg has little or nothing to say. There is help for an understanding of the transmission of the content of moral rules, for habit formation and the process of identification. But there is above all an account of forms of moral failure especially in the area of character-traits.[75]

In all this one can again see Peters's great skill at using eclectically the achievement of others, in this case shrewdly discerning the philosophical underpinnings of different psychological theories and harnessing these to his increasingly perceptive account of the nature of moral development. From time to time he has gone on to make practical recommendations for moral education in schools. But he has always expressed caution about these suggestions, preferring to emphasise as a philosopher his prime concern with the nature and justification of rational morality and the necessary features of its development.[76] Peters's work in this area can of course be critically considered from many different angles, though there is no space to go into details here. His heavily Kantian account of the nature and justification of moral principles is open to many questions and his general ethical position is, to say the least, unfashionable at a time when many moral philosophers seem to favour either some form of utilitarianism or some form of Aristotelianism. To the latter his emphasis on the virtues is to be welcomed, but he gives them no significant standing in the justification of morality. They are now increasingly being seen as providing some form of 'naturalistic' base for just that and moral rules and principles are sometimes seen as but a codification of the life of virtue. In line with this approach, Peters's account of the relationship between reason, passion and motivation seems to put too much emphasis on the force of cognitive appraisals about which we come to care. What the driving force in all this is in our wishes, desires and wants, and what distinctive character these elements of their nature bring with them into the moral life, is by no means clear. His view of autonomy can be questioned as rooted in too restrictive a notion of authenticity. Reject Peters's concept of morality or the basic features of his concept of a person and his account of moral development must go as well. But that is hardly the state of affairs right now. In fact, this elaborated study of the philosophical bases of moral education stands alone as a coherent and comprehensive statement of what the enterprise involves. In this controversial area of education, as in so many others, Peters has pioneered a mapping of the fundamental philosophical questions that arise whilst giving a highly illuminative positive account of how those questions might be answered.

Conclusion

This outline of Richard Peters's contribution to philosophy of education has sought to bring out his distinctive view of the nature of philosophical analysis and argument and to illustrate the application of this in his work on the concept of education and the philosophical foundations of moral education. What this shows above all else is his unrelenting concern to elucidate the fundamental considerations that lie beneath educational thought and practice. To this end he has drawn widely on contemporary and traditional work in most of the major areas of philosophy. Whether or not one agrees with his substantive conclusions on any particular issue it cannot but be recognised that he has introduced new methods and wholly new considerations into the philosophical discussion of educational issues. The result has been a new level of philosophical rigour and with that a new sense of the importance of philosophical considerations for educational decisions. Richard Peters has revolutionised philosophy of education and as the work of all others now engaged in that area bears witness, there can be no going back on the transformation he has brought about.

Notes

1 'The Philosophy of Education', in Tibble, J.W. (ed.): *The Study of Education* (Routledge & Kegan Paul), 1966.
2 Ibid., pp. 63-4.
3 See Haack, R.J.: 'Philosophies of Education', *Philosophy*, vol. 51, no. 196, April 1976.
4 *Ethics and Education* (George Allen & Unwin), 1966.
5 'The Philosophy of Education', op. cit., p. 60.
6 *Ethics and Education*, op. cit., pp. 15-16.
7 See *Ethics and Education*, op. cit., p. 18; Peters, R.S. (ed.): *The Philosophy of Education* (Oxford University Press), 1973, p. 4; Peters, R.S.: *Psychology and Ethical Development* (George Allen & Unwin), 1974, p. 20; Peters, R.S.: 'Philosophy of Education', in Hirst, P.H. (ed.): *Education and its Foundation Disciplines* (Routledge & Kegan Paul), 1983, p. 53.
8 In his very significant paper 'Analytic Philosophy of Education at the Crossroads', in Doyle, J.F. (ed.): *Educational Judgments* (Routledge & Kegan Paul), 1973, Abraham Edel critically attacks this approach in philosophy of education, though without directly attributing this procedure to Richard Peters. See also Dearden, R.F. 'Philosophy of Education 1952-1982', in Dearden, R.F. (ed.): *Theory and Practice in Education* (Routledge & Kegan Paul), 1984.
9 See particularly Gilroy, D.P.: 'The Revolutions in English Philosophy and Philosophy of Education', in *Educational Analysis*, vol. 4, no. 1, 1982.
10 'Motivation, Emotion and the Conceptual Schemes of Common Sense', in Peters, R.S. (ed.): *Psychology and Ethical Development*, op. cit.
11 See *The Concept of Motivation* (Routledge & Kegan Paul), 1958, pp. 154-6.
12 See *Ethics and Education*, op. cit., pp. 16, 23.
13 'Education as Initiation', in Archambault, R.D. (ed.): *Philosophical Analysis and Education* (Routledge & Kegan Paul), 1965, p. 89.
14 'The Development of Reason', in *Psychology and Ethical Development*, op. cit., p. 122.
15 See *Ethics and Education*, op. cit., Part 2.
16 Körner, S.: *Categorial Frameworks* (Blackwells), 1970, p. 72.
17 See Taylor, C.: 'The Validity of Transcendental Arguments', in *Proceedings of the Aristotelian Society*, vol. 79, 1978-9, pp. 151-65.
18 Ibid., pp. 163-5.
19 Ibid., p. 165.
20 Gilroy, D.P., op. cit., pp. 82-3.
21 Edel, A., op. cit., pp. 232-57.
22 'The Philosophy of Education', in Hirst, P.H. (ed.), op. cit., pp. 41-3, 53, 55.

23 Edel, A., op. cit., p. 252.
24 See for example Adelstein, D.L.: 'The Wit and Wisdom of R.S. Peters—The Philosophy of Education', in Pateman, T. (ed.): *Counter Course* (Penguin), 1972, and Harris, K.: *Education and Knowledge* (Routledge & Kegan Paul), 1979.
25 See Hirst, P.H. and Peters, R.S.: *The Logic of Education*, Preface and Ch. 1 and 'The Philosophy of Education', in Hirst, P.H. (ed.), op. cit.
26 See for instance Haack, R.J., op. cit.
27 See 'The Philosophy of Education', in Tibble (ed.), op. cit., pp. 60-2.
28 Cohen, B.: 'Return to the Cave: New Directions for Philosophy of Education', in *Educational Analysis*, vol. 4, no. 1, 1982.
29 'Education as Initiation', in Archambault, R.D. (ed.), op. cit.
30 *Ethics and Education*, op. cit.
31 'Education as Initiation', in Archambault, R.D. (ed.), op. cit., pp. 87-103; *Ethics and Education*, op. cit., pp. 23-45.
32 *Ethics and Education*, op. cit., pp. 49-51.
33 See Peters, R.S.: *Psychology and Ethical Development*, op. cit., papers on 'Reason and Passion', 'The Education of the Emotions' and 'Subjectivity and Standards'.
34 *Ethics and Education*, op. cit., p. 164.
35 'Education as Initiation', op. cit., p. 107.
36 'Education and the Educated Man', reprinted in Peters, R.S., *Education and the Education of Teachers* (Routledge & Kegan Paul), 1977, p. 13.
37 Ibid., pp. 18-20.
38 See Adelstein, D.L., op. cit., and Harris, K., op. cit.
39 'The Justification of Education', in Peters, R.S. (ed.): *The Philosophy of Education*, op. cit.
40 Ibid., pp. 254-8.
41 'Ambiguities in Liberal Education', in *Education and the Education of Teachers*, op. cit., p. 55.
42 'Freedom and the Development of the Free Man', in Doyle, J.F. (ed.): *Educational Judgments* (Routledge & Kegan Paul), 1973.
43 'Democratic Values and Educational Aims', in Peters, R.S.: *Essays on Educators* (Allen & Unwin), 1981.
44 Ibid., p. 32.
45 Ibid., p. 33.
46 Ibid., p. 33.
47 Ibid., p. 34.
48 *Ethics and Education*, op. cit., ch. 11.
49 'Democratic Values and Educational Aims', op. cit., p. 37.
50 Ibid., p. 39.
51 Ibid., pp. 42-8.
52 Ibid., p. 46.
53 *Ethics and Education*, op. cit., chs 4-8.
54 'The Justification of Education', in Peters, R.S. (ed.): *The Philosophy of Education*, op. cit.
55 'Nature and Convention in Morality', in *Proceedings of the Aristotelian Society*, May 1951.

56 'Freud's Theory of Moral Development in Relation to that of Piaget', in *British Journal of Educational Psychology*, November 1980.
57 See especially Peters, R.S. (ed.): *Psychology and Ethical Development*, op. cit.
58 See Benn, S.I. and Peters, R.S.: *Social Principles and the Democratic State* (Allen & Unwin), 1959; Peters, R.S.: *Authority, Responsibility and Education* (Allen & Unwin) Revised Edition, 1973.
59 Peters, R.S., *Moral Development and Moral Education* (Allen & Unwin), 1981. Most of the papers in this volume are also to be found in *Psychology and Ethical Development*, op. cit.
60 'Moral Development and Moral Education', op. cit., p. 63.
61 Ibid., p. 62.
62 Ibid., pp. 63-5.
63 Ibid., p. 68. See also *Psychology and Ethical Development*, op. cit., pp. 152-6.
64 *Psychology and Ethical Development*, pp. 162-6.
65 See ibid., pp. 168-9.
66 See ibid., pp. 169-71.
67 *Moral Development and Moral Education*, op. cit., pp. 118-22.
68 Ibid., pp. 69-70.
69 Ibid., p. 85.
70 Ibid., p. 86.
71 Ibid., pp. 88-92.
72 Ibid., pp. 177-8.
73 Ibid., pp. 171-7.
74 Ibid., pp. 92-110.
75 Ibid., pp. 11-22, 112-14.
76 See particularly ibid., pp. 147-63.

Richard Peters: a philosopher in the older style

R.K. Elliott

> Speaking with understanding they must hold fast to what is
> shared by all, as a city holds to its law, and even more firmly.
>
> *Heraclitus*, D.114

Richard Peters is widely regarded as an analytical philosopher,
and, at least in the earlier days of his career as a philosopher of
education, he seems to have seen himself in the same light. In his
inaugural lecture *Education as Initiation* he writes:

> Philosophy . . . means different things to different people. To the
> general public it suggests directives for living derived from deep
> probings into and ponderings on the meaning of life: for the
> professional philosopher it consists in a rigorous exploration of
> questions to do with the disciplined demarcation of concepts
> and the patient explication of the grounds of knowledge.[1]

He says that his predecessor, Louis Arnaud Reid, a metaphysician
and aesthetician, was sympathetic to the layman's view that the
task of the philosopher is to provide some kind of synoptic directive
for living, whereas he, Peters, was more concerned with becoming
clear about relatively concrete issues. In comparison with Louis
Reid, he says: 'I feel a very mundane fellow whose eyes are more
likely to be fixed on the brass-tacks or under the teacher's desk
than on the Form of the Good.'[2]

In the Introduction to *Ethics and Education* he says that
professional philosophers are embarrassed by the layman's
expectation of philosophy that it will provide high level directives
for education or for life: 'indeed, one of their main preoccupations
has been to lay bare such aristocratic pronouncements under the
analytic guillotine.'[3] He goes on immediately to say that professional philosophers 'cast themselves in the more mundane Lockian
role of underlabourers in the garden of knowledge'. It seems that,
from the professional point of view, pronouncements like Plato's
account of the Good are fit only for the tumbril or the
wheelbarrow, thence to the scaffold or the garden incinerator.

Peters accurately describes attitudes which were prevalent in analytical philosophy at the time he was writing, but it is questionable whether he properly understood his own.

Peters has produced a substantial body of analytical work on relatively concrete issues, chiefly in philosophical psychology: his book *The Concept of Motivation*,[4] for example, and the seventeen papers which comprise the first two parts of his anthology *Psychology and Ethical Development*.[5] This hammering in of brass tacks, none of them too far from the teacher's desk, amounts to a distinguished contribution to contemporary 'professional' work in philosophical psychology, and I suspect that many would consider it to contain his best and keenest philosophizing. I would not say, however, that his chief contribution to Philosophy of Education is to be found either in his treatment of relatively concrete issues or in his use of the analytical method. It is located, rather, in his reflections on the general nature of education and its relation to very general questions concerning 'the human condition', the nature of truth, the meaning of 'God', and the nature of the world; and, against this metaphysical background, in his reaffirmation of the Stoic ideal as the most appropriate attitude to life. In short, his work is most memorable and most stimulating in so far as he philosophizes according to the layman's conception of philosophy, rather than the professional philosopher's.

In a review of *Ethics and Education*, quoted by Peters in the preface to his anthology,[6] Abraham Edel suggested that Peters's thinking of himself as an analytical philosopher is one of the things which prevent him from properly understanding his own philosophical position. Peters replied that conceptual analysis is one philosophical instrument among others, and that its functions are strictly limited. He added that, in his opinion, whatever merits *Ethics and Education* may have, they derive more from his interest in psychology than his adherence to what Edel had called the 'British analytical school'—an opinion Edel would not have contested, since he had said as much himself. Edel had also asked whether Peters did not take his idea of what is worthwhile for granted, out of the Oxbridge educational tradition, without subjecting it to critical analysis, but this question did not attract Peters's serious attention. It seems that at the time of writing the Preface, in 1973, his self-understanding was no different than it had been when he wrote his inaugural lecture, and *Ethics and Education*. Yet the anthology contains 'Subjectivity and Standards'; and his Swarthmore Lecture had been delivered in 1972, and published the same year, in book form, under the title *Reason, Morality and Religion*.[7]

Neither of these works was written for a specialist audience of philosophers. 'Subjectivity and Standards' was a contribution to an interdisciplinary symposium about the role of the humanities in the universities.[8] The Swarthmore Lecture was delivered to a Quaker audience, and was offered, according to the terms of the Lectureship, as 'relating to the meaning and work of the Society of Friends'. Since both works were addressed to lay audiences Peters felt free to write them in a manner appropriate to laymen, rather than in the 'rigorous' analytical manner. He describes the analytical method, with approval, in the opening paragraph of 'Subjectivity and Standards', but says that to do the analytical job properly would require a whole book, which 'would be somewhat remote from the spirit and concerns of this group'. He decides, quite deliberately, to employ a different manner of philosophizing:

> I therefore propose to attempt something more synthetic and hazardous, to revert perhaps to the older style of philosophy in trying to discern some more general attitudes to the human predicament which lie behind our approach to the humanities.[9]

The pieces in the 'older style' are not mere popular versions of things already worked out in the rigorous technical mode. The Swarthmore Lecture, in particular, is very impressive, not the greatest of Peters's works on education, perhaps, but the least dispensable. Together with 'Subjectivity and Standards', it presents a framework of fundamental beliefs into which the positions he takes up in his other educational writings fit. On some matters these works in 'the older style' provide clearer statements or firmer indications of Peters's opinion than are obtainable elsewhere. It would be too fanciful to think of them as containing Peters's 'esoteric' doctrines, but they do provide keys which make it possible to see his educational work as a coherent whole. It seems strange that contents of such importance should have been presented to non-specialist audiences, rather than to professional philosophers. No doubt Peters thought it unseemly to offer for professional attention works in which the views stated were not provided with the *quasi*-scientific proofs which the analytic movement demanded.

Peters's views in his later papers on liberal education and the justification of education are closely related to the general position he articulates in the Swarthmore Lecture and 'Subjectivity and Standards'. And, despite appearances to the contrary, his earlier writings purporting to analyse the concept of education also properly belong to his work in 'the older style'. Dray effectively makes this clear in his criticism of Peters's account of education in

'Aims of Education'.[10] Dray argued that although ostensibly analysing the way the word 'education' is ordinarily used, Peters was covertly prescribing what education should be. Peters seemed sensitive to Dray's criticism, and in 'Education and the Educated Man'[11] he made some changes in his account of education in the light of it, acknowledging that the word was used in a broader sense (as 'upbringing') as well as in the narrower 'liberal' sense (as 'development of knowledge and understanding'). This distinction did not motivate Peters to produce an adequate analysis of the concept, however. Instead, he pointed out that in professional circles (i.e. among teachers and other educationalists) the word is now used almost exclusively in the narrow sense; thereafter he proceeds as if the narrow sense is the only sense of the word which is of interest to a philosopher of education as such. This was a strange position for an analytical philosopher to adopt. The argument implied in what Peters says and does is analogous to an argument that because professional psychologists agree in understanding 'mind' in terms of behaviour, the behaviourist sense is the only sense of the word which can possibly concern the philosophical psychologist.

The position Peters takes up in 'Education and the Educated Man' ought not to cause us surprise, however, because he had already adopted it, more explicitly, in his inaugural lecture. There he asks whether his decision to analyse the concept of education may not have put him on the way to essentialism, and replies that he does not much mind if it has.[12] He thinks that from the point of view of the teacher's task in the classroom education is essentially non-instrumental, an end in itself. The argument implicit here, also, is unsatisfactory, for any craftsman in his workshop sees what he is doing as an end in itself, in the sense that *qua* craftsman his overriding interest is simply in doing his job well, whether he be shoemaker, harness-maker, or whatever. Peters thinks that because teachers in practising their craft think of education as their *raison d'être*, and so as a final end for them, education is *essentially* an end in itself. The argument is no more deeply reflected than the argument from 'Education and the Educated Man', discussed above. Peters's declared intention is to clarify the concept of education, but he carries out this intention by articulating his preconception, rather than by seriously enquiring into the way the word is used.

In these early papers Peters does ask about the meanings of words, and so employs a method which can be called 'linguistic', and is broadly of the kind which is integral to the post-war 'conceptual analysis' associated with Oxford and the 'revolution in philosophy' to which Edel refers. There is little in common, however, between Peters and J.L. Austin. Austin used the linguistic method to create problems, which he then tried to solve by further analysis, and valued linguistic nuances as a means to deeper understanding. Peters uses it more to support positions he has adopted on other grounds.

It may look as if what he was doing in his early writings, when purporting to analyse the concept of education, was declaring his allegiance to a view of education (as non-instrumental) which was not in fact well supported by ordinary usage. It was a view which besides being central to the liberal tradition in educational thought, was fashionable among teachers and other educationists, not only in the classroom but in theoretical contexts also, and in public contexts generally. I do not think that he was actually making any such 'existential' commitment, since he does not give sufficiently clear indications of having been aware of what he was doing in that light. On the other hand, we have his declaration that he would not mind being an essentialist, and that is probably the best clue to what the basis of his view was, namely a supposed insight into the nature of education. Despite appearances to the contrary, in his early writings on the concept of education he was engaged not in philosophical analysis of the Oxford kind, but in philosophy of 'the older style'—hardly less so than in the Swarthmore Lecture or 'Subjectivity and Standards'.

In his reply to Edel, Peters intimated that the style of the 'British analytical movement', to which he thought of himself as belonging, was itself an older style of philosophizing than that of the contemporary school of 'conceptual analysis' with which, Peters thought, Edel associated him. It is true that a good deal of Peters's work is analytical in the sense that it seeks to break up an idea or nature or phenomenon into parts in order to obtain a clearer understanding of it, without going any more closely into how the key words connected with the idea, etc. are ordinarily used than would have been done in traditional empirical philosophy. This earlier analytical style is not the 'older style' to which Peters refers in 'Subjectivity and Standards'. Philosophy in 'the older style' is synthetic, comprehensive, directive, concerned with matters of the highest generality and the highest importance, encompassing both a metaphysical 'world-view' and a philosophy of life. Plato's *Republic* exemplifies it.

Peters was influenced by other traditional philosophers besides the British Empiricists—by Plato, Aristotle, Spinoza, Kant and Hegel especially. Of these, Kant seems to have had the greatest influence upon his world-view. His work is post-Kantian, however, in its recognition of the social determinants of mind and knowledge. This makes a great difference. It does not affect Peters's belief that education is primarily for the sake of the individual, but it amounts to shifting the *epistemological* centre of gravity outside the individual soul. This shift is made with considerable rhetorical emphasis, but Peters does not provide it with an adequate rationale.

In the inaugural lecture he makes an obscure and implausible claim that the infant's possession of even an 'embryonic' mind depends on its initiation into public standards.[13] In *The Logic of Education* he contents himself with the (tautological) claim that objectivity becomes possible only when experience and thought involve concepts shared in a public world,[14] a claim which signals both lack of interest in the pre-objective and rejection of the subjective-relative. In 'Subjectivity and Standards', he suggests, again implausibly, that the fundamental principles of the various forms of knowledge were established by generalizing certain (active and passive) shared responses, such as the feeling of pleasure and the tendencies to assimilation and accommodation.[15] None of this takes him very far towards justifying the shift of epistemological emphasis from the individual to the public.

Although his writings contain original work in ethics and philosophical psychology, Peters's interest in epistemology and philosophy of language is slight in comparison. There is nothing in his work remotely resembling Wittgenstein's critique of the possibility of a private language, nor is there evidence of any close acquaintance with Wittgenstein's work, or of a general reliance upon him in which his general positions, or some of them, are taken for granted. Consequently, because of the great emphasis he places upon public standards, the notion of 'what is shared' acquires a character, in his work, rather like that of a fundamental principle in a metaphysical system.

Peters makes it clear in his Swarthmore Lecture that his philosophy of life is founded on the Stoic precept that one should remedy such ills as can be remedied and accept without complaint those which cannot.[16] More than this, his work is pervaded by Stoic moods, attitudes and values: individualism, for example, universalism, faith in truth and reason, respect for autonomy, distrust of utopianism, a keen sense of the human predicament, compassionate detachment, the advocacy and practice of self-control, reverence for the world and for the individual experiencing it. What in Peters we superficially take to be Kantian is often more profoundly attributable to a temperament of the same general kind as Kant's, and to a mind which was nourished directly by the classical past.

His work also exhibits something akin to the dogmatism for which the Stoics were so persistently criticized by the Platonists in antiquity. Peters's educational thought is based on a group of principles which were foundations of Greek philosophical ethics at least from the time of Socrates. They are: (i) that there is a universal human good; (ii) that the good for man is immanent in, not transcendent of, human life; (iii) that it is immanent in the *individual* life; (iv) that there is no separation between education and life, of which education is a part: in the process of obtaining the educational good the learner is already living the good life.

By keeping in mind how fundamental these principles are to Peters's thought, we can better understand some aspects of it which would otherwise seem strange. An example is his perfunctory treatment of Marxism. He criticizes Marxists on the ground that they lack a proper perspective on time, sacrificing the present to the future.[17] But intelligent and devoted furtherance of the Marxist end would normally satisfy all Peters's criteria for an activity's being worthwhile. It is not even true that satisfaction would be indefinitely postponed, since people normally derive satisfaction from achieving proximate ends, and there are plenty of intermediate stages along the way to working-class hegemony. As for proximate failures, and uncertainty about ultimate success, these are obstacles just as much for those engaged in theoretical pursuits, but are not considered prohibitive of human good to them. Peters's real objection to Marxism is that for Marxists the good of the individual is subordinate to a transcendent (collective) good. This subordination legitimates the suppression or diminution of individual good for the sake of the collective, and is fundamentally opposed to one of Peters's deepest beliefs. It is hard to grasp why such a comprehensible point of view should have been expressed in a way which seems to trivialize it; but Peters has, in effect, disguised his dogmatic individualism as a rational refusal arbitrarily to prefer one of the ecstasies of time to another. Unfortunately, this abstract argument lacks motivational force.[18]

In the following section I shall compare Peters's philosophy—in so far as it is a world-view and philosophy of life—with that of Heraclitus, not in order to establish direct influence (though there was some) but as an aid in constructing an exegesis of these aspects of Peters's philosophy, and in bringing out their 'older style'. Stoic philosophy is too voluminous and diverse to be easily put to the same uses, but I shall sometimes refer to it also. The Stoics were deeply indebted to Heraclitus, however, and comparison with him will bring out some of Peters's similarities with them. Heraclitus' work, though it concerns the individual, is addressed not to the

47

individual himself, in the intimate manner of Epictetus or Marcus Aurelius, but to a more public audience ('society in general'), and this is the case also with Peters, though he has in mind, particularly, those responsible for educating the young. Finally, Heraclitus' metaphysics, like Peters's, is only sketched: the greater elaboration of Stoic metaphysics makes it less useful for the purpose of elucidating Peters by comparison.

Heraclitus urges his hearers to 'hold fast to what is shared', the *logos*. A similar injunction lies at the heart of Peters's philosophy of education. Nothing is of greater importance, in his view, than that civilization should be preserved and enhanced. Civilization is constituted by language, within which 'forms of knowledge and understanding' like science, religion, etc. are 'more differentiated' developments. He stresses that learning 'the language and concepts of a people' is not just a matter of learning how to use words correctly:

> It is a grave error to regard the learning of a language as a
> purely instrumental matter, as a tool in the service of purposes,
> standards, feelings and beliefs. For in a language is distilled a
> view of the world which is constituted by them. In learning a
> language the individual is initiated into a public inheritance
> which his parents and teachers are inviting him to share.[19]

In his inaugural lecture he remarks that children 'start off in the position of the barbarian outside the gates',[20] and that the task of education is to get them on the inside of the activities and modes of thought and conduct which define a civilized form of life. He defends his use of the initiation analogy by saying that 'education consists in experienced persons turning the eye of others towards what is essentially independent of persons'[21]—not towards the Form of the Good, but the objects of the public world, and the objective realms correlated with the special languages of the forms of knowledge. Having objects of the various categories which belong to the public world, and to the special domains, as objects of one's consciousness—being intentionally related to them, in other words—is what Peters means by 'being on the inside' of language and the forms of knowledge. The same opinion, and even the image he uses are found in Heraclitus: 'Eyes and ears are poor witnesses for men if their souls (*psychai*) do not understand the language' (literally, 'if they have barbarian souls').[22]

What we ordinarily think of as 'the language and concepts of a people' does not include the various specialized languages (of the sciences and humanities) to which Peters attaches such great educational importance. That the child's very humanity depends on his learning a native language is plausible, but the powerful arguments which can be employed to justify education at the primary level do not also justify initiation into the sciences and other academic disciplines.

Since Peters, in effect, defines democracy as a way of life in which differences on matters of policy are resolved by discussion, education as initiation can be seen to be essential for and conducive to the preservation of democracy, as he understands it. Learning a native language involves, to some degree, the learning of 'morals' also, the fundamental principles of which are truth-telling, respect for persons, and impartial consideration of interests. Hence learning a shared language creates the possibility of a level of impersonality at which disputes can be settled by discussion without either party having merely to surrender its interests to the other.

Essential to moral argument, Peters maintains, and indeed to rational discussion in general, is that the participants should abandon their egocentric perspectives and rise to the impersonal level of the universal. He believes that the greatest hindrance to this ascent are certain passions, like fear, anger and pride, which, when they are expressions of self-love, tend to install those who suffer them in narrow perspectives from which they tend to misunderstand the situations they are in, and are unable to recognize that other people's interests are as worthy of consideration as their own. He has a deep and painful sense of the danger inherent in unreflected passion. In his paper 'Education and Justification: a Reply'[23] he defends his conception of the educated man against the criticism that it is too limited to be inspiring as an educational ideal, by expressing his conviction that in our society we are as far from achieving this limited and allegedly uninspiring ideal as England are from regaining the World Cup—a remark which owes its disturbing effectiveness not to the banal comparison, but to the allusion it makes to football hooliganism, and through that to the whole violent tenor of the present age. Even more revealingly, in his Swarthmore Lecture he draws attention to: '. . . the awesome spectacle of human beings trying to make some sort of sense of the world and trying to sustain and cultivate a crust of civilization over the volcanic core of atavistic emotions.'[24] He seems here to be alluding to the threat of an outburst of passion on an enormous and terrifying scale. It would not be an exaggeration to say that in Peters's view the survival of humanity, as such, depends upon the general development of self-control, since the non-violent resolution of conflicts of interests depends on it.

Heraclitus asserts that *hybris* must be quenched quicker than a blazing fire,[25] his idea being that lawless violence is a threat to social unity and the common good.[26] He says that it is hard to fight against anger (*thymos*) because it 'buys whatever it wants at the expense of soul',[27] i.e. by carrying the individual away, to the detriment of his own life and the lives of others.[28] Both philosophers express the same abhorrence for practical wilfulness and recklessness, the ancient more fiercely, the modern more perturbedly, but who can wonder at that, granted the fearful predictions that seem so reasonable now?

For Heraclitus, 'what is shared' is not just language and the objective world it subtends, but also truth. Peters uses the expression 'forms of knowledge' advisedly, because, in his case also, what is shared, ideally, and what the parties in a rational discussion accept as their common aim, is truth. He recognizes that each form of knowledge could employ concepts different from those it actually does, but whatever concepts it uses, acceptance by its practitioners of propositions of the sort it seeks to establish rests upon the consonance of these propositions with what is given to sense; and what is given to sense is also, and necessarily, given in terms of whatever concepts are used. In 'Subjectivity and Standards' he makes it clear that all the forms of knowledge are alike in this respect. They all rest upon an external 'given' which is received, in some conceptually organized form, by what Peters calls 'shared responses'. These include sense-perception, as we ordinarily understand it, but also the responses through or by which we recognize values in moral, aesthetic and religious contexts. These 'responses' are thought of as senses, or as close analogues of senses, and the relevant forms of knowledge as capable of formulating and establishing truths, or such close analogues to truths that it would be misleading to call them by any other name.

If morality, aesthetics and religion are inferior to science, which Peters regards as the paradigm of knowledge, it is not because they are not forms of knowledge at all, but because the special senses upon which they depend are not so reliable as the senses of sight and learning, on which science is able so predominantly to rely. This is why, in the Swarthmore Lecture, Peters says that he would feel nervous in the presence of people who had 'chosen' to think that suffering is bad or unfairness intolerable. At first sight, Peters's remark seems strange, for he had been saying that at some point in the regression upon principles we come down to considerations which are *not* chosen.[29] What he means, however, is that fundamental moral principles are not *normally* chosen; and the reason for the uneasiness he would feel in the presence of exceptional persons who *have* chosen them is that, in his view, these will be persons who lack moral sense. Similarly, a person who lacks a capacity for aesthetic response, and simply chooses what he will consider beautiful, is unlikely to inspire confidence among lovers of the Arts. In the Preface to his anthology he remarks that in both morals and religion he remains 'unrepentantly a crude fellow', objecting to the contemporary tendency to side-track 'awkward questions about the truth of religious beliefs' by providing an analysis of the role of religious beliefs in the life of the believer.[30] In the Swarthmore Lecture he provides an account of the religious as a form of knowledge founded upon a religious sense (a sense of awe), which has as its appropriate objects such things as the human situation and the contingency of the world. Presumably, statements attributing substantial existence to a God or gods do not belong to the religious form of knowledge at all.

In *Ethics and Education* Peters says the 'attitude of passionate concern for truth' lies at the heart of any system that is based on discussion and argument.[31] In his Swarthmore Lecture he quotes with approval E.M. Forster: 'Yes, for we fight for more than Love or Pleasure: there is Truth. Truth counts. Truth does count.'[32] Earlier in the Lecture, speaking in his own voice, he says:

> A man who uses his reason must feel, first of all, that he must get to the bottom of things; he wants to find out what is the case, what the right thing is to do or think. . . . Truth matters to him.[33]

These remarks would be misleading if we were to infer from them that Peters attaches any great educational importance to theoretical enquiry simply for its own sake. His interest is primarily in the development of practical reason, only secondarily in theoretical studies, which are necessary to illuminate practical choice and, in general, to assist us in determining what to do. Consequently, the strong emphasis on enquiry—the *pursuit* of truth—which is so characteristic of Dewey, is replaced, in Peters, by an emphasis on *concern* for truth. Peters writes of this concern as 'passionate', but the epithet is descriptive rather than intensive. A person has concern for truth if he has passions such as love of clarity, consistency, order and precision, and hatred of their opposites. The fundamental passion is love of truth itself, but it is to be understood from the point of view of the individual in his practical situation. It does not include love of speculative thought, or theoretical study in general, or of any theoretical study simply as such.

Admittedly, in his early work Peters argued that a commitment to 'what is internal to worthwhile activities, be it the pursuit of truth for its own sake or the determination to make something of a fitting form'[34] is a necessary condition of being educated; and he tended to confuse pursuing truth as an absolute end *within* a discipline with having no ulterior motive in practising the discipline. In his later essays, however, this demand for purity of heart in worthwhile activities is explicitly relinquished, and with it the last trace of the earlier view that the development of a love of theoretical enquiry entirely for the sake of discovering theoretical truth, without reference to practice, is an aim—even a minor aim—of education. The primacy of the practical in Peters's philosophy of education may seem surprising, but it is characteristically Stoic, and Heraclitean.

Heraclitus remarks that 'although the account (*logos*) is shared, most men live as though their thinking (*phronesis*) were a private possession.'[35] In exegesis of this passage, Charles H. Kahn writes as follows:

> In sum, the *logos* is 'common' because it is (or expresses) a structure that characterizes all things, and is therefore a public possession in principle available to all men, since it is 'given' in the immanent structure of their shared experience. The *logos* is also shared as a principle of agreement between diverse powers of understanding between speaker and hearer, of public unity and joint action among the members of a political community. The *logos* is all these things because the term signifies not only meaningful speech, but the exercise of intelligence as such, the activity of *nous* or *phronesis*. The deepest thought of *xynos logos*, more fully expressed in [D.114], is that what unites men is their rationality, itself the reflection of the underlying unity of nature.[36]

Kahn concludes that in Heraclitus *logos* means not simply language but rationality as experienced in thought, speech and action. The importance Peters attaches to rationality is abundantly evident in his work, as for example in his advocacy of 'concern for truth' discussed above. By the time of the Swarthmore Lecture, however, he was operating with an enriched concept of rationality, broader than Heraclitus's, broader even than that of the Stoics, and containing a good deal that one might be inclined to attribute to faculties other than reason.

He does not conceive reason as merely an inferential faculty. Neither does he confine it to thought (cognition), but argues that it depends upon and is unthinkable without certain passions such as love of clarity and truth and hatred of confusion and error. On this ground he rejects the common antithesis between reason and passion, maintaining also that one of the functions of reason is to convert and control the emotions. The force of wayward emotions is confronted and defeated by the calm but strong rational passions; it is by virtue of our desire to see things as they really are and our hatred of self-delusion that we strive to prevent our vision from being confined within narrow egocentric limits. Thus Peters incorporates into reason what Plato calls 'spirit' (*thymos*).

He also attributes to reason certain creative functions. Chief among these is meaning-giving, whereby our merely natural life is raised to a more civilized level. Sex, eating and fighting, for example, have been transformed by being brought under standards, so that exercise of these activities has come to involve skill, taste and moral sensitivity. Such transformations serve to improve the quality of life, which Peters considers to be the fundamental concern of education.[37] There is an obvious analogy between transforming natural activities by incorporating standards into them, and the invention of language in general and the various differentiated forms of knowledge. According to Peters, these also were produced by introducing standards into primitive responses and behaviour, and he considers them, more than anything else, to be constitutive of civilization.

He makes the analogy explicit in 'Subjectivity and Standards', and in doing so draws attention to the forms of knowledge as products of human creativity. This makes his account seem very like that given by Nietzsche in a piece which he wrote originally as an Introduction to the *Birth of Tragedy*, but which was published only posthumously in *The Will to Power*.[38] In it, Nietzsche classifies all the various 'forms of knowledge' as Art, and sees them as inventions by which man, cast into an otherwise desolate and meaningless existence, succeeds in making his life seem to him worthwhile.

Nietzsche represents the arts and sciences as being not forms of knowledge but forms of illusion, and ascribes value to them precisely on that account: 'We possess Art lest we perish of the truth.'[39] Peters goes so far as to describe the physical sciences as 'perhaps the finest product that yet exists of the sustained and controlled imagination of the human race',[40] thus paying a tribute to creativity, but he is far from regarding science, or any of the other disciplines, as less than forms of knowledge in the full traditional sense of the word. Unlike Nietzsche, he does not see overcoming nihilism as the supreme challenge to human creativity, because there is no trace in him of the kind of intense and radical scepticism one finds in Nietzsche. Instead, there is unclouded faith in the beneficial power of truth, and in the truth-bearing character of the traditional disciplines. It is impossible to imagine him knowingly glorifying illusion as a means of enhancing the quality of life. So, even here, where he is concerned with the creative power of reason, and where his position seems so close to that of a great modern 'existentialist' philosopher, his true affinity is much more with a Stoic philosopher like Posidonius, concerning whom Ludwig Edelstein writes as follows:

> In the writings of the younger Stoics . . . a new tone becomes noticeable. The human arts are said to create a second nature, as it were. Posidonius traces in detail the triumph of the human mind that has led man from the most primitive life at the dawn of history to the height of civilization; and he glories in the achievement of man, who by his own efforts alone has overcome the hardships and shortcomings of the situation in which nature, his stepmother, has placed him. The god who speaks through reason has achieved the miracle against all obstacles that nature put in his way.[41]

Another creative function Peters attributes to reason, and considers as a means of improving the quality of life, is that of enhancing the individual's conception of activities in which he is engaged. He points out that in Spinoza's opinion 'the important thing for a man is to grasp the patterns and relationships which structure his life.' This is part of what Spinoza meant when he said that it is the hallmark of Reason to view things 'under a certain aspect of eternity or necessity'.[42] In his own treatment of this capacity for broadening one's view, Peters construes it as a more general capacity, rather than as a contemplative power specifically relating to eternity and necessity. He says that human activities are largely constituted by the conception men have of them:

> . . . a person committed to reason will tend to transform many mundane activities by conceptualization, and by linking them up with other things in life, which will make them much more absorbing and interesting.[43]

In this way, also, as well as by introducing standards into them, we determine what activities like sex and smoking are to be for us.

This transforming of activities by connecting them up with other things is Peters's version of what earlier liberal educationists like Arnold and Newman called 'expansion of the intellect'. The difference is that in the earlier thinkers broadening of outlook was associated with the idea of cross-cultural comparisons acting as incentives to critical reflection. In Peters, the expansion envisaged is entirely constructive, a matter of loading activities with significances, and so with values, and at the same time contributing towards the individual's gathering his life into a synthetic unity. It is one of the ways in which the individual 'makes sense of his life', and, indeed, makes a whole life of it. The notion of the individual as the artist of his own life was a commonplace among the Stoics, and can be found also in Aristotle.[44]

Finally, for Heraclitus, 'what is shared', the *logos*, is understood not just as language, truth and reason, but also as the unifying formative aspect of Being, of the universe and the psyche alike.[45] The *logos* is also this same principle *qua* object of reflective thought,—'existing in the understanding', so to speak. Peters does not have so determinate a metaphysic as Heraclitus—for whom 'this universe is an ever-living fire, with measures of it kindling and measures going out'[46]—but there is a more general similarity between them. Peters's appreciation of the importance for 'world-making' of shared concepts leave his sense of the reality of independent Being undiminished. He stresses that the variability of concepts does not make Nature conducive to our present wishes and purposes. We cannot, simply by changing our concepts, make flesh impenetrable by steel, or even change the consistency of putty.[47] The shared world in which we live is one into which Being everywhere obtrudes. It discloses itself constantly as that which has to be reckoned with, and cannot be got round or fixed up—in death, for example, but also, as we have seen, in every kind of physical necessity, in our having to experience the world as it appears to our senses, for example, without being able to determine what impressions we experience merely by willing them to be such and such. Peters refers to all this as 'contingency' or 'givenness'. Though contingency is met with everywhere in ordinary life, reflection can make us aware of the contingency of the universe as a whole. Peters describes this awareness in Kantian terms, as the recognition that no explanation of the existence of the universe is available, or even possible for us.[48] He goes on to assert the givenness not only of the universe but of certain powers of the subject, including shared senses and other responses such as assimilation and accommodation (the natural basis of our shared concept of causality.)[49] Language and the world come into being simultaneously through the coming together of the being of the subject and the being to which the subject is intentionally related, in a context of being with others—the 'social dimension', which Peters rightly stresses. Hence the world is constituted not by entirely separate individuals, nor even by 'consciousness', but by a *collective* subject; and because of the historicity of language and other 'traditions', by a *historical* subject—in other words, by what the Marxists call 'species man'.

Peters does not make this last aspect of the ontological basis of his position explicit, however; nor is he interested in any further analysis and development of his metaphysical views. His most fundamental response to Being is not speculative, but religious:

> Religion, as I understand it, is grounded on experiences of awe, an emotion to which human beings are subject when they are confronted with events, objects or people which are of overwhelming significance to them but which seem, in some important respect or other, inexplicable and shot through with contingency.[50]

He goes on to say that the appropriate response to a situation in which one feels awe is worship, and that worship is the attempt to express the sense of the impressiveness and significance of the object of awe. Thus one may use the word 'God', as Whitehead does, to express the awe one feels when appreciating the ultimate contingency of the world. Peters thinks that it is unnecessary, however, to express this awe by creating a picture of a 'friend behind the scenes': 'What extra work does the postulation of a spirit behind the phenomena do?'[51]

The feeling of awe is most keenly aroused in Peters when he contemplates 'the predicament of any man trying to make something of his life'.[52] It dawns upon us, gradually, he says, that 'we have to make something of the brief span of years that is our lot', and the pathos of the human situation increases when we take into account the pointlessness of human life.[53] By calling life 'pointless' he means that man has no teleological 'function', natural or metaphysical, which determines how he ought to live.

Nowadays there are very many people who share this view, and Peters may be thought to have expressed it too dramatically by using the word 'pointless', which creates a suggestion of despair. I do not think either that he was being over-dramatic, or that the contemplation of the human situation induced in him any deep and lasting sense of despair. It is not just the fact that man's being-in-the-world is inexplicable, with no personal God or impersonal Destiny to give it meaning, that Peters finds overwhelmingly significant, but that man has to 'make sense' of the world and of his life in it. What Peters feels is awe, not despair, and the feeling of awe is accompanied by what seems like the immediate acceptance of a responsibility to discern and create significance within life.

Unlike Sartre, Peters does not even consider the possibility that the universe might be thought and felt to be redundant, and the invitation to find value in it refused. Unlike Nietzsche, he does not deliberately affirm life for the sake of its joy which is worth more than all its pain. It does not occur to him to ask whether making sense of life is worth what life will cost in suffering, either for the individual or for mankind. He neither chooses to give meaning to life, nor 'plumps' for it, because the possibility of an alternative never presents itself to him. His response to Being-in-totality and to human being-in-the-world, on the contemplation of them, is one of piety. It happens to be inconsistent with his declared opinion that significance, including value, can only be discovered or created *within* life, for he attaches what is, according to his own account, a religious significance to that which gives and discovers meaning and that which receives and discloses it. These are not life, as Peters uses the expression, but the grounds and conditions of it.

Nevertheless, it is difficult not to believe that what makes the thought of the genesis of meaning overwhelmingly significant for Peters are the meanings already created and discovered in the public traditions. It is in the light of what has already been accomplished and handed on that he responds to the thought of Being with a feeling of piety. It is hardly surprising, therefore, that he believes that the public traditions are themselves proper objects of humility and reverence.[54] In terms of his own account, it would not have been inappropriate if, using religious language in a manner characteristic of the later Stoics, he had said that God was incarnate in them.

There is a certain blandness and complacency about Peters's thought which is distasteful to those who identify with the excessively critical and resentful tendencies of the present time. Reverence is hardly fashionable now, and destruction and reconstruction of intellectual traditions seems more attractive than patient submission to them. These are only accidental temperamental differences between him and his younger contemporaries. But, irrespective of questions of temperament, we regard a refusal to go to the limit in asking questions as a deficiency in a philosopher. Whether our attitude is justifiable in his particular case is problematical, however, for how many of us are any more capable than Peters is of answering, without preconception, the question whether human life is worthwhile? If our answer is already given when the question is asked, what advantage do we have over him, which justifies us in criticizing him? We could perhaps say that at least we acknowledge the existence of the question, and so admit that there is a worm at the heart of the rose. But a person of Stoical disposition, as Peters is, cannot be expected to attach any importance to making an acknowledgment which would be emotionally disturbing and yet lack point. What work would it do? Though his writings are not addressed to the individual, it is the individual whom Peters has always in mind, and the life he has to lead. From the standpoint of his benevolent practical concern, he cannot blamelessly allow himself to be distracted by idle speculations. Whether it is to our taste or not, we need to recognize that he is a philosopher in an older style, and the style is Stoical, as he himself acknowledges.

Peters's enrichment of the concept of reason gives rise to ambiguity and creates the possibility of tensions within it. There is a possibility of conflict between the dispositions which make up 'concern for truth'. Hatred of error, for example, may incline us towards vagueness and obscurity, over-riding our love of precision and clarity. According to Peters, love of order and consistency are central to reason, but they are not sufficient for truth, and have often been preferred to it. A mode of life in which values internal to concern for truth are extensively preferred to truth itself is readily conceivable. This is one thing which makes it difficult to grasp exactly what Peters's 'reasonable level of life' would be like.

Another is the ambiguity in Peters's key word 'reasonable', when it is used in practical contexts. So far as his explicit theory goes, his conception of practical reasoning is of deliberation which seeks to discover what is to be done. It aims at truth and is dominated by concern for truth. It is not a separate and distinct form of knowledge but a combination of the moral and empirical forms. Since in concrete contexts moral reasoning is of this same mixed type, Peters tends in effect, to identify the practical with the moral. Stoic philosophy had the same tendency, from which in some part its sublimity derives.

Practical reason serves different purposes in different situations, but when there are conflicts of interests it may enable disputants to settle their differences without recourse to violence, a function which Peters recognizes and values. But to decide what *shall* be done in situations when the primary aim is accommodation of interests it is not normally necessary to discover what *is to be* done (i.e. the truly just thing to do). It is systematically unclear whether Peters's concern is to raise the semi-barbarous majority to the ordinary civilized level at which interests are harmonized through discussion, or to raise the ordinary civilized standard closer to the moral ideal, which is approximation to moral truth. These two ends do not form a continuum and are not always compatible. Peters gives the impression that practical reasonableness is the quest for moral truth *whereby* differences are resolved by discussion. But a general increase in degree of concern for moral truth will not necessarily mean an increase in the democratic capacity for accommodating conflicting interests, especially if there are sharp differences about what the moral truth is. Moral progress is not *ipso facto* progress towards social harmony.

Starting from what is realistically accomplishable, and attributing that kind of accomplishment to 'reason', Peters goes on to envisage a more ideal state of affairs, as if that is accomplishable by more of the same 'reason', without closely considering what in fact the nature of the intervening stages would have to be. The strain of idealistic puritanism so evident in his work is as basic in him as it is in Milton, and, as suggested above, has similarly strong classical, as well as Christian, antecedents.

Peters makes considerable use of a notion of 'demands of reason'. This notion is unproblematical so long as we understand by it such logical principles as the laws of non-contradiction and excluded middle. But he conceives reason also as demanding that questions be asked and answered for the sake of ascertaining truth. Originally, he construed these demands in an extreme manner, and on this basis provided a somewhat intimidatory 'justification' of education. In his later work he seems to have replaced this justification with a gentler and more credible version, and to have modified his notion of the demands of reason correspondingly. The new justification is, however, associated with a further and more serious problem, which calls into question Peters's hitherto confident orientation of education towards objectivity and away from the subjective-relative.

In *Ethics and Education* he argues that seriously to ask 'Why do this rather than that?' means that the questioner, having willed knowledge as an end, is already committed 'embryonically' to the means to its attainment, and the question is such that some degree of mastery of all the various 'forms of knowledge' is necessary for answering it.[55] Hence a need for, and a justification of, education as initiation into the public traditions. The impression Peters gives is that reason not only has jurisdiction over the individual soul, directing it to ends as well as regulating means, but also exercises a continuous psychological constraint upon it to engage in enquiry of ever-wider scope and greater depth. But the notion of embryonic commitment is ambiguous. Peters might have meant *prima facie* commitment, revocable when the full extent of what was involved in answering the question became clear or on some other ground.

In fact, he seems to have meant *unlimited* commitment, the infinitude of which the serious individual discovers only gradually as reason makes further and further demands upon him—a Faustian kind of commitment, to be sure. Escape from this state of bondage can be gained only at the cost of not seriously asking this or any other practical question. So the choice, for every individual, is between being either more reflective than Hamlet or less reflective than Laertes.

Fortunately, the predicament supposedly created by reason and its demands is illusory, because the seriousness that would have to be abandoned is that of the scientist or philosopher or other person who has made a profession of enquiry, not that of the ordinary person. How far the ordinary person should pursue his enquiry does not depend simply on whether further relevant questions can intelligibly be asked, but on what best serves his interest, and prudence is unlikely to counsel him to spend too long a time on theoretical enquiry.

It looks as if, in his later work, Peters abandoned the view that reason makes unlimited demands universally. In these later papers he develops his notion of the human predicament, and considers its consequences for education. In 'Education and Justification: a Reply' he mentions a region of concern—most commonly known, perhaps, as 'the human condition'—which, he says, is 'the region in which the demands of reason should operate', and 'whose boundaries should determine the extent to which questioning should be pressed'.[56] In 'Ambiguities in Liberal Education' he writes of 'questions arising from the general conditions of human life', answers to which 'provide a general framework of beliefs and attitudes through which particular ends are sought and particular puzzles arise'.[57] He provides examples of the kind of question he has in mind:

> What is he [the educand] to make of objects in the natural world and of phenomena such as the dark, thunder, the tides, time and the changes of the seasons? What is he to make of other people and of their reactions to him and to each other? What is he to think about himself and about questions of ownership? What attitude is he to take towards the cycle of birth, marriage and death? In what way is he to react to authority and violence?[58]

Peters thinks of these questions concerning the human condition as relevant to everyone, including those who are not presently interested in reflecting on them. To answer them, the employment of all the 'forms of knowledge' would be required. This constitutes a new justification of education as initiation into public traditions, and it is one which does not need to presuppose that the individual is subject to limitless rational demands. Thus a way of retreat from the earlier, untenable, position is opened up.

It seems that Peters came to adopt the view that reason does not demand that questions concerning the human condition should be raised, but that if they are, then 'the demands of reason should operate'. He might be taken as meaning that if learners do raise such questions, reason demands that they pursue them without limit. If so, then they are little better off than they were under his earlier dispensation. I think, however, that all he means is that enquiry within the various disciplines into general questions concerning aspects of the human condition should proceed in the manner which is normal for those disciplines. Specialists in them will engage in the pursuit of truth with that passion for enquiry which we presume to be their dominant disposition. Non-specialist learners, however, are no longer thought of as conscripted by reason into unlimited intellectual activity but, more realistically, as freely engaging in their interdisciplinary studies with whatever degree of seriousness they naturally have, or their teachers can induce in them. Peters says that a major contemporary educational problem is that of finding a way of presenting to non-specialist learners knowledge which has been developed in the disciplines, which is highly relevant to the human condition, and which is likely to influence their beliefs concerning it.[59] This is consistent with what I take to be his later view. I think, therefore, that although he did not enquire into the matter specifically, he nevertheless modified his beliefs concerning the demands of reason. At least, he reached a point from which it would have been very easy for him to have done so.

Peters elucidates what it is to 'make sense' of life partly in terms of the creative, connective activity of reason discussed above, and partly in terms of asking and answering questions about the human condition. In both cases there is ambiguity or tension between the individual and the universal. Is it the individual who conceptually connects his activities, or the public culture which connects these kinds of activities? Are the questions about the human condition answerable within the public traditions or only by private decision? This tension constitutes a threat to the very close connection Peters made in his earlier work between education and objectivity.

In 'Ambiguities in Liberal Education' Peters writes of the need to develop beliefs and attitudes which will help a person 'to make sense of and take up some stance towards the various situations and predicaments that he will inevitably encounter as a human being'.[60] In 'Education and Justification: a Reply' he says of the human condition, as an area of significance and concern, that it 'will combine areas of concern common to any human being with individual emphases and idiosyncrasies'.[61] In these remarks there is a suggestion that an aim, or hope, of the educator is that, on the basis of what he learns in the disciplines, each learner should begin to form a coherent personal world-view and life-philosophy. Strength is lent to this suggestion by Peters's claim, in the Swarthmore Lecture, that various attitudes to religion, including both faith and the rejection of religion altogether, are open to a rational man, and by the fact that his own attitude is different from both of these. Thus Peters seems to have acknowledged the incapacity of the disciplines, including morals, philosophy and religion, to determine adequately what ought to be believed about matters of the highest importance, and what attitudes ought to be adopted towards these things. He seems to have envisaged the creation of incompatible and even mutually antagonistic personal interpretations by individuals of their being-in-the-world, of which his own Stoic view of life is one. This lends his philosophical endeavour a somewhat tragic aspect: 'The world of the waking is one and shared, but the sleeping turn aside each into his private world.'[62]

Love of truth demands of Peters that he recognize that the only justifiable attitudes to many of the questions which arise out of reflection on the human situation and condition are agnostic ones. It cannot acquiesce in the construction of non-objective personal world-views and views of life, and there is no form of knowledge recognized by Peters and Hirst in which these constructions could be made. In the Swarthmore Lecture, however, prominence is given to the creative functions of reason, and by the criteria which are relevant to *these* functions, even the personal decisions by which the individual *Weltanschauung* is formed would count as rational choices. They would be choices of the sort artists make, however. Thus the passionate concern for truth is subordinated to the values involved in 'making sense' of things and giving order and unity to one's life.

I doubt whether Peters has fully grasped the magnitude of the departure from his earlier position which is involved in his later tendency to emphasize the educational importance of reflection on the human condition. What is clear is that in his later work he is anxious that individual learners should construct their world-views out of materials which have satisfied the discipline's criteria of truth or probability, or of having some warrant, or at least of not being demonstrably false or invalid or incorrect. (Alternative materials might be derived from myths, *pseudo*-sciences, wishes, and prejudices of various kinds.)

But if the truth, etc. of these materials is of the first importance, it is imperative that the disciplines themselves should be free, so far as is humanly possible, from hindrance and distortions which would reduce their capacity for the establishment of truth. Peters's and Hirst's failure to elaborate their account of forms of knowledge beyond the very primitive sketch they supply in *The Logic of Education* is one of the most serious weaknesses in their educational philosophy. They emphasize, however, that the forms are historical institutions, which have undergone a long period of evolution. Peters praises Hegel and Marx for their vivid awareness of the 'social dimension of mind', specifically mentioning Hegel's notion of objective mind, articulated in institutions.[63] It is surprising that, having so stressed the social and historical character of the forms of knowledge, he should provide such an *a priori* account of their character in 'Subjectivity and Standards', where besides arguing that truth is what gives them all point, he argues that the standards of each are formed by the generalization of particular responses. But the aims and procedures of historical institutions, especially if these have the character of languages, will tend to be extremely complex, and to be discoverable only by resolute and sensitive empirical enquiry. An educational theory which does not even try to look and see what they are, but takes an idealized conception of science as the measure against which the other disciplines appear, in their various degrees, to fall short, is likely to have unfortunate educational consequences, not least in the aesthetic domain. For it will underwrite and advocate standards and procedures which are inappropriate to disciplines whose ends it has misconceived.

One would have expected a philosopher who proclaims the social and historical character of the forms of knowledge to have been sensitive to the work of sociologists of knowledge, such as Schutz, for example, to philosophers like Husserl and Scheler who have produced important work in this area, and to some of the able contemporary sociologists of knowledge working in the analytical and phenomenological traditions. Among these thinkers some are deeply concerned with the relations of the special disciplines to their sources in ordinary language and the 'natural attitude'. Many are keenly aware of the complexity of the procedures and motivations of the disciplines, and of the discrepancies which frequently exist between the aims actually being pursued and those which the practitioners believe their discipline to be pursuing. Peters shows very little interest in the sociology of knowledge, however, and what interest he does show is unsympathetic.[64] He does not anywhere acknowledge that the disciplines stand in need of thoroughgoing interdisciplinary investigation and critique. His attitude seems to be that they are self-correcting and should be trusted absolutely.

This may be because he tends to think of the forms as objective mind, teleologically directed towards the faithful and adequate reflection of a reality which is itself orderly; and developing, in accordance with its own principle, towards the fullest possible articulation and internal differentiation. This Hegelian picture is imaginatively attractive, but not really conducive to the health of the disciplines. Peters may also have been influenced by the thought of the circularity involved in the idea of reason criticizing itself. The specialized disciplines are not identical with reason itself, however, and are demonstrably capable of being illuminated by historical, sociological and philosophical enquiry.

Peters shows excessive reverence for standards generally, not only in the disciplines, but also in connexion with improvement of the quality of life. He does not ask, in some cases, whether the introduction of standards into 'natural' activities may not be worth the price it exacts. The standards introduced into sexual relations in the Middle Ages, for example, by the Arab poets of Andalusia and the troubadours, and the connexions they made between sex, love, honour and religion, may have given rise to a sweet new style in behaviour as well as in poetry, but they were also responsible for a great deal of guilt, anguish and despair. Standards cannot be relied upon to make life worthwhile, any more than they can be relied on for the establishment of truth and the proper ends of the disciplines generally. Continuous critical reflection upon them is required if the quality of life and the health of the discipline is to be preserved and improved.

Reverence for standards prevents Peters from appreciating the strength of the progressive educationalists' case. He refutes the extreme view that no standards whatever shoud be applied to children's work, and that they should be allowed simply to express themselves and 'do their own thing'. Less extreme progressivists do not reject standards altogether, however, but object to the use of too rigorous standards, by which they mean standards whose enforcement tends to stifle creativeness and destroy enthusiasm for the subject being studied. Many teachers of English, for example, have believed that insistence on high rhetorical standards tends to be detrimental to individual self-expression and the child's enjoyment of writing. Even in undergraduate study of philosophy such high critical standards may be set that students become afraid to say anything in the least adventurous. In such circumstances, studying the subject can become a miserable affair, even for persons with good aptitude for it, and lead to stultification rather than development. What is needed, pedagogically, is a sort of dialectic of freedom and constraint, and, at least in so far as that is what they are insisting upon, the progressivists' case is a good one.

In the preceding pages I have tried to provide a sketch of Peters' philosophy of education, in so far as it is a philosophy of 'the older style', and to indicate what I take to be certain inadequacies in it. These seem to spring, for the most part, from his keen interest in construction, which hardly allows him to submit his own ideas, enthusiastically conceived, to remorseless critical scrutiny of the kind practised by, say, Plato in his later dialogues. These presumed inadequacies notwithstanding, Peters's work is exceptional for its time, and needed by it.

Those parts of Peters's work which deal with 'relatively concrete issues' fit into the framework of his world-view and philosophy of life, and make a large contribution to the substance and general impressiveness of the whole. I shall not comment on the value they have entirely in their own right, but continue to consider Peters's work in so far as it is a philosophy in 'the older style'. From this perspective it appears as having qualities which lift it above ordinary professional philosophizing and give it an aspect of greatness. First, it is 'authentic' in the sense that the philosopher reveals himself in it, an essential feature in a philosophy of life if it is to warrant serious attention. Secondly, it instantiates and gives a fresh and powerful expression to the Stoic cast of mind, which perennially compels respect. Finally, it is not a latter-day imitation of a once-admired mode, but a new creation in the grand style. This is partly because Peters was to some extent unaware of himself as creating a philosophy of this kind, but thought himself to be doing something different; and partly because in addressing lay audiences he allowed himself to follow his bent. Whatever the causes and conditions, he succeeded in producing something like a 'system', expressive of him in the kind of way that the great traditional philosophies of education are expressive of their authors.

What his work teaches us, in particular, is that philosophy of education cannot properly confine itself to 'relatively concrete issues', and that to understand education we need to 'place' it in the total context of human being. In effect Peters recognizes that he was mistaken in his earlier belief that philosophy of education

65

exists primarily, if not entirely, for the sake of helping the teacher in the classroom. Philosophy did not free itself from domestic service to theology in order to become, in the sphere of education, little better than the odd-job man of pedagogy.

In his later work, Peters not only advocates but exemplifies what he came to regard as the final end of education—not 'the educated man' with his 'O' and 'A' levels and his BA or BSc, worthy though he is, but the person who is a philosopher of a kind everyone can be, and which very many people have at least some interest in being. Furthermore, Peters shows in his own work that this end is not quickly and easily attained, but occupies a lifetime, not as a continuous process of enquiry, however, but as a broadening and deepening of reflection in the light of personal experience, and in receipt of further relevant information and fresh stimulation from the public culture.

Peters reaffirms the educational importance of the personal view of life, and therefore the need for a variety of emphases in philosophy of education. His Stoic perspective is a noble one, but other admirable perspectives are possible—the Christian perspective of Simone Weil, for example, or the Marxist perspective of Antonio Gramsci.

The understanding of education will remain incomplete if it is not related to the intellectuals, both with respect to the producing of them, and the influence they have upon education itself. Peters compares unfavourably with Gramsci in this respect; although he explains what education is, he fails to account for himself, the educator of the educationalists. But he and Gramsci and Simone Weil all agree in the belief that a principal part of the schooling of the young should be their introduction to the humanities and the sciences. Peters's best service to education—as distinct from his service to philosophy of education—has been his powerful affirmation, and repeated reaffirmation, of his secure faith in the formal intellectual tradition.

Notes

1 R.S. Peters (1967), *Education as Initiation: an inaugural lecture delivered at the University of London Institute of Education, 9 December 1963* (London, Harrap, for University of London Institute of Education), p. 7.

2 Ibid., p. 8.

3 R.S. Peters, *Ethics and Education*, (Allen & Unwin), 1966, p. 15.

4 Routledge & Kegan Paul, 1958.

5 Allen & Unwin, 1974.

6 Ibid., p. 19.

7 Friends Home Service Committee, 1972.
8 W.R. Niblett (ed.), *Science, the Humanities and the Technological Threat*, University of London Press, 1974.
9 *Psychology and Ethical Development*, p. 19.
10 R.S. Peters, J. Woods and W.H. Dray, 'Aims of Education—a Conceptual Enquiry', in R.S. Peters (ed.), *The Philosophy of Education*, Oxford University Press, 1973.
11 *Proceedings of the Philosophy of Education Society of Great Britain*, Jan. 1970.
12 Ibid., p. 11.
13 *Education as Initiation*, pp. 34-5.
14 P.H. Hirst and R.S. Peters, *The Logic of Education* (Routledge & Kegan Paul), 1970, p. 62.
15 *Psychology and Ethical Development*, p. 426.
16 *Reason, Morality and Religion*, p. 88.
17 Ibid., pp. 64-5.
18 Peters has a further argument, *viz.* that the Marxists will have nothing (worthwhile) to do when the Marxist end has been attained. See, e.g., *Psychology and Ethical Development*, p. 416.
19 *Ethics and Education*, p. 53.
20 *Education as Initiation*, p. 43.
21 *Ethics and Education*, p. 54. See also *Education as Initiation*, p. 40.
22 Charles H. Kahn, *The Art and Thought of Heraclitus*, Cambridge University Press, 1979, p. 106. The fragment (D.107) translated by Kahn is: ΚαΚοι μαρτυρες ανθρωποιοιν σφθαλμοι Και ωτα βαρβαρονς ψνχας εχοντων.
23 *Proceedings of the Philosophy of Education Society of Great Britain*, vol. II, July 1977, pp. 28-38.
24 *Reason, Morality and Religion*, p. 87.
25 D.43: 'One must quench violence quicker than a blazing fire' (trans. Kahn).
26 See Charles H. Kahn, op. cit., p. 241.
27 D.85: 'It is hard to fight against passion; for whatever it wants it buys at the expense of soul' (trans. Kahn). Kahn argues that *thymos* is to be understood as 'anger' in this fragment. Op. cit., p. 242.
28 See: Charles H. Kahn, op. cit., p. 243.
29 *Reason, Morality and Religion*, p. 38.
30 *Psychology and Ethical Development*, p. 21.
31 *Ethics and Education*, p. 165.
32 *Reason, Morality and Religion*, p. 70.
33 Ibid., p. 48.
34 *The Philosophy of Education*, p. 18.
35 D.2, trans. Kahn.
36 Charles H. Kahn, op. cit., pp. 101-2.
37 *Psychology and Ethical Development*, p. 416.
38 F. Nietzsche, *The Will to Power*, ed. W. Kaufmann, Weidenfeld & Nicolson, 1968, sect. 853, pp. 451-3.
39 Ibid., sect. 822, p. 435.
40 *Psychology and Ethical Development*, p. 421.

41 Ludwig Edelstein, *The Meaning of Stoicism*, Harvard University Press, for Oberlin College, 1966, p. 68.
42 *Reason, Morality and Religion*, p. 68.
43 Ibid.
44 Peters cites Aristotle in this regard. See: *Ethics and Education*, p. 155.
45 See Kahn, op. cit., pp. 21-2.
46 D.30.
47 *Psychology and Ethical Development*, p. 415.
48 *Reason, Morality and Religion*, p. 82.
49 *Psychology and Ethical Development*, p. 417.
50 *Reason, Morality and Religion*, pp. 80-1.
51 Ibid., p. 83.
52 Ibid., p. 84.
53 Ibid., p. 99.
54 *Psychology and Ethical Development*, p. 424; *Reason, Morality and Religion*, p. 67.
55 *Ethics and Education*, p. 164.
56 'Education and Justification: a Reply'., pp. 35-6.
57 'Ambiguities in Liberal Education and the Problem of its Content', in R.S. Peters, *Education and the Education of Teachers*, Routledge & Kegan Paul, 1977, p. 54.
58 Ibid.
59 Ibid., p. 55.
60 Ibid., pp. 55-6.
61 'Education and Justification: a Reply', p. 35.
62 D.89, trans. Kahn.
63 *Ethics and Education*, p. 49.
64 E.g., *Psychology and Ethical Development*, p. 415.

Education, training and the preparation of teachers

R.F. Dearden

Richard Peters's views on education, training and the preparation of teachers were a very important formative influence in the reconstruction of education courses which took place widely in the 1960s. Most of the articles indicative of this influence are conveniently gathered together in the collection of papers entitled *Education and the Education of Teachers*,[1] but an important contribution omitted from that collection appeared in the volume edited by J.W. Tibble entitled *The Study of Education*.[2] The period in question was one in which the teaching profession's aspiration to become a graduate profession was endorsed by the Robbins Report, which recommended that what had formerly been known as training colleges should be retitled 'Colleges of Education' and that a new degree, the Bachelor of Education, should be introduced.[3] With the introduction of a Bachelor's degree into initial training there was a correlative move towards providing more Master's degree courses for the advanced study of education. Peters was prominent amongst those who determined the character which the content of these new developments would be given. In a nutshell, what he proposed was that the 'undifferentiated mush' which he saw educational studies as largely being should be replaced by the differentiated study of the several disciplines which bore most obviously on education, four of which became canonical: psychology, history, sociology and of course his own subject the philosophy of education. In this development, as in several others, it was not always easy to distinguish the contribution which was primarily due to Richard Peters from the contribution due to Paul Hirst, the two working closely together as they did and presenting arguments which were in many ways complementary.

Peters's views on education and the training of teachers were an application of his views on education and training more generally, so that an appreciation of those views is inseparable from, and presupposes, what became one of his most celebrated doctrines: the analysis of the concept of education. This doctrine was an organising principle for a great deal of his work, both academic

69

and institutional, and in some of the many senses of that most ambiguous of terms it became a Kuhnian paradigm. Critics rightly saw the analysis of the concept of education as the central point on which they had to be satisfied, while research studies channelled their efforts into tracing more particular implications or tackling some of the further questions that were raised. The analysis itself did not remain unchanged. Presented in his inaugural lecture *Education as Initiation*[4] it underwent further important qualifications in 'Education and the Educated Man'[5] and a gathering shift in emphasis became fully explicit in 'Democratic Values and Educational Aims'.[6] As well as being subjected to extensive criticism by others, the analysis did not escape criticism by Peters himself. And as with his views on the education and training of teachers, so too with his analysis of the concept of education, there is an important relationship to the work of Paul Hirst that has to be taken into account. This is most evident in the way that Peters's rather formal analysis is nevertheless constantly pulled in terms of content in the direction of Hirst's 'forms of knowledge' theory of liberal education. The question whether Peters was analysing education in general, or liberal education in particular, or whether there was in fact any important distinction to be made between the two, is one that must later be considered.

The plan of the present contribution will therefore be as follows. Firstly, a reminder of the salient features of Peters's account of education and training will be given. Some of his own objections to his earlier analysis will also be reviewed and some of the strains and tensions in his account will be identified. Next, the implications of the analysis for teacher education will be traced, including Peters's account of the situation that made differentiated study a necessity. As with the concept of education, so also with teacher education, Peters's views underwent a development, and his plea for differentiated study was later supplemented, though not supplanted, by a plea for a closer integration of the disciplines with practice. Finally, it will be necessary to consider the relevance of Peters's position for the strongly emerging vocationalism that is proving to be the dominant note of the 1980s.

In his inaugural lecture, Peters mentions how it caused him some surprise to find that while so many were in one way or another concerned with education, so few could be found who offered any sort of account of just what education is. A massive omission had been identified and it would be his first task to provide the remedy. While it was never expected, indeed it was explicitly denied, that an analysis of education would settle all disputes as to what pupils should be taught, nevertheless there was a clear expectation that guidance of some kind would be forthcoming. One engaged in such an analysis in order to clear one's head on matters of great importance. In coming to see things more clearly one would also, perhaps, come to see them rather differently.

In the analysis that was presented, a whole family of processes of teaching and learning was allowed, under certain conditions, to be educational. What identified the members as being of one family was their coming up to certain standards. First, the processes had to lead to the development of states of mind that were valuable, worthwhile, or desirable. They had to be valuable not just in serving such further ends as improving one's life chances in the social mobility stakes, or in meeting the need for trained manpower; they had to be valuable for their own sakes, as enhancing the quality of life for the individual being educated. Not every valuable state of mind resulted from an educational process, for example compassion and courage often do not, but that a process should lead to the development of a state of mind valuable in itself was a necessary condition of being educational. This 'for its own sake' presented the characteristic difficulty that nothing further could be cited by way of justification for it. The aims of education were therefore all intrinsic to the activity. They were, if not definitional of what it is to be educated, then no more than statements of priority or emphasis within the category of the worthwhile in itself. If justification were demanded, then it could not be other than in terms of a transcendental deduction, this being a pattern of argument which combines the two features of refusing to justify in terms of something further, while at the same time claiming to remove the apparent arbitrariness of stopping just there.

A further very important necessary condition was that the family of educational processes should produce knowledge and understanding, but not just any knowledge or understanding. Knacks, rules of thumb, and discrete items of information were not educational. Education was a matter of coming by principles, conceptual schemes, awareness of the reason why of things, understanding in breadth and depth. In short, it was coming to acquire a characteristic cognitive perspective. This acquisition was no mere loading up with inert information. As a result of being educated, one's experience was transformed and one travelled with a different view. The knowledge and understanding thus acquired were ingredients in one's perception and revelatory of reality.

The procedures of education had not only to look forward to certain achievements but also to incorporate at least a minimum of wittingness and voluntariness. Below a certain level of awareness and consent what was taking place might be justified but it would not be education. It would be conditioning, hypnosis or perhaps medication. Sometimes these minimal conditions, which in any case were probably derivative from the achievement aimed at rather than truly independent conditions, were strengthened into a requirement that a critical attitude, even autonomy, should be developed. This brought out that aims can be embodied in procedural principles as well as in content.

The whole account of the educational process was summarised in terms of the metaphor of initiation. Children are born outside the gates of civilisation and the teacher, who possesses the relevant desirable knowledge and understanding, should lead them inside to share in what he knows. In that way a middle route was thought to be found between the erroneous and misleading metaphors of moulding and of growth, each of which overstressed one side of the educator's task.

Training, by sharp contrast, was an altogether meaner thing. It aimed at specific ends and sought a limited competence in relation to those ends. Education could not be tied down so specifically. One was not educated in, or for, or as anything, whereas this was just what happened with training. Training aimed at certain kinds of efficiency in conventional situations, whereas education enlarged the mind and was valuable for its own sake.

The arguments by which these points were established were mainly linguistic. Appeal was made to what we would or would not say, what it would be contradictory to say, what the dictionary recorded and also what the term suggested. These linguistic points were taken as the clues to conceptual distinctions which underlay them. But there was also a very revealing historical claim involved in the argument. This was the claim that our concept of education had taken on its present form in the nineteenth century, in the context of the industrial revolution and the felt need to distinguish between education and trade training. Both the historical and the linguistic claims were well illustrated in an interesting set of contrasts between education and training to which Peters drew attention. His examples included the contrasts between moral education and character training, colleges of education and training colleges, physical education and training, the education of the emotions and the training of the will, and the contrast which we were invited to imagine between sex education and training. In each case the cognitive condition was strongly corroborated, since the education side of the contrast implied awareness of principles and conceptual schemes whereas the training side implied narrowly focused competence.

The linguistic arguments were subjected to the variety of criticisms which were being directed at linguistic philosophy generally. Critics asked whose use was being described, what the criterion for a correct analysis was and whether some version of the naturalistic fallacy was not being committed. References were made to Wittgenstein's family resemblance argument about games to suggest that there was no reason to think that instances of education implied common criteria anyway. Some of these arguments failed to carry full conviction because they pointed to what was generally the case, whereas the concept of education might just have been an exception. Peters himself had stated that such arguments could not secure a commitment to valuing education as so characterised. All he hoped to do by these arguments was to clarify, and so to present as an issue for serious consideration, a certain historically evolved ideal. Further questions would then arise but at least we would have been brought to confront something that called for important decision.

A major doubt which I myself always felt, and which I will later try to justify, was that Peters was really describing not education as such but one admittedly very important and historically primary conception of it, namely liberal education. He was himself aware of this criticism. His reply was that 'liberal' simply served to underscore in various ways that what was under consideration was indeed education, and not training, or indoctrination, or conditioning. A putative account of education might be deficient in each of the three conditions necessary for a process to be educational. It might, like industrial training, be deficient in respect of the value condition by being simply of instrumental value. Again, it might be deficient on the cognitive condition by being over-specialised and so lacking in breadth, or by being concerned with knacks and bits of information and so lacking in depth. Finally, it might employ dogmatic or uncritical methods and so be deficient in respect of manner or procedure. To call education 'liberal' was simply to underscore the fact that none of these deficiencies was present and therefore that we did indeed have a genuine case of education.

Paul Hirst had presented a very influential argument for a modern form of liberal education, so did Peters's analysis mean that anyone clear-headedly concerned with education must be committed to accepting Hirst's 'forms of knowledge' thesis? Undoubtedly there was a powerful complementarity between the two theses, which became fully explicit in their jointly authored volume *The Logic of Education*.[7] Nevertheless, Peters drew back from the full equation, on at least three counts. First, Hirst was regarded as altogether too bold in referring to forms of 'knowledge' in several cases, such as the moral, aesthetic and religious domains, though something a little weaker such as awareness or understanding was acceptable. Secondly, Hirst was only interested in the development of the rational mind, or the exclusively intellectual aspects of his forms. Peters wished to claim that education was as much concerned with attitudes, actions, emotions and desires, though a leading role would no doubt attach to the cognitive core in each case. Finally, Peters did not equate his breadth and depth of awareness with the development of mind in each and every one of the Hirstian forms. The educated person would have to be capable of seeing different sides of a question, or different aspects of a situation, but not to the extent of having been extensively initiated into each of the forms of knowledge. Whether all of this satisfactorily resolved the doubt about equating education with liberal education, however, will need to be considered further later.

Doubts of a more general kind about the correctness of the analysis persisted. For instance, it was plainly just not true that 'we' use the term 'education' just in the manner described or, as it seemed, prescribed. In 'Education and the Educated Man' Peters confronted the accumulating counter-claims. On the value condition he dealt with the neutral use of education by such social scientists as economists, sociologists and anthropologists by distinguishing between descriptive commentary on somebody else's activity and that activity as it appears to the person engaged in it. It is to the latter's point of view, the agent's, that his analysis was said to apply. As to poor or bad education, that use reflected a dispute over emphasis or priority amongst values.

On the cognitive condition, he accepted that we speak of specialised education but dealt with that by saying that in peripheral uses one condition is often dropped from the central use of a term, whereas it was the central use that was his concern. The Spartans gave him much more difficulty. We might wish to refer to Spartan education though they lacked the kind of cognitive perspective that was characteristic of the educated Athenians. The case of the Spartans was solved by distinguishing an undifferentiated rag-bag sense of education, which somewhat indiscriminately referred to up-bringing in general, from the sense which referred to the nineteenth-century ideal of the educated man. Two senses of educated were thus allowed. Formally, however, there were not two but four possibilities, as he saw in one place.[8] Both the value and the cognitive conditions might be met, as in the specific concept he wished to defend, or neither might be met, as in the meanest sorts of upbringing, or one condition but not the other might be met.

This fourfold and not just twin possibility was never subsequently developed and has not been generally noticed. The neglected intermediate possibilities, however, would have allowed a more comfortable accommodation of some serious anomalies. The whole sphere of professional or vocational education would appear to satisfy the cognitive but not so obviously the value condition, while music and physical education would appear to satisfy the value but not so obviously the cognitive condition, especially if that condition is allowed to be pulled in a theory-loaded Hirstian direction. He could thus have avoided the bizarre justification of physical education as making us fit for tackling the question 'why do this rather than that' in a non-sluggish way, and the scarcely less bizarre relegation of music to a hived-off game because it did not make a contribution to theoretical knowledge.[9]

The equation of education with liberal education, even after the denial that this implied a commitment to the concrete form which Hirst gave to the concept, continued to cause difficulties, sometimes recognised and sometimes not. Practical subjects, such as carpentry, toolmaking and cookery, were allowed to be educational. This not only weakened the cognitive requirement but led to the equation of the intrinsic value condition with sensitivity to the intrinsic standards of an activity. But every activity has standards intrinsic to it (forgery, bicycling, playing snap) and its having such standards is by no means the same thing as being worthwhile as an activity. In a fascinating piece on ambiguities in liberal education, Peters himself pointed to several possible confusions that lurk in the notions of a practical end and in being valuable for its own sake.[10] For example, he pointed out how an institutionally 'pure' activity may be pursued by individuals engaged in it for all sorts of practical ends, whereas an institutionally practical activity might be intrinsically motivating to those who practised it. The paper drew no conclusions for liberal education and indeed Peters confessed, with characteristic candour, that he had begun to feel increasing dissatisfaction with the dichotomies in terms of which liberal education is generally interpreted.

In his 1979 paper 'Democratic Values and Educational Aims' a very interesting shift in emphasis strongly emerged. Even in 1966, in the celebrated chapter in *Ethics and Education* on worthwhile activities, there had been some uncertainty as to the nature of the worthwhile. Did it refer to activities to be engaged in, the serious equivalent of pastimes, or was it the perspectives from which activities might be viewed? No doubt the two conceptions are not mutually exclusive, but there is an important difference of emphasis between them which would result in very different criteria of relevance in constructing a curriculum. In the 1979 paper the ambiguity was implicitly resolved in favour of the perspective interpretation. Education was there seen as giving us a perspective on the human condition as we find ourselves in the natural and social world. This move also decisively marked off Peters's conception from the Hirstian emphasis on formal differences based on epistemological irreducibility. Again, there might well be overlap but the intentions would be different. Peters's latest conception was in terms of our coming to grasp how we are placed in the world and hence of our having a better vantage point from which to determine what to become. To this end we needed to be acquainted with the natural world in such manifestations as the seasons, electricity, birth, death, ageing and disease; with the interpersonal world in terms of love and hate, friendship and loneliness; and with the social and political world in terms of authority, wealth, law, crime, violence and dissent. Work, however, was not amongst the topics listed. What had become apparent was not that liberal education was only one possible conception of education, but that there were various possible conceptions of liberal education itself.

Did Peters succeed in giving us an adequate analysis of the concept of education? I want to suggest that he did not, but that he did do something else that was more worthwhile. But first, how far can one follow him in his initial enterprise? Clearly not just anything can count as an educational process. If I say that education is a chemical process occurring in the Sun, or a mode of transport used in New Guinea, then I am certainly wrong. To be a concept at all there must be some things that are ruled out and education does rule out many things. We might begin to approach what is ruled in by considering the following contrast. Suppose that the community's health were suffering and measures were sought to combat this ill. Which would be the educational ones amongst the many sorts of measures that are possible? They would not be, or would not in a direct way be, the provision of extra medical-care facilities, or the passing of restrictive laws. Rather they would comprise such measures as the issuing of pamphlets on your health, taking televisions slots or programmes to inform and advise, providing lessons on health in schools, and so on. In short, they would address themselves to securing their ends by means of learning. Similarly, the specifically educational arguments for opening a new nursery would not be that mothers would be freed for work, or that the children would be safely occupied, or that a redundant building could be brought into use, but that the children could benefit from the learning made possible. Again, a sixth form conference on industry would be educational in intent if its primary purpose were to give insight into industry but not if it were to recruit (though that might, as indeed anything might, yield educational benefit incidentally). If overseas students' fees are lowered for trade reasons, again that is not the educational argument for lowering those fees. That argument would refer to the learning benefits.

But is just any learning educational? Clearly it would not do to specify here the learning that takes place in educational institutions. Some of the learning that occurs in such institutions is not educational, such as learning that room 15 has been repainted. Some learning that occurs outside such institutions is educational, such as the impressions gained from a first visit to a zoo or an engineering factory. And how are the educational institutions to be identified without circularity anyway? The point is important not only to leave room for education to occur in a de-schooled society, or under the auspices of 'Education Otherwise', or in workplaces and homes, but also to preserve the same sort of critical possibility in relation to formal educational institutions as is preserved in relation to legal institutions by distinguishing between morality and positive law. The institutional capture of concepts needs to be guarded against.

Can one go any further than saying that education is simply a matter of learning? I have always thought that Peters's second condition, the cognitive condition, was very near to the mark. If anything distinguishes a learning sequence as educational it is that there is a benefit to understanding to be gained from it. Teaching by rote, learning meaningless formulae, learning discrete items of information such as telephone numbers which in no way extends our understanding, are none of them educational, whereas when we take the trouble to explain the reason why of things, fitting them into a wider scheme, then educational benefit accrues. Understanding, of course, is a matter of degree, but that also very much accords with the judgments that we make.

Most of Peters's discussion implicitly refers to general education. But of course there are many specific kinds of education, such as those concerned with specific subjects (mathematical education), specific topics (cancer and alcohol education) and specific activities of people (medical, consumer, technical and driver education). Peters's cognitive breadth condition fits general education much more happily than it does these more specific forms, but the requirement of understanding connoted by the depth condition is still there. This is not to say, of course, and Peters himself explicitly denies it, that education is only concerned with understanding. As he pointed out against Hirst, education is often as much concerned with attitudes, actions, emotions and desires, but in these cases understanding would still be a leading string through modifying the cognitive core of each of these additional aspects.

What of Peters's value condition? He said repeatedly that education has no aims beyond itself, in that respect being like life. In so far as it has aims they are intrinsic to it, being either definitional points about what it is or else priority claims within the worthwhile. This seems to me to be an error which stems from the equation of education with liberal education, for liberal education is indeed an end in itself. It may also be true when we consider learning as educational, that there are intrinsic standards operating, determined by what it is that is to be understood and what counts as an understanding of it. But that does not mean that the project of understanding can have no further aim, or that the project must be worthwhile in itself. The many more specific forms of education, such as consumer education, medical education and management education, have further aims written all over them. But what would be true is that, since education typically calls for time and other resources, anyone engaging in it will think it valuable in some way.

Does this, if correct, lead to a breakdown of the distinction between education and training? It is certainly possible to draw a sharp contrast between liberal education and a narrowly conceived trade training. There is also a difference in the immediate point of each: education aiming at the growth or reconstruction of understanding whereas training aims at an operative efficiency. But acquiring an operative efficiency may be a necessary part of coming to understand, while conversely operative efficiency may not be possible without understanding. For example, having been trained in some mathematical procedure may be a precondition of successfully understanding some more advanced topic, while a precondition of successfully being trained to cure people of a certain affliction may be an understanding of the life-cycle of some parasite. In certain cases there is indeed a sharp contrast between education and training, but in many cases there is extensive overlap. Students could attend the very same course and for some of them the learning would have general education as its point, while for others training was its point. A course in the grammar of a foreign language, for example, could be undertaken by some as part of military training (to be translators) but undertaken by others as part of a liberal education. The sharp contrast which

Peters drew goes back to the Greeks, for whom the liberal studies of the gentleman were opposed to empirical and untheoretical technical skills. But, as Dewey saw, very many technical activities have now come to be informed by extensive bodies of knowledge, often theoretical knowledge, as we see in a whole range of technologies and the professions. After all, Peters himself wished to draw attention precisely to this in connection with teaching and the disciplines of education.

If we pursue a general analysis of the concept of education, therefore, it is doubtful whether much of substance will emerge beyond a reference to learning which satisfies the requirement of developing understanding, that being very much a matter of degree. This is unsurprising if we reflect that concepts are relative to interests, for who would have an interest in such a general concept? Education, whether general or specific, is a practical field. The important issues relate not to a perfectly general concept of education but to different and typically competing conceptions of it. There is a close parallel with morality here. What is common to Nietzsche and Kant, or to the Mundugumor and the Muslims, is likely to be of much less interest at the level of commitment than their differences.

In distinguishing between the general concept of justice and more determinate conceptions of it, Rawls drew attention to a contrast that is very relevant here.[11] Whereas the general concept of justice implied a 'proper' distribution of benefits and burdens, or some set of principles for assigning rights and duties, rather more particular determinations of this general concept were given by different political philosophies, such as the socialist, the liberal or perhaps the fascist. In much the same way, I suggest, we can usefully distinguish between a thin and uncontroversial general concept of education and the *many* more particular determinations of this envisaged by different educational philosophies, each offering a version of what it is to be 'an educated man'.

In this way there would be Marxist and Nazi conceptions of education, Christian and Islamic conceptions, Gandhi's and Dewey's conceptions, conceptions appropriate to moulding a sense of unitary national consciousness and conceptions which accept pluralism in society. There would also be liberal and vocational conceptions. The antagonism which would undoubtedly exist between these different conceptions would often find expression by one saying of another that is 'not education'. But this is an evaluative 'not', as in saying 'I don't call a Ford a car', or 'Picasso's work is not art'. From this perspective, an answer can be given to those who might say that several of my listed conceptions of education are not educational at all but indoctrination. That charge is made from inside a particular liberal conception of education and is internally connected with the values of that conception. The conception under attack would characterise itself in quite other ways, and obviously not pejoratively, such as seeking the salvation of souls or securing equality and happiness for the people. An entirely parallel example drawn from competing conceptions of work would be that of a Marxist characterising work under capitalism as being 'alienated'.

In some of his statements, Peters allows for all this. I referred earlier to a passage in *The Logic of Education* where he mentions four and not two formal possibilities. In his discussions of aims of education he refers to differences of emphasis and priority within the worthwhile. In his 1979 paper he refers to his own account of education as contestable. Nevertheless, I think that two broad impressions stand out from his writings on the subject. First, the impression is given, especially in his earlier writing, that the analysis of the concept of education is something of considerable moment and the absence of such an analysis has been a very serious omission. Secondly, the later impression is given that, apart from ragbag upbringing (the 'undifferentiated' concept), education means liberal education, though he implicitly distinguishes two varieties of this: the worthwhile activities account and the perspectives on the human condition account. I suggested earlier that Peters did not give us an adequate analysis of the concept of education but that he did do something more worthwhile. The inadequacy, I now want to say, was in not sufficiently recognising the diversity of educational philosophies, and in overestimating the usefulness of an account of a supposed general concept. What was much more valuable was his elaboration upon, drawing of distinctions within, and justification of, one very important conception of education, namely that of liberal education.

Preparation for practising one of the professions, such as teaching, does not obviously exemplify a liberal education in the sense of something worthwhile in itself, with none but intrinsic aims. When Peters turned to the education and training of teachers, therefore, it was not surprising that his cognitive rather than his intrinsic value condition was most in evidence. Before elaborating further on this, however, it is necessary to describe something of the situation in teaching and teacher training as he found it.

Controversy was one of the striking features of the educational scene when Peters surveyed it in the 1960s. He described a state of affairs in which a fairly settled tradition was breaking down.

Whereas teachers had previously been able to teach largely as they had themselves been taught and could learn their craft more or less on an apprenticeship basis, in the 1960s aims were no longer agreed and procedures were in question. Parents were questioning what the schools did as never before and the basis of the teacher's professional authority was insecure. In such circumstances, Peters argued, teachers are forced to become more reflective, more intellectually resourceful, more critical and alert to questions of justification. And they needed to stand on their own feet not only in relation to parents but also in relation to government.

Educational studies, or educational theory, would be a principal instrument in enabling them to do this. It would stand them on their own feet as independent-minded or autonomous critical thinkers, with some capacity to evaluate new trends, gimmicks, advice, exhortation and parental and official pressures. Of course, 'education' is here being used in a double sense. It refers on the one hand to a range of studies which have as their subject matter the processes of learning, and on the other hand to the personally educative effect which engaging in such studies was hoped to have on the teachers themselves. Perhaps it was with both senses in mind that the Robbins Report recommended the change in the title of training colleges to 'Colleges of Education'. Whereas the training of teachers had implied a narrowly focused development of competences related to uncriticised specific ends, the education of teachers would include more attention to principles, concepts, and theory generally. And here it will be useful to distinguish two broad senses of 'theory' in education.

Educational theory may mean, in the first place, a set of instructions, prescriptions or practical judgments which are entertained, reflected upon or considered apart from their actual application. A great deal of the talk addressed to teachers is of this exhortatory kind, indicating what they must, ought, should or need to do, typically without any reference to justifying considerations or any explanatory framework. Often, however, there is the tacit assumption that the speaker's experience or role are themselves of a kind sufficiently potent to validate everything that he says. One danger of such theorising is that it will fail to take account of the full range of relevant factors actually operating in the real situation, and then theory gets a bad name. 'That's all right in theory but it won't work in practice.' When educational theory is disparagingly referred to, it is usually the case that practical prescriptions are being issued divorced from a realistic appreciation of the factors actually operating in the schools. The same divorce can affect prescription in every practical field: nursing, engineering, policing, car maintenance and so on.

But there is a second sense of educational theory and it was this sense that Peters had in mind. This second sense refers to enquiries which seek to find the truth about, or to deepen understanding of, some aspect of educational practice. Usually such enquiry is undertaken from the point of view of a specific discipline, such as psychology, sociology, history or philosophy, to name the four that became best established (though economics, comparative studies, management studies, literary studies and even anthropology have made some contributions). Though such enquiry may have a bearing, indeed a very important bearing, on some aspect of practice, its immediate object is knowledge and understanding and therefore it does not immediately issue in recommendation or prescription. It reveals how things are, or how they might be, in some respect. Thus a comparative educationist may explain how church and state accommodate to each other on education in various countries; a historian may disclose some of the conceptions and influences that have governed the education of women; a sociologist may reveal a hidden curriculum and a philosopher may draw attention to different kinds of knowledge. From none of this does any practical prescription immediately follow and hence the complaint against this kind of theorising will be that its practical relevance is unclear. What is its use?

Hirst saw the possibility of hierarchically ordering these two senses of theory in such a way that practical prescription had disciplined commentary as its backing.[12] In this way practical judgment was revealed as being logically hybrid and Peters was led to say that educational studies are necessarily a mess. The 'mess' resulted from the diversity of kinds of backing which practical prescription must necessarily have, for example aims or values to give point and a criterion of relevance, commentaries on the nature of learners and the settings from which they come, explanations of the processes of learning and the characteristic courses of developments, and so on.

With this broad account in mind, Peters then concentrated on giving an outline of the nature and role of philosophy of education. He identified three erroneous conceptions of it: as a set of practical principles, often in reality highly ideological in character; as the history of educational ideas, which, like the enunciation of principles, was still too undifferentiated and uncritical; and as the implications for education of various 'schools' of philosophy, which was more respectable but which left the relevance of the philosophy very unclear. Instead of any of these he put forward a conception that applied philosophical techniques and insights directly to educational questions and problems. In this conception, the key questions were: what do you mean? how do you know? and what are you presupposing? The main areas of general philosophy to have a bearing were ethics, social philosophy, epistemology and philosophy of mind. His model for this approach was Dewey (the relationship between Peters's work and that of Dewey would be a very interesting one to explore, there being many striking points of resemblance as well as important differences).

If there is a point on which Hirst and Peters would differ here, I suggest that it would be over Hirst's tendency to see educational theory as potentially monolithic, or as approximating to an uncontroversial unity. Since truth is presumably one, this does not at first seem to be an unreasonable aspiration. But Peters was always conscious of the extent of controversy both within and between the disciplines. For example, there are rival schools of sociology, psychology and philosophy and there are sociological critiques of philosophy and philosophical critiques of psychology. Furthermore, I have already in the course of distinguishing between the concept and conceptions of education drawn attention to the diversity of value-judgments which bear fundamentally upon education. Educational theory is, no less than education itself, a controversial matter.

One of the most striking features of recent official policy statements is that controversy is hidden by them, whereas it is one of the most important functions of educational studies to bring out something of the alternative conceptions that exist. In fact, unnoticed incoherences exist between these policy statements themselves. It is assumed in *Teaching Quality*, for example, that the curriculum is to be thought of in terms of a very traditional core of academic subjects, whereas the Secretary of State has constantly expressed the view that this curriculum fails the lower 40 percent of the school population.[13] There is also a strong current stress on the vocationally useful, both generally and specifically, which does not necessarily cohere well with a stress on traditional academic subjects. Thus controversy is concealed both in what official policy includes and in what it excludes. The concealment of controversy in the document *Teaching Quality* is strikingly highlighted if one sets it beside Peters's UNESCO article 'The Meaning of Quality in Education'.[14] In that article, he pointed out the multidimensional nature of quality and the problems in trying to compare it in product as against process, in intrinsic aim as against extrinsic purpose, and in the many dimensions of the product and stages of the process.

Peters's views on the education of teachers were expressed in a series of papers mostly written in the period 1964-73, the keynote one of which was his 1964 paper to the ATCDE/DES conference at Hull. This was entitled 'The Place of Philosophy in the Training of Teachers'. In this paper he set out the educational scene as he saw it, gave an account of educational theory in general and the case for the replacement of 'undifferentiated mush', and finally identified and located the place of philosophy in a sound scheme of educational studies. Three principles governed his account of the role which each of the disciplines should play. The first was that the disciplines should mesh with each other on common themes. The second was that the studies should take practical problems or topical themes as their criterion of relevance. The third principle was that the study should constantly intimate the more funda-mental problems in each of the disciplines.

Subsequent papers broadly followed this outline, though differences of emphasis did emerge and he became more conscious of the rather different accounts one might give in relation to initial training as contrasted with advanced studies for experienced teachers. One emphasis that emerged more and more strongly was related to what sociologists sometimes call the 'etherealisation' of studies, or their tendency towards abstraction from their original practical contexts. The logic of educational judgments is one thing but institutionalisation in courses is another. That raises questions about the division of departments, who is to be responsible for what, and how logically related features are to be kept in institutional contact. A healthy layout of the one can be compromised by a pathological development of the other. To some extent Peters saw this as happening. In his later papers on teacher training, he constantly urged starting with actual problems, especially in initial training, and the necessity for foundations people to work together with subject tutors. But he never urged a reduction to a narrowly conceived survival training such as we presently hear advocated.

A second emphasis which emerged was on the importance of subject matter, or having something to teach. A teacher, he argued, must be an authority on something, at least relative to those who are to learn from him. In this respect his views strikingly anticipated one emphasis of the 1980s. But what should the teacher have to teach? Do educational studies have no bearing on this, as recent official statements such as *Teaching Quality* seem to imply? It is one of the illusions of recent policy statements that subjects just present themselves for teaching in the schools quite uncontro-versially. Yet one can ask of any subject why it should appear on the curriculum at all and in what form. Granted that the subject is to make an appearance, one can go on to ask what selection of topics is to be made, with what emphases these topics are to be taught and how they are to be assessed. Take a subject such as religious education, for example. Should that be conceived of in terms of the teaching of a particular faith, as in Catholic or Jewish schools or as is sometimes requested by immigrant religious communities? Or should it be conceived of in some more detached and pluralistic liberal way as a comparative study, or a sympathetic study of several major religions? A Marxist conception of education would presumably exclude religion altogether in accordance with its atheistic convictions. As soon as such questions are raised, it becomes apparent that it is an illusion that subject matter can be separated from a consideration of the concept of education or better still from a consideration of alternative conceptions of education.

On one important point Peters's views remained unchanged. This concerned the bearing of the disciplines on practice. It was a further consequence of the greater looseness than in Hirst of the connection between the two senses of theory which I earlier distinguished. Peters always saw theory in the truth-seeking sense as indeed having a bearing on practice but not as immediately issuing in prescriptive practical judgment. Such theory illuminated practice, and might slowly transform the teacher's general outlook, but it does not tell him what exactly he is to do. As with education generally, it leads one to travel with a different view. Thus one might be led to see learners as organisms which emit behaviour, or as agents with purposes, beliefs, emotions and intentions. One might view the curriculum in terms of some liberal conception or as the ways in which capitalism prepares its needed workforce. One might see individual differences in ability to learn as genetically determined or as socially learned. All of this has practical bearings but it needs supplementary information, values to serve as aims, and a creative synthesis into a procedure, method or pattern of organisation before it can bear on the detail of practice. The narrowly focused and persistent question 'what is the use of it?' is therefore in an important way misplaced when addressed to theory. Even the concessionary admission of theory, provided that it is 'integrated' with practice, is frequently too facile. 'Integration', like 'bridging' and 'applying', is, as Hartnett and Naish have recently pointed out, an unclear metaphor.[15] What these terms are supposed to stand for is rarely exemplified by a convincing example. An adequate answer would take some time, and the use-questioner is characteristically in a hurry.

In the light of all this, what can we now say about the bearing of

Peters's analysis of education and training on the preparation of teachers? Expressed in another way, was it appropriate for training colleges to be re-titled Colleges of Education? Certainly the preparation of teachers must be primarily conceived under the aspect of training, or measures which will result in an operative efficiency. Teachers are engaged in a practice and only secondarily in reflection on that practice. But if Peters's analysis of the situation is broadly correct, they must indeed be engaged in reflection on that practice. They will need not knacks, rules of thumb, discrete items of information or simply an accurate memory of what their own teachers did, but an understanding, indeed various kinds of understanding.

This is already sufficient to warrant the title 'education' in the general sense earlier distinguished. That title would be earned in respect both of understanding of subject matter and of those parts of educational theory which are closest to practice, such as researches into reading and the effects of various kinds of grouping. But for Peters education is necessarily a liberal enterprise and so more than this would be needed. In fact teacher training was seen by him as in need of liberalising in both of the ways in which he conceived of liberal education: as initiation into worthwhile activities and as illumination of the human condition. He argued that the disciplines of educational theory should constantly have their fundamental problems intimated, even though this was to tempt attention away from the immediacies of practice. The disciplines were to be seen as forms of inquiry worthwhile in themselves, participation in which was the best way to become independent or autonomous in one's judgments. He also argued, more obviously and more often, that the disciplines were liberalising for the light which they cast on the educational situation, as so to speak one aspect of the human condition.

There are evidently several overlapping tensions in such a conception of preparation for teaching, which in any case needs supplementing by reference to 'method' studies and practical experience. One obvious tension is between these liberalising tendencies and the urgently practical preoccupations of the trainees themselves. Another, strongly felt by Peters himself, is between loyalty to the parent university discipline and its standards (the 'super-ego' of the education lecturer, as Peters called it) and, once again, being seen to be relevant to and found intelligible by practitioners. Neither Peters nor anyone else has satisfactorily resolved these tensions, which seem inevitably to require some sort of compromise between, or balancing of, claims.

One thing does seem clear. Recent official statements which

think of preparation for teaching simply in terms of academic subject knowledge and some professional skills maintain an illusion of uncontroversiality only by politically pre-empting some of the most open questions about education: questions which it is part of the function of educational studies to bring out. I have already tried to substantiate this with reference to subject knowledge. But 'professional skills' are no less controversial. Even such apparently neutral and narrowly defined 'skills' as working with a blackboard, moving groups of children around a school or collecting and distributing materials are all loaded with educational value-judgments and permit of alternative conceptions. Much of the new hard-headedness is not so much progress beyond the disputes of the 1960s and early 1970s as a throwback to the elementary school tradition, with the teacher as technician or craft apprentice learning the one right way of doing things.

Suppose that Richard Peters were to emerge from his retirement and comment on the education and training of teachers today, what might he say? So far as one can extrapolate from his published writing, he would see no reason to abandon the analysis of educational theory in terms of various disciplines which provide commentaries on each other, on the subject matter of education and on the forms taken by practice. The differentiation of the disciplines, at least at the level of logical analysis, would seem to be incontrovertible. But he might well have different things to say about the institutionalised forms which educational studies ought to take, both in initial and in in-service training. He was well aware of the unintended consequences of setting up large and powerful education departments, though it is doubtful whether a fully satisfactory alternative model has yet emerged. The logic of the case does not readily map on to personal interest, professional development and institutional divisions. But what I think that Richard Peters would firmly set his face against, as being contrary to the whole thrust of his work on education, training and the preparation of teachers, would be a narrow vocationalism in educational subject matter and an equally narrow pressing of the question 'what is the use?' in relation to educational theory. His work on liberal education in its different modes serves to highlight by stark contrast the inadequacies of such approaches.

Peters ended his introduction to *Education and the Education of Teachers* by writing 'The interesting question for the future is whether the emphasis on theory of the 1960's will tighten up and give depth to the more practical concerns of the 1970's.' A likely answer that is emerging, the possibility of which he also foresaw, is that theory will be resolutely excluded from the preparation of teachers as a preliminary to the assertion of a much tighter central political control over teaching. Snibborism, or the reversal of Robbins, could well lead some future Peters to illustrate the difference between education and training by asking what happened when the few remaining Colleges of Education went back just to being training colleges.

Notes

1 R.S. Peters, *Education and the Education of Teachers*, Routledge & Kegan Paul, 1977.
2 J.W. Tibble (ed.), *The Study of Education*, Routledge & Kegan Paul, 1966.
3 *Higher Education* (Robbins Report), HMSO, 1963, paras 341 and 351.
4 R.S. Peters, *Education as Initiation*, Evans, 1964.
5 R.S. Peters, 'Education and the Educated Man' in *Proceedings of the Philosophy of Education Society*, vol. 4, 1970.
6 'Democratic Values and Educational Aims', 1979, reprinted in R.S. Peters, *Essays on Educators*, Unwin, 1981.
7 P.H. Hirst and R.S. Peters, *The Logic of Education*, Routledge & Kegan Paul, 1970.
8 In *The Logic of Education*, op. cit., p. 25.
9 In R.S. Peters, *Ethics and Education*, Unwin, 1966, p. 163.
10 R.S. Peters, *Education and the Education of Teachers*, op. cit., Ch. 3.
11 J. Rawls, *A Theory of Justice*, Oxford University Press, 1972, pp. 5-6.
12 See for example P. Hirst, 'Philosophy and Educational Theory' in *British Journal of Educational Studies*, vol. 12, no. 1, 1963 and Hirst's contribution (chapter two) to J.W. Tibble (ed.), *The Study of Education*, op. cit.
13 *Teaching Quality*, HMSO, 1983.
14 R.S. Peters, *Education and the Education of Teachers*, op. cit., ch. 2.
15 A. Hartnett and M. Naish, 'The PGCE as an Educational Priority Area' in *Journal of Further and Higher Education*, Autumn 1981.

Education and rationality

Anthony O'Hear

A quality of life is not the prerogative of an intellectual elite.
R.S. Peters, *Ethics and Education*, p. 178

One of the most characteristic themes of R.S. Peters's writings on education throughout his career is an insistence on the centrality of the development of the understanding to any worthwhile education. Such development requires the imparting to the learner of both cognitive content and the ability to handle theoretical justifications. In Peters's view, respect for the learner as a person requires no less. The learner is a member of a community of beings who raise questions about the worth and justification of what they do. It would be irrational for an individual to close off such questioning at any arbitrary point, and a failure of respect on the part of teachers for their pupils if, in their teaching, they were to answer requests for rational justifications by appeal to tradition or some non-rational allegiance. Democracy, indeed, is a form of life which is (or should be) concerned with uncovering principles for proceeding in the extirpation of prejudice, superstition and error, and in which each citizen has to be taught to look for evidence for his beliefs and to be critical of what he hears from others and acquires through the media:

> Of particular importance in education . . . will be those beliefs about the attitudes towards the human condition that will confront any man, whatever his occupation. To expect any final truth about such matters is a chimera; but at least the individual can improve his understanding and purge his beliefs and attitudes by ridding them of error, superstition and prejudice.[1]

Education has a central role to play in equipping the individual for such a self-transformation, through the intellectual virtues of consistency, precision and a respect for the facts and through a breadth of understanding of the types of grounds there are for beliefs and attitudes.

Peters himself has said that referring to values such as those just described as aims in education may sound 'a bit mundane and unexciting'.[2] Regrettably, it does not sound like this to me; although it may have done at one time, we have now moved into an era where such ideas are by no means taken for granted, and where some concerned with education do not feel the need even to pay them lip-service. Indeed, those who put them forward are constantly told to be 'realistic', to live in the real world of long-term or so-called 'structural' unemployment, ineradicable social deprivation, racial problems and the rest. How do you expect teachers to cultivate a love for intellectual virtues in a crowd of unwilling and recalcitrant adolescents in Toxteth or Brixton? It is as much as can be done to control them. The wheel has turned, and it is now the rationalists in education who have been pushed on the defensive. The onus now appears to be on the rationalists to demonstrate what Peters may have taken for granted in *Ethics and Education*, that education is 'not simply for the intelligent . . . not a question of some being capable of it and others not, (but) a matter, rather, of how far individuals can progress along the same avenues of exploration'.[3]

The dispute between rationalists and 'realists' over education is often taken to be basically a practical one, that it is impractical and unrealistic to expect the mass of children to benefit from an education, in Peters's sense. But, I shall argue, this is ultimately an illusion, generated no doubt in part by the social and political role of control schools are actually called upon to play; but these demands themselves are simply part of our current socio-political ethos.

Whether education is or is not to be an initiation into rational activity—for all—is not a practical question. It is a moral question, as Peters sees clearly, and also a political question, as I shall suggest in the bulk of this paper. What is basically at issue is how we intend to treat each other and what we expect from each other, and these are pre-eminently moral and political questions. Of course, given that we organise our society in a way that effectively denies the actual and potential rationality and control over their own lives of the vast mass of the population, it is not surprising that too many schools and teachers find it 'unrealistic' to attempt to inculcate in pupils a respect for intellectual virtue. Given that in our cities particularly, we tolerate large groups of people being written off as superfluous to economic needs, it is hardly surprising that school is seen as itself part of the machinery whereby people are processed as superfluous or not, and I think that this view of school is going to be only reinforced by the current emphasis on education for work, the idea that the installation of computers in classrooms is going to be some sort of panacea and all the rest of the trashy thinking of businessmen dabbling in education and educators reinforcing the prejudices of the very people who have despoiled our town centres and our lives. If school is for work, and there is no work . . .

It occurs to me that in speaking of rationality in the context of education, what I intend might be misunderstood by people whose concept of rationality, perhaps because of their own belief in an impoverished account of scientific thinking as the paradigm of rationality, is confined to a Weberian means-end rationality (*Zweckrationalität*). On this view, goals are simply treated as given, and rationality consists simply in adopting means that are likely to produce the goals, just as science itself is seen as simply the deduction of testable consequences from universal theories, and technology the means of producing the consequences from your theories which are best suited to your goals. Reason, then, is and ought to be the slave of the passions, but where the passions come from, what they are and what they should be is beyond rational investigation. Indeed, as we shall see shortly, the setting of goals and perhaps even the means to attain them are sometimes regarded as best left unexamined, because of the supposed limits of human reason. Peters's conception of rationality, and the one being advocated here is, of course, not one which regards the unexamined life as a rational life, or even as a fully human life. Nor can any simplistic positivistic view of science and its technological applications as the paradigms of rationality be sustained, in part because of the incapacity of positivistic analysis to say anything significant on the way we formulate scientific theories and assess their comparative probability prior to testing. Yet, in some ways the most striking fact about scientific reasoning is the way that infinite numbers of equally falsifiable theories are consistent with whatever observational base we care to choose. Some informal sense of what is reasonable or likely must be used to sift the plausible from the implausible among what is observationally possible. Even in the choice of scientific theory, then, we operate with an unformalisable sense of insight and equally unformalisable senses of what is the simplest, most coherent, least existentially promiscuous explanation. Without these senses, we would never get as far as opting for one specific scientific theory against its competitors, actual and potential.[4]

Like Peters, then, I am construing rationality widely enough to allow historical and literary studies to count as rational, as well as mathematical and scientific ones. Indeed, I am suggesting that these types of distinction are themselves quite suspect once one looks at just what scientific reasoning is like. Science is as much based in intuition and interest and ideas of what is good and worthwhile and constitutive of human flourishing as any other form of human reflective activity, and not, of course, less rational because of that. As Peters sketches the role of reason in human life . . .

> human beings do not just veer towards goals like moths towards a light: they are not just programmed by an instinctive equipment. They conceive of ends, deliberate about them and about the means to them. They follow rules and revise and assess them. Assessment indeed has a toe-hold in every feature of this form of behaviour which, in this respect, is to be contrasted with that of a man who falls off a cliff or whose knee jerks when hit with a hammer. Words like 'right', 'good', and 'ought' reflect this constant scrutiny and monitoring of human actions.[5]

Peters goes on to suggest that an unreflective reliance on authority and custom in any sphere of life is an inappropriate way to behave for beings whose life has the demands of reason written into it from the start. The demands of reason are not, he says, just an option available to the reflective, but are inherent in the quest everybody engages in in deciding what to do and what to believe.

As I have already indicated, Peters's emphasis on and explication of the place of reason in human life informs his writing and thinking on education, which could be characterised as humane, democratic and libertarian, in the way he expects each person to scrutinise and monitor his or her beliefs and plans. As such, Peters's position stands in sharp contrast to those who see education as primarily a way of moulding people to fit into a certain sort of society and to enter the workforce in one or other of the niches prepared for them by the operation of market forces. In order to bring out what social and philosophical presuppositions might be used to defend such a view of education, we will now examine the educational consequences of F.A. von Hayek's ideas on society. Their importance and centrality lies not simply in their great influence—which could be a fortuitous historical accident—but more in the fact that in the spirit of the time, Hayek manages to combine what at first sight might seem opposed, namely, a highly conservative and anti-rationalistic attitude to behaviour and social mores, with a passionate belief in the benefits to be gained in the operation of the free market. Both these aspects of his thought, I shall argue, flow from his fundamental mistrust of reason, and both, I shall also argue, flow quite logically into his own views on education, which I shall then contrast briefly with those of another more explicitly authoritarian strain of conservative thinkers before returning to the humanism of Peters.

Hayek's conservatism, despite the fact that he disavows the use of the term and explicitly repudiates colonial adventurism and the use of state power to shore up ageing social systems of privilege, as well as the instinctive resistance of conservatives to new ideas,[6] is actually extremely deep-rooted, more so perhaps than that of some of those who call themselves conservatives, but who are actually simply upholding comparatively recent power-structures. For Hayek's conservatism is based in a belief in the importance and efficacy of irrational evolutionary forces and their beneficial effect, contrasted with a deep scepticism of the powers of human reason, especially in the sphere of planning. Indeed, although he is often regarded as primarily an economist, it is possible and perhaps even necessary to see his ideas on knowledge and on the evolution of social order as providing the theoretical underpinnings of his economics. For Hayek, fundamental to the analysis of society is the concept of a spontaneous order, whereby anything we may call a system naturally maintains itself in equilibrium through responding and adjusting to changing circumstances. Examples of spontaneous order are found in many spheres, in physics and chemistry, in biology and, of course, in social set-ups. Perhaps the most famous applications of the idea are those by Darwin in his theory of the evolution of species and by Adam Smith with his theory of the invisible hand.

Smith's ideas on systemic stability not only pre-dated those of Darwin, and may, according to Hayek, even have influenced biologists such as Darwin, but they are also more immediately pertinent to Hayek's social philosophy. The concept of the invisible hand operating in society is invoked to illustrate the way in which a man might, through his social and economic activity, promote ends that were no part of his own intention. Thus, to adapt an example of Karl Popper, a man putting his house on the market tends—against what he wants—to push the price of houses down. But in doing this, he no doubt contributes effectively to the smooth running of the housing market, which is presumably in the general interest. Smith is, of course, optimistic about the operation of the invisible hand. A well-structured social whole will be the continuing outcome of its operations, so long as they are untrammelled by state intervention. What Smith calls the great society, or that in which people no longer knew all those they lived in community with on a face-to-face basis, was made possible by individuals directing their efforts not towards the wants and needs they observed in those around them, but by the abstract signals of the market, the prices at which labour and commodities were bought and sold. If we all respond to these abstract signals, then both labour and capital will be drawn to their most productive uses, and we will all become richer and so, in the end, able to do more good than if we or some planners had attempted in the first instance to deal rationally and intentionally with the needs we perceived in those around us. Such rationalistic planning will have the effect only of diverting limited resources to less productive functions.

Smith's invisible hand is not, of course, a person or a mind (or even a god). What is revolutionary in his analysis of the growth of the great commercial centres of his time is the way he is enabled to account for facts of social organisation in non-rational, non-intentional and non-psychological terms. Whether or not he entirely shared the cynicism of Mandeville's *Fable of the Bees* (1705), which depicts a realm in which

> every part was full of vice,
> Yet the whole mess a paradise,

Smith's stress on the workings of the invisible hand led him to be highly suspicious of attempts to plan or manipulate society for the better, even for the best of reasons. We just do not know enough about the likely effects of even the best-meant acts in the great society, or about the way its balance is in fact maintained. In fact, allowing the invisible hand and the abstract signals to do their work can best be seen as a rational response to our incorrigible ignorance of the complexities and sensitivities of great societies. The market itself is a means for overcoming our ignorance, and retrieving and transmitting knowledge dispersed among millions of people.

This indeed is how it is seen by Hayek.[7] And it is a stress on our ignorance rather than on our acting in self-interest that is paramount in Hayek's development of Smith's invisible hand doctrine. For Hayek, any individual agent in a large and increasingly complex society such as ours will be ignorant of many of the consequences of his or her actions. This ignorance affects public planners as much as people pursuing purely private ends. How, then, does society remain in one piece, without dissolving into fragments and chaos? Hayek follows Smith's lead in suggesting an invisible hand explanation of many aspects of social order which are not economic in the narrow sense: Hayek sees spontaneous order as having a crucial role in the development of law, custom, morality and other social institutions. In all these areas there is (or ought to be) free scope for the play of the evolution and natural selection of the determinants of social order in response to changing circumstances. As he puts it in *Law, Legislation and Liberty*,

> the cultural heritage into which man is born consists of a complex of practices or rules of conduct which have prevailed because they made a group of men successful but which were not adopted because it was known that they would bring about desired effects.[8]

So our social arrangements and institutions do hold our society together because they have evolved through a type of Darwinian natural selection, by which they themselves have contributed to the stability of the society in question, which has led to both their survival and that of the society. These structures evolved non-rationally and will continue to develop non-rationally. We attempt to alter them by rational interference at our peril, because of ignorance of the effects of our reforms and of the fabric of society. Indeed, Hayek actually justifies individual freedom in the market and elsewhere precisely because it provides a context in which new spontaneous orders may arise and be maintained and old ones be modified appropriately. As he puts it in *The Constitution of Liberty*,

> it is because every individual knows so little and, in particular, because we rarely know which of us knows best that we trust the independent and competitive efforts of many to induce the emergence of what we shall want when we see it.[9]

The emergence, naturally, will be unforeseen and unplanned for. It is worth underlining here that Hayek does not think that social or economic equilibria can be achieved once and for all. He conceives spontaneous order as a continuing re-balancing of a system in response to changing environments. This indeed is why, in the market, he is so concerned to stress the positive role of competition and entrepreneurship (and even monopolies where these arise naturally although here he departs from Smith who took perfect competition as the background for the invisible hand). For Hayek, only through unfettered entrepreneurship will opportunities for further trade be fully exploited, by the dragging of manpower and resources to their most productive uses. Hayek sees inequality in society as an essential part of the competitive process, claiming that egalitarian societies naturally stagnate, through a blunting of the competitive drive, ingenuity and willingness to take risks that he sees as the condition of material progress.

In extending the idea of spontaneous order from the market to human conduct more generally, a new aspect of order appears. For while at least some of the order that arises in the economic sphere might not seem to require any more to its enforcement than the economic controls of reward and punishment for responding or failing to respond to the signals of the market, when we speak of the rules governing practices and customs which are not narrowly economic, we are talking about rules on which people will act even when they are not being constrained from outside in any way. Indeed, did people not act in regular and predictable ways, even in their voluntary behaviour, social life would be impossible, because no one would be able to predict with any probability what anyone else would do.

The practices and rules of conduct which Hayek sees as existing in any spontaneously ordered society and as necessary to any viable social order at all are, then, internalised, governing the agents from within. But, in Hayek's view—and this is a crucial step in his argument—a rule on which we act without coercion does not have to be a rule which we can justify or are even necessarily aware of. To defend the idea of acting on rules without being aware that we are doing so, Hayek appeals to ethology and linguistics as areas in which there are examples of behaviour which is rule-governed, but not consciously rule-governed, such as our immediate and untutored sense of what is grammatically deviant. He does not appear to be aware of the difficulties involved in this way of talking, at least if we want to spell out the content of these rules (for how do we know which of the multitudes of sets of rules consistent with our behaviour we are actually obeying?), but goes on to stress that identifying and naming the regularities that govern our actions is something that may be possible only at a very late stage of intellectual development.[10] Even when we, either individually or collectively, do reach this late stage and formulate the rules we have hitherto been unconsciously following, we should respect them, because of their evolutionary ancestry and their role in keeping society stable. 'Paradoxical as it may appear', he writes, 'it is probably true that a successful free society will always in a large measure be a tradition-bound society.'[11] This is because if we question and dispense with our traditions, our society will fall apart. If it is a free society, it will not be free much longer, because into the resulting chaos will rush as the inevitable consequence dictatorial forces re-imposing order.

I do not know how much Hayek's thought was conditioned by the events of Weimar Germany, but in an essay published shortly after World War II, entitled 'Individualism, True and False', Hayek contrasts contemporary Anglo-American conformism in habits and dress very favourably with what he claims is the characteristically Germanic and, he says, Goethe-inspired quest for the 'original personality', in which the individual sets himself up as the judge of the right and the true. Fantastically, Hayek blames the rise of Nazism on this. A contrast, and one germane to the theme of this paper, can be made here with Thomas Mann's 'Germany and the Germans' of 1945 in which Mann argues that it was precisely the failure of the cultured to bring their culture and rationality into public affairs that opened the way to Nazi irrationalism. In their 'musical-Germanic inwardness and unworldliness' they neglected the essential, outward and in the largest sense 'political' obligations of the true humanist. According to Hayek, though, it is not difficult to destroy the 'spontaneous formations that are the indispensable basis of a free civilization'; to avoid doing this and having the ensuing calamities thrust upon us, each individual must submit to existing moral rules and conventions that are not the result of intelligent design, 'whose justification in the particular instance may not be recognisable and which to him will often appear unintelligible or irrational'.[12] Reason in Hayek's view can determine what to do only in combination with non-rational impulses, 'its function is essentially to act as a restraint on emotion, or to steer action impelled by other factors.'[13] In other words, Hayek accepts the means-end view of rationality, arguing that we must simply submit to the evolutionarily guaranteed virtues of tradition; we are powerless to understand their point or to construct anything as good in their place. If we want social stability and freedom, we should simply recognise the demands of economics and absorb traditional values.

Clearly, ideas on society, such as those of Hayek, will have educational implications, and although it would be easy enough to guess what these might be, we do not have to do this, as Hayek himself has spelled them out in ch. 24 of *The Constitution of Liberty*. Quite a lot of what he says there is to point, very pertinently in my view, at the dangers of systems of education whose control is centralised in the hands of the state, and at the social problems involved in a single system of assessment and certification. There are also passages recommending educational vouchers and student loans for vocational courses. In general, he accepts the Millian view that the State should provide parents with the means for a basic minimum education for their children but not the education itself. All these points can be argued quite independently of Hayek's general views on society and knowledge, and from rather different premises. Where, however, Hayek's views on knowledge and society do play a significant role, is when he tackles the basic question of the nature of the compulsory education he thinks is needed in an advanced society. He says that:

> general education is not solely, and perhaps not even mainly, a matter of communicating knowledge. There is a need for certain common standards of values. . . . If in long settled communities with a predominantly indigenous population, this is not likely to be a serious problem, there are instances, such as the United States during the period of large immigration, where it may well be one. That the United States would not have become such an effective 'melting-pot' and would probably have faced extremely difficult problems if it had not been for a deliberate policy of 'Americanisation' through the public school system seems fairly certain.[14]

He goes on to question whether there is much value in attempting to make available to all the 'best knowledge which some possess', as there is little evidence that the differences in knowledge between the most and the least educated in a society makes much difference to the overall character of the society.[15]

When we go beyond the minimum education needed to produce in people shared values and beliefs and an ability to contribute reasonably to the common needs, however, we are faced with the 'really important issue' of how people should be selected for higher education. Hayek's answer is that however we select these people, grants or even subsidies in the form of loans should only be given to those who promise the best return from such an investment. He goes on to question whether all those intellectually capable of higher education have any claim to it, or whether it would even do them any good. And, then, most strikingly and significantly of all, we find that:

> there is also another problem which has assumed serious proportions in some European countries . . . the problem of having more intellectuals than we can profitably employ. There are few greater dangers to political stability than the existence of an intellectual proletariat who find no outlet for their learning.[16]

So, access to education beyond the minimum, whatever it is agreed to be, is, unless one pays for it, to be signalled by the abstract demands of the market in terms of employment needs. Educating people beyond the demands of the jobs they will get is seen as a potential threat to the spontaneous formations which underpin the delicate order in which we live. All this fits depressingly well with the quotation from Guglielmo Ferrero with which Hayek begins the introduction to *Law, Legislation and Liberty*:

There seems to be only one solution to the problem (of preserving order): that the élite of mankind acquire a consciousness of the limitation of the human mind, at once simple enough and profound enough, humble and sublime enough, so that Western Civilisation will resign itself to its inevitable disadvantages.

In a similar way, Hayek stresses over and over again, neither progress nor stability can be achieved by rationalistic constructions or analyses of procedures, but only to the extent that we preserve and imitate those rules and practices which have—despite reason—proved themselves successful.

What are we to make of all this stress on tacit knowledge and the displacement of the rational? It might be argued, and indeed Hayek does argue, that we can never make explicit all the knowledge we have, because in all our researches and expositions, we will be presupposing something which cannot itself be formulated at the same time. This sort of argument is sometimes linked to Gödelian considerations concerning the incompleteness of arithmetical systems and to Quine's demonstration that logical truth cannot be entirely a matter of conventionally adopted rules, because in the very application of the conventions to concrete cases we will be presupposing some of the bits of logic that are supposed to be introduced by the conventions. But as Hayek himself recognizes, Gödel's proof does not show that there is any arithmetical truth which cannot be proved in *some* system, nor does Quine's argument show that we cannot submit our most basic logical intuitions, on such matters as contradiction and *modus ponens* inference, to rational scrutiny. (We can indeed do better than that, and actually prove the consistency and completeness of systems using these intuitions). In any case, even the acceptance of a sense in which some logical principles can only be shown and not said would be of doubtful relevance to those areas of conduct and custom in which Hayek most stresses the limits of reason. Hayek has recently used an argument to the effect that because our moral intuitions have evolved by group selection, they will not be intelligible to individuals but this seems just mistaken. The effects of group selection elsewhere are open to individual scrutiny. Can't we as individuals put our basic moral intuitions, say, to the test, to see if they are livable, if they are consistent with other intuitions, if they are generally respected by all peoples or whether they are simply local and parochial expressions of interest and, above all, if they are suitable for new circumstances? Isn't it just the sort of thing we should do? Doing this sort of thing does not imply what

Hayek sometimes seems to expect rationalists to do, namely, to construct or choose a new ethics out of the blue, but it is nevertheless a highly rationalistic and potentially revisionary approach to ethics, totally at variance with the intellectual abdication Hayek recommends in the face of the traditional.

The possibility (and duty) of undertaking a rational examination of moral and other values is relevant to another fundamental aspect of Hayek's thought, which looks like a matter of purely factual claims, but which turns out in fact to be highly value-laden. This is the assumption that social equilibrium is necessarily the result of unplanned and organic developments in that society. One wonders, though, what short of chronic banana republic instability, would go to show that a society is not in some sort of functional equilibrium. But, can we assume that any society that survives a given period of years relatively unchanged has reached the type of delicate and responsive balance so valued by Hayek? Presumably not, because there can be hardly a single society anywhere in the world today that does not have considerably more state inteference and planning than would be consistent with Hayek's preferred model of the free operation of the invisible hand in both its economy and its institutions. Let us suppose, though, that there was such a society, have we any guarantee that, particularly in current world conditions, there might not be chronic large-scale unemployment in that society? That this is just what would happen seems increasingly likely as it becomes progressively cheaper for entrepreneurs to do without human workers altogether. Indeed, some have questioned whether, now that direct human labour is no longer the main source of riches, the free market model (of labour being pooled to its most productive use) is at all applicable in present conditions if we want full employment. Even among those employed in a totally free market economy, have we any assurance that large numbers would not have to sell their labour at or below subsistence level, because of the fundamental inequality in bargaining position between a rich and possibly monopolistic employer and a needy worker who is only one of many after the same subsistence wage? Would such things be an acceptable price to pay for the benefits of stability and material progress a free market is supposed to bring? Here, I think, we begin to see the essentially value-laden nature of the idea of the social equilibrium as envisaged by Hayek. What might seem a delicate equilibrium, and something desirable in a society, to some members of that society might look very different to those in different positions. Would they necessarily be convinced by Hayek's arguments about the inevitably deleterious effects of interfering in the naturally selected social and economic arrangements? One can, of course, like Popper, stress the inevitability of unforeseen consequences of social policies, without at the same time ruling out social and economic engineering on principle. The rational thing to do might well be to attempt to remedy obvious cases of deprivation and poverty by intervention, the effects of which one monitors carefully. Of course, such monitoring has not exactly happened, in part, I believe, because of the fundamentally irrational conduct of politics in most countries, West and East. Politicians do not monitor the effects of their policies with a view to correcting their mistakes, because they are afraid that they will lose votes or standing if they admit that what they have done has led to unforeseen and unwanted consequences (i.e. mistakes). Indeed, that rationally one would predict mistakes from anything one does is perhaps the greatest unlearned and untaught lesson in the theory of rationality, and a fundamental reason for trying in a democracy to transmit something of the rational attitude in schools. However, this aside, many Western states have intervened very considerably in the social and economic orders without this producing the breakdown of spontaneous order that Hayek predicts, or indeed leading to the road to serfdom, total loss of individual liberty and dictatorship. Whether one prefers a society with more or less state interference cannot be decided as if one were deciding for or against order and freedom as such, which is why I am suggesting that aiming for a society in a Hayekian state of equilibrium which should not be disturbed by state interference might have a lot more to do with where one stands in society, than with any general principles about knowledge and social order. Hayek is, of course, aware that the result of the operation of the free market will necessarily be that many will have 'much more than their fellows think they deserve, and even more will have much less than their fellows think they ought to have'.[17] But he says that material progress is actually due to the operation of the market which rewards without regard to desert or needs, and that as the market increases the total product, everybody will in the end be materially better off. Against this, one could, of course, question whether material progress is so important that the (inevitably uncertain) quest for it should be allowed to override one's sense of revulsion at, say, the conditions of the poor in Western cities, to say nothing of Africa and South America.

In any case, it is unclear why Hayek thinks that the essentially random development of spontaneous order will lead to the sort of liberal society he favours. As Norman Barry points out, social evolution has in fact produced many non-liberal, highly interventionist institutions.[18] Barry goes on:

> the period of the dominance of the open society, the market
> economy and minimal government may then be regarded as
> perhaps a chance mutation in a course of evolution which is
> proceeding in quite another direction. Yet if we are intellectually
> tied to tradition, and if our 'reason' is too fragile an instrument
> to recommend satisfactory alternatives, how are we to evaluate
> critically that statist and anti-individualist order of society
> which seems to have as much claim to be a product of evolution
> as any other social structure?

Barry here, I think, touches on the fundamental weakness in
Hayek's thinking about evolution and society. Reason is, and ought
to be only the slave of evolution, on Hayek's view, but how can we
tell what evolution requires? Why is it more in accordance with
evolution not to plan than to plan? Is there not a sense in which
anything we do, given that we are products of evolution, is itself a
product of evolution? Hayek will no doubt reply that inteference in
natural evolutionary processes is bound to be irrational, because
we have no idea where such interference might lead. But is it any
more rational not to interfere as a policy? We do not on Hayek's
view have any more insight into where evolution will lead us. The
argument from ignorance cannot extend solely to ignorance about
the effects of planning. Certainly there is a sense in which some
sort of equilibrium will result from allowing evolution to take its
course, but we have no guarantee that what emerges will be to our
advantage. It might involve the extinction of the human race, or
the perpetual domination of one part by another. Are we simply to
acquiesce in such outcomes on the grounds that we should allow
the non-rational forces of evolution to establish whatever equilibrium results? What would Hayek say if highly dictatorial regimes
arose 'naturally'? What I am suggesting is that we need reason in
the first place to decide what is required by evolution, and that we
should then use reason to assess its desirability. Reason ought to be
the judge of evolution, and not its slave.

In his writings on tradition and evolution, Hayek treats social
customs and rules as if they were specific adaptive behaviours,
selected by means of natural selection, but in two crucial respects,
the analogy with biological evolution fails. First, human cultural
evolution is not genetic. There are no genes peculiar to members of
society A with rule R1, which members of societies B . . . N, with
rules R2 . . . RN in place of R1 do not have. (There are actually
only minuscule genetic differences between all human races and
societies, an interesting and possibly significant contingency.) So

there is no genetic base to differences in culture and tradition, nothing selected and reinforced by biological natural selection, nothing fixing our cultural patterns in any biological way. Far from it, in fact, and this brings us on to a second and more significant aspect of human culture. Unlike other developmental processes in nature, human cultural evolution can be directly adaptive to changing environments, and is potentially highly flexible and reversible. Biologists such as Sir Peter Medawar and Stephen Jay Gould are fond of speaking of human social evolution as Lamarckian in nature, with the environment imprinting non-genetical information on us in adulthood, and we passing this on non-genetically to our off-spring through teaching and writing. In contrast to the slow and undirected development of species immured in purely biological or genetic modes of development, human cultural evolution is rapid, cumulative and, above all, flexible. This last point is what gives us our great evolutionary advantage: we, unlike other animals, are not stuck with modes of behaviour that worked in one type of situation, but which may be fatal in another. While there are biological constraints on human behaviour and survival, such as rate of maturation and physical strength, the behaviour that promotes survival in one set of circumstances may need modification in others (here hawkishness, there dovelikeness), an we can use our intelligence to modify our responses as circumstances change.

It is just this specifically human form of adaptiveness that Hayek's downgrading of the rational appears to rule out. He wants us, it seems, to be as foredoomed in our social behaviour as is a species whose genetic constitution makes it unable to cope with a new environment. In so doing, he may even be wide of the mark biologically, as our comparatively large brain would appear, from the perspective of evolution, to be advantageous mainly in respect of the flexibility of response it allows its owner.

Furthermore, it is not the case that all human behaviour and customs, even ones deeply embedded in a culture, were embedded to promote survival. Here again, biology leads Hayek astray. For in the development of a human society, there is no clear way in which the environment can get to weed out a potentially useless or debilitating custom, as Professor J.W.N. Watkins has pointed out to me. Cultures have long survived with clearly debilitating customs, such as the Catholic custom of enjoining celibacy on the most intelligent members of the Church. But even if we accepted that social survival is more like genetic survival than it is, it would not follow that every custom in a long-standing society was actually useful to it, or had ever been so. Against the panselectionism of Wallace and other Victorian evolutionists, according to which nature moulded each aspect of a surviving species precisely to promote its survival, contemporary biologists will now argue that the mere existence of a limb, organ or capacity in a species does not guarantee that that limb, organ or capacity has anything directly to do with the survival promotion of members of that species. All that natural selection teaches us is that individuals as a whole, and the species to which they belong, survive, not that everything about them directly promotes their survival. And so it must be with human customs and societies, if we are to accept biological analogies. How do we know whether a limb, organ, capacity, or even a custom has survival potential for its bearer? The fact that it exists does not show this, and so we are led once more to the need for an intelligent appraisal of its functions and capacities in order to decide. It is worth remarking, too, that changes in biological structure introduced in one set of circumstances may have capacities and uses of quite different sorts—again a biological commonplace, but one that, contra Hayek, might once more suggest the place for an intelligent appraisal of any customs or rules of conduct we are looking at from an evolutionary perspective, to see what new possibilities they might open for us.

So although it is true that we, including our reasoning and planning abilities, are products of an irrational evolution, there is no reason, even from an evolutionary point of view not to reason about our situation and customs, and plan for the future. This indeed is the possibility evolution has given us. What our reason allows us to do is to propose and plan, and to test those proposals and plans, in order to avoid the disastrous consequences that would arise for us if we simply waited until old solutions to old problems and the holders of those old solutions were weeded out by new problems. Indeed, the clearest lesson evolution offers us is that past solutions are not always future solutions, and this is surely as true in the social sphere as it is in technology and nature. Unless we reason about our values and traditions there is an ever-growing danger that our technological innovations will destroy us. Hayek himself has very little sense of this, arguing not only that ever higher contributions to productiivty are the only road to international peace, but that these advances will be made only if people in the West continue to advance materially at a high rate.[19] Against this, however, it is surely no longer necessary to stress the need for planning and control on a world scale in an attempt to save the world from the unfettered exploitation of competitive entrepreneurs and monopolists. Indeed, it might be argued that we ourselves need rationally to re-appraise our own tacit acceptance of the virtue of material progress. To take a perhaps less-controversial case of a traditional set of values, however, it might well be that at one time the attempt on the part of parents to have large numbers of children definitely helped the societies to which they belonged to prosper. In many parts of the world, having large numbers of children is now a traditional and unquestioned value. But, because of better medicine and child-care and the exponential growth of populations, this is a value which should now be questioned and changed. Is Hayek suggesting in neo-Malthusian fashion that we should not attempt to change this rationally, by educating and informing the peoples concerned, but that we should allow a change in it to arise quasi-naturally through the effects of famine and land-hunger? Similarly, one might argue that the sort of aggressive machismo that might arguably have been appropriate in pioneering days in the Americas, and indeed the very Americanisa-tion extolled by Hayek, are in present circumstances highly dangerous to the whole world. (Those who do not like this example could ask themselves similar questions about pan-Slavism.) Again, there seems to be a strong case for attempting to transform these traditional values through reason and education, before the values destroy us.

To sum up these reflections on Hayek's general position on knowledge and society, beyond pointing out the admitted diffi-culties inherent in social planning, he has not given any cogent reason for abandoning all attempts to plan our institutions on a rational basis or to reason about our values. Appeals to the evolutionary growth of our faculties and organic developments of our traditions cannot show that planning or reasoning should not be attempted. Indeed, I have suggested that the repudiation of rationally inspired intervention in our institutions and scrutiny of our values is itself something that needs rational defence, that it cannot simply be justified by an appeal to evolution, for evolution itself is silent on the matter, and that such a repudiation is likely in any case to be suicidal in changing circumstances. Without the evolutionary prop, Hayek's position is little different from any standard exaltation of the irrational over the rational. But when we turn to Hayek's specific educational proposals, we have to ask what their political consequences are likely to be, because they seem to bring his position on education close to a very different brand of conservatism.

Education, on Hayek's view, should be universal, but only up to a minimum standard and, then, in large part, to inculcate the tacitly accepted values and customs of the society. Combined with his insistence that public policy should not be diverted from allowing the invisible hand to take its ineluctable course by attending to the perceived needs of sections of society, we have a picture of a state acting with extreme conservatism, upholding traditional values through education and allowing the status quo to continue unchecked, whatever the social and human cost of doing so. How, though, can we ensure that the 'right' values are transmitted through general education? Will there not have to be people claiming special insight into what these values are, in order to monitor what is happening in schools? It is hard to see how Hayek's non-interventionist conservatism does not pass imperceptibly into a more authoritarian brand altogether. Despite his expressed liking for a Millian pluralism in education, the whole tenor of his thinking on both education and value has a much more authoritarian seam. Indeed, his 'Individualism, True and False' is as much an attack on Millian experimentation in living as it is on Goethian original personalities; his insistence on the promotion of common standards of national values and tradition in education sounds curiously like the demands other conservative thinkers make from time to time, for example, that English (or British) history form the core of history teaching in schools. I am not saying that Hayek himself would endorse anything of this sort, but simply that his ideas lend themselves rather naturally to such an interpretation.

Roger Scruton is a representative of the authoritarian strain of conservative thinking, while Hayek would claim to be a liberal. Scruton is less persuaded than Hayek about the inherent value of the free market and extremely hostile towards any displacement of rational thought by consumer calculation. He also, as we shall see, is quite prepared to speak about the traditions and institutions for which Hayek has such respect as myths. Nevertheless, he is as insistent as Hayek on the need to play down the role of reason in human affairs. In particular, Scruton is unable to envisage a viable society as being based on the free choices of free and rational individuals. He is especially dismissive of social contract theorising, which seems to him to deprive social arrangements of their necessary legitimacy and objectivity. In a typical passage in *The Meaning of Conservatism*, he writes:

> the bond of society—as the conservative sees it—is just such a 'transcendent' bond (as that whereby children are placed under their parents whether they like it or not), and it is inevitable that the citizen will be disposed to recognise its legitimacy, will be disposed, in other words, to bestow authority on the existing order. . . . The conservative places his faith in arrangements that are known and tried, and wishes to imbue them with all the

authority necessary to constitute an accepted and objective public realm.[20]

In another passage, Scruton writes:

society exists through authority, and the recognition of this authority requires the allegiance to a bond that is not contractual but transcendent, in the manner of the family tie. Such allegiance requires tradition and custom through which to find enactment. But tradition is no static thing. It is the active achievement of continuity: it can be restored, rescued and amended as grace and opportunity allow.[21]

Hayek would surely not dissent from this evaluation of the nature of tradition and its importance to society.

Scruton insists that the authority of the state cannot play its necessary role in bonding society if it appears to be arbitrary or unfriendly. It needs to be mollified by adherence to what he calls a constitution, those rules and customs through which men engage in the exercise of power, and through those autonomous or partially autonomous institutions, such as the family, the monarchy, parliament, the judiciary, the church and the army, which preserve the constitution from abuse, particularly abuse by legislative statute, and which give expression to the objectivity, continuity and stratification of society and exceeding what could be written down.

Of great importance in establishing allegiance in people's minds to the institutions of the constitution are the ceremonies and myths which endow these bodies with a sense that they are more than the chance union of particular participants. Scruton speaks of the 'symbolic depth' of the ceremonies of state, of the way that through them, participant and spectator find themselves taken up into something greater; thus, he says, there emerges the myth of the 'glory' of the nation, of its unqualified right to allegiance. He goes on:

in referring to 'myth' I by no means wish to disparage these beliefs. On the contrary, they constitute the great artifact whereby institutions enter the life of the state and absorb the citizen. In a sense the Marxists are right in saying that bourgeois man robs the world of history by creating myths which represent as natural and inevitable what is in fact historical and subject to change. But they are deeply wrong in supposing that it is only *bourgeois* man who does this, and that there is some other form of man for whom the necessity would not arise.[22]

And he goes on, although himself an atheist, to extol the need for an established religion, both because secularisation hinders the recognition of social bonds and because into the religious vacuum left by the decline of organised religion is likely to rush a horde of idiotic, destructive and anarchic cults.

Scruton's position is that of a hyper-sophisticate (to use a term of his), a conservative who sees the authority and objectivity of the state as constituted and sustained by means of myth and ideology and yet, at the same time, wanting the social order that would result. The trouble is that in seeing the sustaining forces as myth and ideology:

> he has set himself apart from things. The reasons that he
> observes for sustaining the myths of society are reasons which he
> cannot propagate; to propagate his reasons is to instil the world
> with doubt. Having struggled for articulacy, he must recom-
> mend silence.[23]

I have rarely seen, since Plato, a more explicit and honest statement of conservative realpolitik, of the belief that one is in a position to recommend, for the good of all, the propagation of ideas in which one does not in one's own heart believe or in which one does not believe in the way one preaches them. Scruton claims that all politics depends on this sort of mystification of the masses, but I do not see why this should be so, unless he is taking the view of V.S. Naipaul that politics is the opium of the people. If so, the time has come to move beyond politics. In any case, the consequences of Scruton's policy are frightening.

For who is going to decide on which set of beliefs is the appropriate myth, and how will it be upheld against the questioning and criticism it will inevitably face? This is, of course, from one point of view an educational issue: whether we, the hypersophisticates reading Scruton are prepared to recommend an educational policy of indoctrination. It is also totally irrational and very probably counter-productive in human terms, apart from leading inexorably to repression and thought-control, in that it denies a basic principle of rationality, that knowledge grows through criticism and criticism from any quarter must be recognised. There can be no distinction in reason between the hypersophisticates who know the truth, and the common men who have simply to be formed through the myths of the ruling classes.

Both Hayek and Scruton, in their own ways, recommend faith in and preservation through education of values and traditions they believe are fundamentally non-rational and incapable of defence on their own terms. They both recommend systems of schooling which for the majority will do little more than instil these values and give them apprenticeships. Scruton actually says that it is a mark of disrespect to force education on those who do not desire it, or cannot acquire it.[24] But how is he so sure that there are people like that? Sure, there are people who will resent being certified and processed as the dregs of society, the new and very probably permanent lumpen-proletariat, which I have already suggested may well be the effect of work-orientated education. Against this, however, I would set a passage from Saul Bellow's *The Dean's December* about the account his hero Corde wrote for *Harper's* about the Chicago ghettoes:

> In a class of black schoolchildren taught by a teacher 'brave enough to ignore instructions from downtown', Shakespeare caused great excitement. The lines 'And pity, like a naked newborn babe, Striding the blast' had pierced those pupils. You could see the power of the babe, how restlessness stopped. And Corde had written that perhaps only poetry had the strength 'to rival the attractions of narcotics, the magnetism of TV, the excitements of sex or the ecstasies of destruction'.[25]

Of course, education will not by itself solve the problems of contemporary life. What I am objecting to is its being made an accomplice in the filling of people's minds and spirits with authoritarian myth by those who consider themselves their betters.

What we are confronted with is a choice between, on the one hand a vision of education as that initiation into rationality and its procedures which is consistent with respect for individual persons and a belief in human rationality as such, one which, in effect wants to give people control over their lives, and a concept of education as simply an initiation into traditional values and myths, about whose truth we must be silent and to whose authority we must submit. I hope in this paper to have shown that, perhaps surprisingly to some, the struggle between these visions is very much a live one, and to have exposed some of the arguments that might nowadays be mustered to defend what will in effect be divisive and largely indoctrinatory forms of education, R.S. Peters has been tireless and consistent in his defence of the right of everyone to an education which will enable them to take responsibility for their own beliefs and attitudes. Peters's vision is neither mundane nor unexciting. It is revolutionary in its implications and its vision, and very probably inconsistent with the way we organise society and the roles we expect people to fill. It deserves continual re-statement and defence against the forces of irrationality and reaction, which, politically, appear to be in the ascendant.

Notes

1 Peters, R.S., *Essays on Educators* (George Allen & Unwin, 1981), p. 40.
2 Ibid., p. 49.
3 Peters, R.S., *Ethics and Education* (George Allen & Unwin, 1970), p. 178.
4 Cf. Putnam, H., *Realism and Reason* (Cambridge University Press, 1983), pp. 298-301.
5 Peters, R.S., 'The Justification of Education' in *The Philosophy of Education* edited by Peters, R.S. (Oxford University Press, 1973), p. 254.
6 Cf. Hayek, F.A., Postscript to *The Constitution of Liberty* (Routledge & Kegan Paul, 1960), pp. 397-411.
7 Cf. Hayek, F.A., 'Adam Smith's Message in To-day's Language' in *New Studies in Philosophy, Politics, Economics and the History of Ideas* (Routledge & Kegan Paul, 1978), pp. 267-9.
8 Hayek, F.A., *Law, Legislation & Liberty*, vol. I (Routledge & Kegan Paul, 1973), p. 17.
9 Hayek, F.A., *The Constitution of Liberty*, p. 29.
10 Cf. Hayek, F.A., 'The Primacy of the Abstract' in *New Studies*, pp. 35-49 esp. pp. 46-7.
11 Hayek, F.A., *The Constitution of Liberty*, p. 61.
12 Hayek, F.A., 'Individualism; True and False', in *Individualism and Economic Order* (Routledge & Kegan Paul, 1948), pp. 1-32. The quotations are from pp. 22 and 25.
13 Hayek, F.A., *Law, Legislation & Liberty*, vol. I, p. 32.
14 Hayek, F.A., *The Constitution of Liberty*, p. 377.
15 Cf. ibid., p. 378.
16 Ibid., p. 383.
17 Hayek, F.A., 'The Atavism of Social Justice' in *New Studies*, pp. 57-68, p. 64.
18 Barry, Norman, 'The Tradition of Spontaneous Order' in *Literature of Liberty*, V, Summer 1982, pp. 7-58, p. 46.
19 Cf. Hayek, F.A., *Constitution of Liberty*, pp. 52-3.
20 Scruton, Roger, *The Meaning of Conservatism* (Penguin, 1980), p. 33.
21 Ibid., p. 45.
22 Ibid., p. 169.
23 Ibid., p. 191.
24 Cf. ibid., p. 159.
25 Bellow, Saul, *The Dean's December* (Secker & Warburg, 1982), p. 187.

Personal authenticity and public standards: towards the transcendence of a dualism

Michael Bonnett

One of the central issues in education is surely that of how we are to think the relationship between the mind of the pupil and that which he is to learn. Indeed this issue is perhaps the definitive one for education, embracing as it does the nature of mental development, the nature of knowledge, the nature of learning and the nature of educational values. And from such considerations flow implications for the whole gamut of the educational enterprise: from curriculum aims, content, and methods, to the exercise of authority, discipline, and pupil-teacher relationships. It is a crucial task, then, for philosophy of education to work towards an adequate understanding of this relationship and it is with respect of this core problem that I wish to consider the work of Richard Peters, for he is a philosopher who has always been highly apprised of its importance.

In his writing his own position is often elucidated in the context of a critique of two opposing views of education which are loosely termed the 'traditional' and the 'progressive', both of which are vitiated in his view by their adherence to misguided assumptions concerning the nature of mental development. The traditional approach seemed to view the mind as essentially passive—an empty receptacle to be filled from without with recipes and information, or as malleable material to be moulded in accordance with external directives. By contrast the progressive reaction was to see the proper development of mind in terms of some sort of natural growth from within according to innate principles, an internal dynamic which merely required a suitable external environment to facilate its flowering. Thus for the traditionalist the typical mode of teaching would be formal instruction and rote exercises to 'stamp in' what was to be learnt, whereas for the progressive the very notion of *teaching* would be viewed with suspicion, the emphasis being on the pupil's self-initiated learning out of natural curiousity and interest fostered in a rich environment.

Such characterisations are familiar enough and, though clearly over-simplified to the point of caricature, have the virtue of pointing up a significant dichotomy of view which extends well beyond the horizon of purely educational concerns, viz. the relative importance of the 'inner' as against the 'outer', the private as against the public, the subjective as against the objective, the individual as against the cultural, nature as against nurture, romanticism as against classicism. It may well be objected that such a list conflates a number of distinct issues, and of course there is a sense in which this must immediately be conceded. Yet beneath the diversity there is distinguishable a common sentiment which sometimes discloses itself in seemingly perverse and tortuous ways, but which remains intelligible as such nonetheless. I refer to a dualism of 'subjective' internal order and 'objective' external order.

The traditional and progressive views of education stand on opposite sides of this divide, the one therefore emphasising the teacher's responsibility to provide external direction to mental development, the other emphasising methods by which the internal order of the individual pupil would be respected. And each feeling constrained to ignore or reject the demands of the other as inconsistent with its own view. Peters's response to this dichotomy is, broadly, to suggest that each side contains a certain germ of truth but makes its point in too extreme a fashion. The problem then, is to reconcile them—to show the proper relationship between 'inner' and 'outer'—in effect, to deny the dualism which holds them apart and distorts them. He attempts to achieve this by proposing a certain 'holy ground' of education whose recognition is essential to a proper understanding of mental development in both its 'internal' and 'external' aspects. For Peters, only by reference to such a ground does individual mental development become intelligible and teacher intervention become justifiable. His elaboration of such a 'holy ground' of education seems to me to be one of Richard Peters's major contributions to the philosophy of education. It is a direct response to the fundamental question from which this paper took its start, and it is clear that Peters sees his solution as having implications as extensive as those claimed.

In what, then, does this holy ground consist? It consists in various public modes of experience which are the source of that body of content emphasised by the traditionalists, and are constitutive of the development of mind and therefore of the possibility of individual potential emphasised by the progressivists. For Peters its recognition takes the focus of educational concern away from both a rigid and constraining content to be imposed upon the learner on the one hand, and almost solipsistic notions of

112

personal growth on the other, and moves it into a deeper perspective from which they can be reinterpreted in a way which allows what is of underlying value in each to be preserved and brought into a genuine synthesis.

Education as initiation into public modes of experience

For Peters all characteristically human consciousness involves entering a shared inheritance; it is never a 'naive opening of the eyes'. Thus to quote him in one of his early essays on education:

> No man is born with a mind; for the development of mind
> marks a series of individual and racial achievements. A child is
> born with an awareness not as yet differentiated into beliefs,
> wants and feelings. All such specific modes of consciousness,
> which are internally related to types of object in a public world,
> develop *pari passu* with the pointing out of paradigm objects.[1]

Thus mental development is seen as centrally involving initiation into a world of public objects which itself is in a significant sense a public creation. It is the achievement of shared traditions of thought, that is, shared ways of discriminating and classifying, and shared ways of bringing such categories into relationship and testing for their validity. It is thus the public rule structures—*the standards*—articulated and embedded in such traditions which constitute mind in a very fundamental sense. Only through the acquisition of such standards can man enter a world of human significances. And only by reference to such standards can he in turn contribute to it, for being critical and creative involves more than mere contra-suggestability and self-expression.

Peters, then, in the mainstream of his thought,[2] stresses the highly conventionalised nature of human thought and action, and the way in which the notion of public standards lies at the heart of what education as involving the development of mind must be about. It is for him just such a care for standards that transcends the dualism of inner and outer, for at this level the inner order and outer order seem to be fundamentally at one: the progressives' desire for individual development only being possible in terms of their acquisition, and the traditionalist's desire for the teacher to assume his proper responsibilities for directing the course of this development in terms of an objective external order being subsumed by a notion of initiation into public procedures which allows the pupil the possibility of making his own appropriate response to the human situation.

What is it, then, on Peters's account, to live in accordance with

113

such public standards—to have one's mental life so structured and thereby *gain* a mental life in human terms? Clearly at a very basic level understanding human action at all has typically to make reference to the idea of purposive rule-following. As argued in the early work *The Concept of Motivation*, it is shared rules that at the everyday level pick out human goals and the conditions necessary for attaining them, e.g. buying some tobacco or signing a contract can only be understood from within the framework of a set of conventions and, for example, could never be adequately characterised in terms of either mere bodily movements and their causal antecedents or purely idiosyncratic intentions held by the agent. Yet what would it be to live in accordance with the public standards which are constitutive of the public modes of experience to which Peters draws attention in the educational context?

In the later, and important, essay 'Subjectivity and Standards'[3] to which I will frequently refer in this paper, Peters says of standards that they 'represent the various demands made on us by the use of reason in its different forms'. The development of mind for Peters then ultimately consists in the internalisation of the standards of rationality where rationality itself, as has been indicated, is seen as a phenomenon of social life. Thus reason even when it takes place in the individual's head is an internalisation of public procedures, not the flowering of some inner potentiality, and particular standards in the different areas of rationality represent in detailed form 'the pressure of the givenness of the world and of human responses which is mediated through social traditions . . . a quality of life which takes account of the conditions under which it has to be lived'.[4] Clearly the standards with which we must here be concerned are diverse in kind, ranging from principles of classification employed in sensory perception and understanding, to principles of procedure and evaluation in the area of conduct. They vary, too, according to the different levels at which they have a purchase in human affairs, and therefore the ease with which they might be changed or dispensed with, to wit: basic discriminations in sense experience and 'laws' of thought such as the principle of non-contradiction, as against standards which are more subject to changing social conditions, the current state of knowledge, or fashion, as would be the case with those relevant to matters of hygiene, etiquette, or style of dress. Further, standards are not to be seen as purely cognitive in their force but demand certain attitudes and 'passions' such as the 'rational passions' of care for consistency, relevance, clarity, and humility before the facts. Indeed they may be seen as pervading affective life in general for they both structure, and allow evaluation of, the cognitive appraisals which might be held to be internal to all affect that rises above the level of pure sensation. Thus the 'holy ground' of education is certainly not to be construed as consisting in mere sets of abstract principles, but something more akin to a form of life in which they are embedded and which they enable. Yet despite the great diversity in the kinds of standards and the levels at which they operate within such a form of life, and despite the fact that such a form of life has its affective or 'subjective' side, on the present thesis the whole form of life must take its essential character from the mode of operation of standards which inspire and sustain it.

What, then are the *central* features of the notion of a standard, and their mode of operation in experience? Standards represent definitive measures of quality in experience and thus give it form, determining degrees of appropriateness, adequacy, and excellence in perception, understanding, and behaviour by providing shared fixed and generalizing points of reference. What sort of thing something is to count as and what value, positive or negative, it possesses become a function of established standards of correctness against which things are measured up and through which they are viewed—brought into meaningful relief. Standards, as it were, take a 'stand' in relation to the flux of experience, operating by bringing an element of definition and permanence which enables a transcendence of the here and now. They bring meaning through constancy. It is to these central features of the notion of a standard operating in experience that my discussion later in this paper will be addressed. But first I would like to summarise Peters's position on these and associated matters.

The quality of human experience is the product of living which attains to rational standards which transform primitive wishes, drives, reactions, etc. by making them appropriate to the situation in which we are all placed, i.e. by making them principled. It is in this way that one becomes sensitised to the human condition: a continuity of human experience constituted by those more permanent and all-pervasive concerns in human life which are connected up backwards and forwards from the present in the dimension of time, and through the medium of shared standards which transcend the here and now, the immediacy of instincts and drives and irrational wishes. To live according to such standards, then, involves a radical decentering of the individual both in the sense of transcending egocentricism, and enmeshment in the particular. For Peters, in estimating anything rationally 'identity is as irrelevant as time and place' and he speaks approvingly of G.H. Mead's notion of the reasonable man as one who adopts the view of the 'generalized other'.[5] Here, then, in brief outline, we have the view of a rationalist *par excellence*. The 'holy ground' of education, the fundamental essence of characteristically human experience in whose context all notions of individual mental development has to be understood, are the different public forms of rationality, traditionally thought of as the sciences and the humanities. And the central meaning of education is that of the liberal tradition which goes back at least as far as Plato, and in which the good of the mind is seen to consist in the acquisition of the standards implicit in the rational pursuit of truth. The question now arises as to how adequate a picture of the human situation and the development of mind this account provides.

Because of the fundamental level at which it seeks to operate it can be questioned from many and varied vantage points. As the title of this paper suggests, I shall here be chiefly concerned to question it from the subjective or individual side of the dualism previously distinguished: to what extent does it properly subsume and uphold this aspect and thus open up the possibility of a genuine transcendence of the dualism? Perhaps we can begin to come at this issue by reconsidering the view of Peters expressed earlier concerning the mind of the child as being initially undifferentiated into wants, beliefs and feelings, on the grounds that there is nothing to lend structure to such mental states prior to the acquisition of public classificatory standards through the pointing out of public objects. Several important questions arise here. I will begin with two:

(1) how could such mental developments get underway?
(2) what is the relationship between 'publicity', meaning and reality assumed by this view?

The problem raised by the first question is simply that if public standards are posited as fundamentally constituting mind they form a necessary condition of all perception and yet themselves have to be learnt. How is this possible? If the neonate cannot enter into significant relationship with anything prior to acquiring these structures, how can they be pointed out to him? Peters here speaks of the child having an 'undifferentiated awareness'. But what could this mean? Elsewhere he suggests that the child's 'mind' is ruled perhaps by bizarre and 'formless wishes',[6] but what sense can be made of a 'formless wish' and how could such wishes enable an appreciation of public objects? It almost seems as though Peters is aware of a problem of circularity posed by his thesis but cannot quite bring himself to accept the implication, viz. that we must from the beginning presuppose a definite structure to consciousness which is pre-social in origin. In his concern to provide a necessary corrective to the extreme naturalism of romantic child-centred views by properly pointing out that the child develops by entering a shared world in which social objects loom large, he seems in danger of overstating the case and overlooks the contribution that the child's own *nature* must make in order to gain access to this world. In sum, Peters is correct insofar as he points out that the mark of consciousness is self-transcendence, i.e. intentionality—a directedness on objects which are in a certain sense external to it—but he would be wrong to equate such external objects with publicly elaborated objects.

This leads us to our second question: what is the significance of claiming that the objects to which consciousness relates itself exist in a *public* world? An extreme interpretation—and one which found some favour recently—is to claim that all such objects are pure social constructions and therefore solely the product of, and exclusively sustained by, a particular social milieu. Clearly on this basis the claim that mind is from the beginning a social achievement would be true *ex hypothesi*, but then our problem regarding the initiation of mental development becomes quite intractable. Peters himself rebukes the protagonists of such a view on the grounds that they ignore the brute givenness of the physical world and certain human responses. Human reality is not purely a social construction, as anyone who tries to fly unaided quickly discovers. To use Kant's language, it would seem that Peters grants a form of sensibility which is pre-social, but holds that this remains 'blind' until its presentations are structured by the form of understanding, which is a social product. Certainly he criticises Kant for paying too little attention to the social in this respect. So is it that for Peters a world is somehow present to consciousness pre-socially but only *accessible* to it—becomes part of meaningful experience—through public concepts? With Hirst, in *The Logic of Education*[7] he certainly speaks of all experience being dependent upon the acquisition of the relevant concepts, but now, granted an independent reality in some sense, why should these be public, as his account of the priority of such concepts to mental development suggests? Why should not a child form 'idiosyncratic' concepts, i.e. ones whose genesis in his consciousness is not a product of the pointing out of paradigm objects by his elders? Of course, insofar as the child follows a rule in differentiating out aspects of his experience such objects as he thus relates to would of necessity be *in principle* public in that anyone else following that rule in that situation could gain acquaintance with that object. But this would not seem to do for Peters, for such objects would then not be the 'sole property' of an existing public world, and the child could come at them independently of this and thus achieve a degree of mental structure which was not logically dependent upon pre-existing public standards (though the child may well be *biologically* dependent upon a social situation). In this way the child would acquire a growing individual perspective on the world which would colour subsequent mental development through being the subjective ground from which future development might take its rise and into which it would need to be integrated. And to say that this occurrence would then be part of the public world—occurs *in* it, in that it can be witnessed and described through public concepts—would become an empty truism with no implications for mental development of the kind that Peters claims. In sum the claim that all mental structure is dependent upon the acquisition of public concepts is ambiguous. If by 'public' it is merely meant that such concepts are in principle *publicly accessible*, the claim is probably true but of little consequence. If by 'public' it is meant that such concepts are *publicly generated*, i.e. are necessarily the product of a social tradition and thus only become available to the individual through his being initiated into that tradition, the claim would be of considerable consequence if it were not ultimately incoherent.

What surely has to be granted to make sense of mental development at all—and has been underlined at great length by thinkers such as the 'early' Husserl with his notion of a transcendental meaning-giving subjectivity (though there he no doubt overstated the case for the opposite extreme) is that we have to acknowledge a pre-social subjective vectorial structure to consciousness.[8] From the beginning significant experience involves meaning-giving through intentional acts; nothing comes already endowed with a particular meaning for the subject, but has to be so construed or *taken* by him. This he can only do in terms of some pre-existing intentional structure which, it would seem to follow, must originally be pre-social in order for him to be able to relate to the social in the first place. An essential element of subjective giving is thus presupposed, as is a predisposition to understand the world as shared. To enter any world, including the human world, he must first *inform* it from a certain originary standpoint. This means then, more than that the child is possessed of formal discriminatory powers, but also substantive interests—a certain 'mindedness'—in relation to which such powers may actually come into play and meaning be given. This being so, an account of mental development which focusses almost exclusively on the role of public standards remains seriously one-sided through failing to do justice to the subjective conditions necessary for socially elaborated meanings to enter significantly into the conscious life of an individual.

A full recognition of the fact that mind is substantially more than a reflection of public standards is important not just with regard to the development of mind, but also with regard to the development of the public forms of experience *themselves*. There is a level at which the self-criticism necessary to progress within a mode of experience requires that particular aspects come to be seen in novel ways. Public concepts have to be applied under the guidance of a new conception of the situation which must in turn stem significantly from a corresponding subjective *noeisis*. Here an 'idiosyncratic' element is essential, for before the noeisis such a conception was not part of what Toulmin has aptly termed the 'transmit' of a form of experience, nor were the conditions *sufficient* for its genesis, though the criteria for its acceptability may have been. But more than this, if radical changes in the outlook provided by a form of experience—of the kind suggested by Kuhnian paradigm shifts in the sciences—are not to be purely arbitrary affairs, then we have to acknowledge some acquaintance-ship with the objects of understanding in that form which is not structured purely by the standards which currently constitute that form, and which can inspire, guide, and legitimise such shifts. Thus public standards themselves cannot be what are most fundamentally constitutive of human consciousness. Indeed it may on occasion be necessary to stand out against them, to remain resilient to the pressure of public 'reason'. And unless there is something beyond public standards—some more primordial apprehension of truth, fittingness, etc., there is nothing to appeal to for sustaining fundamental criticism and change.[9] It is in this respect that Martin Heidegger's understanding of truth as revealing—an open dwelling with things prior to judgments of correctness—has much to offer.[10] He suggests that when we truly speak, judge, evaluate, we must in some sense already be *with* that of which we speak, for we could not otherwise form true predicates concerning it and represent it to ourselves as a particular kind of thing. If this is indeed the case—and because of its germaneness to our discussion it is a view to which I shall return at more length presently—it will be this prior dwelling with things and not public standards alone which allows of the possibility of genuine communication and human awareness.

So far in this paper I have attempted to elucidate the framework of the social-rationalist position on the development of mind which underlies so much of Richard Peters's view of education. And I have begun to indicate some serious reservations concerning this view in its ambition of transcending the dualism between the internal subjective order and the external objective order emphasised by educational progressivism and traditionalism respectively. While supporting the notion that a satisfactory grasp of the relationship between learner and that which is to be learnt requires—indeed itself consists in—a transcendence of this dualism (indeed in a sense, and at another level, such transcendence is precisely how one might characterise the enterprise that a genuine learner is engaged in in making what he learns his own) it seems that Peters's notion of a holy ground consisting in modes of experience structured by public standards overcomes this dualism by, in effect, subjugating one aspect to the other. Nonetheless it must be granted that he genuinely points the way forward by proposing the notion of a holy ground in education which goes some way to undermining the long-standing and divisive traditional/progressive framework of reference through suggesting a deeper perspective in which the separate emphases of each need to be reinterpreted. What is in question now, then, is the proper nature of this holy ground, and in the light of the general criticism that has been made of Peters's characterisation of it, this question will now be pursued by attempting to trace further the ways in which a focus upon public rational standards does too little justice to the notion of an inner subjective order.

The demands of authenticity

In the paper 'Subjectivity and Standards' to which reference has already been made, Peters directly addresses the relationship between the holy ground of public modes of experience and the individual. His attachment to rational standards and their elevation as constitutive of human mental development leads him to make the following claim: no value attaches to 'naked mineness'—to authenticity—'Indeed in estimating anything rationally identity is as irrelevant as time and place.' Whilst the rational principle of respect for persons demands that an individual's point of view should not be disregarded '. . . this does not mean that there is any value necessarily in the *content* of his wishes, or point of view.' The value of authenticity comes to lie solely in the fact that mere unthinking conformity to standards of rationality shows insufficient care for them as such.

Now this expression of subordination of authenticity to the appreciation of rational standards has a curious consequence which is illuminative of the nature of the commitment implicit in the social-rationalist view. In company with many others, Peters regards the principle of respect for persons as central to a rational morality. It is very prominent in his extensive writing in the field of moral philosophy and ethical values in education. Yet what, for him, can 'respect for persons' actually amount to? From the foregoing it is clear that it is certainly not respect for individuality as such. But what then are we to understand by the term 'person'? Presumably, following on from previous argument, it refers to a centre of human consciousness where what is meant by *human* consciousness is one structured by rational standards. Clearly, then, on this way of thought respect for persons is no more than a variation of the principle of respect for rational standards, and it follows therefore that the principle does not enjoin us to respect non-rational people or aspects of people such as, say, when they might seek to act out of intuition or love which claims no basis in rational justification. We should respect them in the sense of allowing equal importance to their ends as to our own, only to the extent that they are centres of consciousness where the rational public modes of experience flourish, or perhaps are likely to be developed through such respect. But in this case the suggestion that we should respect them but not necessarily the content of their views becomes vacuous. They can only count as worthy of respect to the extent that such content accords with rational standards. Consistency seems to demand of the rationalist that his allegiance is solely to public reason. This does not of course deny that non-rational entities may not be deserving of *some* sort of respect, e.g. insofar as they are susceptible to pain, joy, etc. it may be proper to give thought to minimise the one and maximise the other, but there can be no admonishment to respect their ends *as we would our own as rational beings*. Now it seems to me that this consequence brings us starkly up against the full force of the position to which Peters is committed, and it may lead one to question whether the transformation of natural sentiments such as sympathy for others into a principled respect for persons is really an unmitigated gain after all. More importantly, it raises the whole question of the fittingness of the elevated position given to rationality by Peters. A position in which it exclusively sets the standard for all thought and value. This, again, is a question to which I will return. First it is necessary to say a little more about authenticity itself.

Peters characterises authenticity in terms of the popular notion of 'doing one's own thing'. As far as it goes this characterisation is undeniably correct. The problem is that it tends to leave more unsaid than said. In particular it makes no reference to the element of personal responsibility which attaches to truly doing one's own thing and which indeed is centrally definitive of it. It is the acceptance of personal responsibility for the expression of one's choices and commitments that makes them one's own. It is through a developing sense of such responsibility that commitments which one may have received unreflectively or even unwittingly from others during one's upbringing, acquire a personal cogency and become truly appropriated by the self— rejecting such responsibility precisely being a way of denying that they are one's own. It is this element of responsibility that has prompted existentialists to speak of freedom as a burden and source of anxiety which we often try to evade by the self-deception of supposing that facets of the situation external to us have totally constrained us, and must therefore bear the ultimate responsibility for our actions: the anonymous 'they', an immutable personality, social roles and background, transcendent fate or Divine Will, etc. The important consequence of this line of thought is that it will be through such genuine self-expression, i.e. expression of those commitments for which we accept personal responsibility, that we each enter into a personally significant relationship with the world—things having personal meaning through the possibilities they hold out in terms of such commitments. And thus it is such commitments, and the precise ways in which they are held, which will come properly to constitute the core of that meaning-giving subjectivity to which reference has previously been made.[11] This being so, while it must surely be granted that 'naked mineness' cannot be the sole value in education, authenticity itself cannot be dismissed as having *no* value as it is a fundamental condition of personally meaningful experience as such, and therefore of making what one learns one's own. For public standards to be truly internalised, and thus actually operative in structuring an *individual* mind, they cannot be sustained there as in the mind of generalised 'everyman', but must be enlivened by the authentic concern of the individual. To abandon this facet would be to condemn human understanding to an essentially thoughtless, though quite possibly 'impassioned', enactment of an external order, and make man a mere functionary of public reason. As will be argued in more detail presently, rational standards alone, through their aspiration to generality, depersonalise the subject, average off the object and thus mechanise the process of thought. And in doing this they would deny themselves a fitting home. Curiously, a care for them, equally, must be a care for what lies *beyond* them, if it is to be the spirit and not merely the letter of the law which prevails. Intelligent application of public standards requires a sensitivity to that which is not standardisable, that is to say, an open and creative response to things themselves. Insofar as authenticity denotes genuine self-expression—the individual living and finding meaning in accordance with his own essence which might facilitate this sensitivity—it would be unfortunate, though not unexpected, for the rationalist to suggest a one-way subordination of authenticity to rationality when what is rather required is something more akin to a mutual appropriation of the two.

It is true that in saying this one is attributing to the notion of authenticity an element of openess which mere 'mineness' might well deny, for, no doubt, the latter can take the form of a self-assertive ownership and power-seeking which is blind to all else. But here, again, too little attention would have been paid to the notion of responsibility which I have suggested to be central to authenticity. Responsibility proper intimates a certain involvement in the world which recognises the negation implied in any thought or act. Actualising one possibility is always at the expense of denying others, and it is only because one is aware of what one has denied in what one has achieved that one can feel responsibility. This is the condition of the possibility of freedom and of having a conscience—an openness to guilt which cannot be assuaged by attempting to take refuge in public standards. Such sensitivity to negation is, then, necessarily an openness to things themselves and is receptive to directives from them. This is to say that authenticity proper aspires to a direct relationship to Being, a relationship beyond the reach of generalising standards as such, and to which they must be referred in their application. Note, that in speaking of responsibility, guilt, and conscience here, they are far removed from the narrowly moral context with which they have come to be conventionally associated. They are rather, as Heidegger would claim, *presuppositions* of notions of moral rightness and wrongness, and the notions of responsibility, guilt and conscience which imply assessment of moral praiseworthiness and blameworthiness.[12]

However, might it not be objected here that, at whatever level, such notions must themselves involve the use of standards of some kind, for example, at the very least, on the present account, the standard of not having standards. This latter formulation seems to me to trade on a mere play on words and in any case quite misrepresents the view that I am trying to express. The essential point is that such notions as responsibility, conscience, and guilt, *properly understood*, demand a certain transcendence of existing public standards through maintaining an awareness of that which a standard denies. They suggest a frame of mind which, as it were, constantly puts up for question those central features of the mode of operation of a standard previously picked out, and which thus provides a context which transforms this mode of operation itself by preserving an awareness of that which is so much more than that revealed in the objects of 'standardised' perception. It is not, then, that a consciousness totally devoid of public standards is being postulated, but rather one in which those measuring, defining, generalising and stabilising motives central to their operation are not allowed to dominate. In sum, what is being suggested here is the possibility that human consciousness needs to be thought as essentially more than merely a home for rational standards and the form of life they inspire; that the necessarily levelled-off quality of a principled way of relating to things is neither the whole of human being nor indeed its most fundamental feature. We are led then, finally, to a more detailed examination of the ideal which runs through so much of Richard Peters's thought: public rationality as the essence of man.

The demands of rationality

It is clear that Richard Peters is far from insensitive to many of the reservations which I have raised concerning the notion of mind as structured by public standards. But he is inclined to view them as qualifications rather than reservations: aspects which his view can consistently accommodate, rather than telling criticisms. For example he himself speaks of 'the dreariness and cravenness of secondhandedness' in one's understanding of public standards, and the need for reason to be 'employed with a certain humility and reverence—with a sense of our shared humanity'.[13] Now while such 'qualifications' seem to show a proper sensitivity to fundamental dimensions of humanness which lie beyond the notion of standards alone, surely they must be seen as damaging to his central position *in that they do just this*. Basically it seems to me that he fails to fully appreciate the enmeshment of thought that his elevation of reason brings in its train, and thus wrongly assumes that he can consistently accommodate aspects of human experience which are not adequately characterised by reference to the notion of standards and yet still overcome the dualism of 'inner' and 'outer' through recourse to such standards. Or is it that he is here feeling towards a notion of reason which is larger than the notion of standards in terms of which he has hitherto characterised it?

For the classical rationalist, rationality represents the sole non-arbitrary pathway to truth. This is not to claim that say, pristine intuition, may not chance upon truth on occasion, but that without reason such truth as it chances upon cannot be *shown* to be truth since the very notion of justification implies reason. Further it is only through reason that truth can be pursued systematically and thus, seemingly, with any good chance of success. Rational standards, then, are the means of overcoming arbitrariness and of bringing things into an order which makes them manageable and thus accessible to thought. It is this order which allows of assessment and evaluation of a state of affairs: *Truth is gained through rational judgment and categorising.* Thus Peters speaks of science as 'the supreme example of reason in action' and of the physical sciences as 'perhaps the finest product that yet exists of the sustained and controlled imagination of the human race'.[14] In some sense they come closer to reality than the arts, for according to Peters in poetry and literature the 'givenness of the world' is less insistent and their products are more truly 'creations' than those of the sciences and philosophy. Now here, it seems to me, is intimated a very singular vision concerning the nature of truth and thought, and thus of the essence of humanness to which an adequate education should be sensitising a new generation. It might prove instructive at this point to contrast this view with that of Martin Heidegger who once made the claim that the sciences do not think.[15]

For the rationalist the development of thought basically takes the form of the acquisition of an increasing range of categories, allowing ever-finer discriminations to be made by means of which we can represent things to ourselves with increasing specificity and develop analytic relationships between them. Such rational cate-gorising, then, in keeping with certain of those features which I have held to be central to the operation of all standards, involves a threefold mastery of things: *fixing* them as of a certain class with certain objective properties, *assessing* them as having met the relevant standards, *evaluating* them according to where we have placed them in our overall order of things. Heidegger points out that recognition of these essential facets of rational thought reveals that it has an essentially self-assertive and calculative nature. Further, its 'success', especially as evidenced in the sciences, has led to it becoming the dominant form of thought in our time such that it is now in danger of setting the standard for thought as a whole. This is not merely because it assuages man's appetite for power, but because it constantly creates and reinforces this appetite such that a thinking which cannot compete on this basis increasingly comes to be regarded as worthless. In short, rational-assertive thinking is coming to condition man's way of relating to Being as a whole, and it is part of its self-assertive nature to eclipse any other way of relating to Being through itself remaining impervious to any such suggestion that there are worthy alterna-tives. From the standpoint of rationality radical alternatives are redundant, and absorption in this framework thus increasingly removes the possibility of seeking any other. Thought becomes essentially a matter of ratiocination, and things themselves are acknowledged to the extent that they can enter into this process and be 'reckoned up'.[16]

In truth, then, rationality entails a lack of openness to Being, a self-preoccupation, despite all the claims of rationalists precisely to the contrary. Herein lies the greatest danger: rationality tranquillises a sensitivity to the need for alternative modes of thought through its plausibility, in its own terms, of encompassing the whole of thought proper. It lays claim to virtues of thought which interpreted in its own way it possesses, but it is precisely its interpretation of these virtues that is at stake, and constantly diverts attention from a more fundamental interpretation of them. It claims above all to deliver thought from idiosyncrasy, narrow-mindedness, and arbitrary self-assertiveness, making possible instead objectivity, openness, and impartiality. Yet there is a sense in which by its very nature as calculative it can itself only flourish by denying these virtues when they are interpreted from a deeper perspective. To refer back for a moment to that 'paradigm of rationality in action'—the exact sciences. Despite the impartiality and openness suggested (and achieved no doubt at a certain level) by the canon of seeking the negative instance—Popperian falsification—it remains the case that the whole enterprise is conducted in the light of a prejudice in favour of the value of levelling and possessive explanation. Thus things are indeed disclosed as *instances* rather than in their own vital uniqueness, and nature is acknowledged only insofar as she puts in an appearance in terms of the theories—categories and general relationships—current within whatever paradigm is holding sway. Science does not think because it cannot. In looking past things as they are in themselves, in refusing to stay *with* things, it forgets Being. It has acquired instead a self-fuelling autonomy which carries it ever forward and away from how things actually *are* in their concrete 'thereness'. In common with all forms of rationality it progresses through representing things to itself through statements (or something analogous) whose correctness is established by means of public standardised procedures. To allow itself to be affected by the individual as such—to participate in its thereness rather than put it at a distance so as to be set up for inspection and evaluation—would be for rationality to turn aside from its quest; to falter; to give thought to Being.

The arts, of course, have often been thought of as less 'objective' than the sciences and more concerned with the individual and the particular, but insofar as they too are appropriately thought of as being centrally structured by rational standards, as involving assessment and evaluation articulated in statements—*insofar* as this is an appropriate characterisation of them, they are subject to similar criticism. Of course, insofar as they are *not* so characterisable, and are not fundamentally dependent upon such features, they seem to fall beyond the notion of rational standards and thus of rationality itself. Though this raises an important issue concerning the extent to which rationality does necessarily involve rational public standards, it is not a question which can be taken up in depth in this essay, the important point for present purposes being that for rationalists such as Peters rationality clearly not only does necessarily involve such standards, but they are definitive of it.

Yet to return to the ambiguity touched on earlier, it is also clear that Peters does not see standards as rules which are merely imposed upon reality and which come in the end to substitute for it, but rather as representing—to hark back to his definition given earlier—'the pressure of the givenness of the world and of human responses'. That is to say Peters himself sees standards as in some sense responsive. The problem arises now, however, as to how this is to be made intelligible in terms of his own account. To what, precisely, are standards to be responsive? What account can be given of the 'givenness' of things on his view? The physical world and characteristic human responses can only be given to human consciousness, but, as previously brought out, the problem here is that consciousness is *ex hypothesi* only capable of meaningful experience in terms of a structure provided by public standards. As it stands on this account there can be no awareness of the givenness of things as such, only a 'standardised' awareness—the standards representing less the pressure of things themselves and more the pressure of rational purposes connected with the processing and manipulation of them.

Yet, surely, Peters touches upon an important point here. Is it not the case that things are always perceived under some aspect and that this aspect will reflect our purposes, i.e. the notion of things as they are in themselves is at worst a nonsense, or at best—as with Kant—such things are the occupants of a world of which human beings can never have direct awareness and are thus a purely metaphysical speculation? Rational standards, then, represent common aspects under which things are viewed which are appropriate to human purposes. I think the response to this seeming rebuttal lies in both a more careful consideration of the notion of human purposes, and an appeal to certain human experiences.

The first thing to be said is that human purposes need not be self-wilful. It makes perfectly good sense for one's purpose to be to enable something to exist in its own right or develop in its own way. With such a purpose one attempts to enter into a receptive-responsive relationship with it in which preconceptions are held in abeyance such that the thing and its needs can be revealed in their true nature. One genuinely attempts to work *with* the thing in an attempt to bring forth what it has in it to be. Heidegger has coined the term 'poetic building' as suggestive of this empathetic response to things and claims that it might be in keeping with the pre-Socratic experience of thought expressed, for him, in Parmenides: 'a letting-lie-before-us and a taking-to-heart' in which the characteristic attitude of thought is one of receptiveness, celebration, and thanksgiving. What we have here, then, is a certain reverence for Being and sense of wonder that things *are* in which their intrinsic strangeness, which is the source of their vitality in thought, is preserved, as against a curiosity which requires that they be explained or justified, and thus made acceptable, i.e. familiar, transparent, and on call. The aspect under which they are perceived is thus one of openness, which is incompatible with standardisation, though it may well be that they are first brought to our attention in the context of self-centred practical purposes, or 'impartial' theoretical purposes in which standardisation is prominent. Indeed it is likely today that our first, though very partial, glimpse of them is afforded through everyday rational categories, but such thinking requires a willingness to shed these categories—to allow a certain dissolution of them such that their significance in experience becomes diminished and the thing itself comes to presence. I have previously suggested that something of this sort may be achieved through an authenticity in which the negation in what we think and do is properly acknowledged, and by means of which our essence to reveal things as they are can begin to hold sway in our relationships with things and thus a genuine harmony be achieved in some degree. But there is also, of course, the fact of human experience in, for example, the contemplation of an artwork. Here it is possible for us to enter a relationship with the thing in which all assessment and evaluating, all aesthetic 'connoisseurship', are put to one side and the thing shines forth as it is through our participation in it. This being so, to speak of artworks as being more truly 'creations' is not to say that they are fictions in which reality is thereby obscured. Quite the contrary, for in the experience of the artwork it is possible for the *given*ness of things, which implies their fixation, to be replaced by a spontaneous *give*ness whose reception preserves us from the ultimate nihilism which self-centred ordering sets in train.

Herein, then, lies the goal implicit in authenticity and, equally, the proper grounding for standards and changes in them— the source of their 'objectivity'. This is to say that it is at this level that we must seek for the transcendence of the dualism of 'inner' and 'outer'. The essence of both is a responsibility towards Being lest artificiality subvert truth and creativity, rootless inventiveness and exploitation borne of the motive for mastery substitute for a genuine bringing forth of things into light.

Conclusion: education and the integrity of thought

The fertility of much of Richard Peters's thought in the philosophy of education lies in his capacity to focus on problems of central importance, and his attempt to derive a unifying perspective on these problems from the standpoint of a manifold rationality which nonetheless has a monolithic base in the notion of public standards which determine the essential character of the 'holy ground' of education. That there are signs of ambiguity and tension surrounding this mainstream of his thought arising out of a sensitivity to facets of human experience which are not readily accommodated to it, only adds to its seminal character. I have suggested that while an attempt to overcome the dualism of 'inner' and 'outer' is central to a proper grasp of the relationship between the learner and that which he is to learn, the social-rationalist position which elevates public standards to the central role in such an enterprise in effect subverts certain crucial considerations which the notion of authenticity, properly conceived, brings to our attention. These considerations, I have suggested, indicate a way forward towards a more adequate overcoming of the dualism in which the 'holy ground' of education emerges as an openness to Being which is both the goal of personal authenticity and the well-spring of human culture, from which its various modes of experience therefore draw. I have claimed that such an acknow-ledgment is jeopardised by a view of man wedded to a standards-orientated rationality whose calculative nature distorts our under-standing of the virtues of thought. Equally it can be seen to distort our understanding of certain excellences of thought— creativity and criticalness—by leading to an interpretation of the former which emphasises masterly inventiveness and ingenuity, and of the latter which emphasises analytic dissection and reconstruction— both in terms of categories which must define the matters at stake in advance. In this way it tends to make them subservient to a public status quo. Creativity proper and criticalness proper, in truth, are of a rather different character. In essence they involve a certain violence to the public ordering of things and its demands for transparency and specificity, such that the original in its strangeness may genuinely break through—be allowed a free space in which to show itself. But this violence is an intimate striving with public standards by means of which we ordinarily and for the most part are made familiar with things, and reposes in a reverence for Being that is withdrawn before such standards when they have thus become dominant. This is not to deny that thinking—*any* thinking—must make distinctions, but rather that they are never allowed a status greater than that of pointer to the openness of what is, and are always thought in terms of those partial motives which are holding sway through them, and thus with remembrance of that which they negate. On this view, then, rigour is not fundamentally achieved by a thinking rooted in defining categories and 'reasoned' connections between them in accordance with accepted standards—a securing and comforting ordering maintained by imperviousness to the spontaneity and uncanniness of existence. On the contrary its source is rather an openness to just this spontaneity and certain inscrutability of things, and thus the fundamental rigour of thought consists in an alertness to, and willingness to respond to, signs on its way, which is uncharted. In this way thought itself may become a poetic building—and this includes that thought involved in the process of education, even though this is a highly practical concern.

It would not be unnatural for a view which understood the development of mind to consist centrally in the acquisition of public standards to advocate a compulsory curriculum designed to achieve this end. In this way the undifferentiated mind would be systematically introduced to the relevant standards and thereby liberated from amorphousness and ignorance into the rule-governed world of human culture. In this would lie the development of individual autonomy, for familiarity with such standards, as well as constituting entrance to such a world, would constitute the means by which one could frame, evaluate, and implement one's own purposes within it. Thus just as the mind is seen as a reflection of public standards, so too, is the curriculum—a process which, while not disdaining to harness children's interests in the advancement of this goal, cannot allow such interests—arbitrary and idiosyncratic as they may well seem to be—to define or condition it. For rationality is the fruit neither of an individual consciousness nor an untutored one. Thus curriculum aims, and therefore to a certain though lesser extent, content and methods, are determined independently of any individual child by reference to the structure of the different public modes of rational experience.

How does such a strategy square with the way of thought which I have been trying to develop in this paper? An education which is concerned to facilitate a thinking which springs neither from the self-assertiveness of modern rationality nor the self-assertiveness of an egocentric individualism, but from an authentic relationship with things themselves, must itself endeavour to spring from this same source and thereby overcome the dualism of 'inner' and 'outer'. It must, in effect, aspire to a poetic building in which an individual learner is brought into contact with that within his culture which will allow *his* thinking to aspire to thought of Being. There may be many obstacles to this. Much which is prominent within contemporary culture—particularly those aspects picked out by the notion of 'mass culture'—would distract him from this path, as too—as I have tried to show—might certain motives implicit in modern rational-intellectual culture. Equally, on the part of the individual, a disposition to essential unthinkingness born of ingrained apathy, timidity, and the absorbing 'busyness' and self-deception of what Heidegger has aptly called the 'they-self' of everyday life would leave him desensitised to any such need. Yet this may well be his starting point. And, to refer back to the dichotomy in educational thought with which this paper began, neither 'traditionalism' nor 'progressivism' as there characterised can make an adequate response to this situation. To attempt to impose a structure on the mind pays too little attention to the role of meaning-giving subjectivity, while allowing merely current wants and interests to provide direction may well be to indulge an essential superficiality. Thus both a compulsory 'standards-centred' curriculum and a 'child-centred' curriculum will take us nowhere with regard to our present need.

The way forward is cued, I think, by the unity which the notion of authenticity can evoke when seen from the perspective of responsibility towards Being, for from this perspective authenticity of the individual and authenticity of standards are complementary facets of the same. Through a growing sense of personal responsibility in the terms previously described, the individual achieves a movement towards openness which at the same time allows him to authentically appreciate, apply, and therefore modify, standards.

The essence of education then, is neither a compulsory curriculum structured by an external order, nor a 'laissez-faire' curriculum structured by a purely internal order, but an *empathetic challenging* of the individual to overcome timidity and take up the risk of his own life. It is in the nature of such a challenge that while an essential element of consent is preserved for the challenge to be genuinely taken up, so too is the element of demand necessary for personal growth. The task of the educator, then, is to challenge the learner to locate and acknowledge his own concerns—what they involve, what they demand as fitting and the personal responsibility that accrues. In thus deepening by disclosing those concerns which are *his*, he becomes individualised and achieves a care for his own being which is the reverse of egocentricism. On the contrary, it is the condition of openness. In becoming aware of the true force of his own concerns in both their enabling and negating aspects, in being thus willing to have a conscience, he is thereby released to a care for the being of things, of whose presencing public standards are both an expression and a denial, for in representing generalised, common—and therefore, in a certain sense, anonymous—concerns, they discriminate by covering over that which they negate. In other words only a genuine individual is predisposed to reveal another, to lighten things in their own vital individuality by being receptive to them as such. This awareness of individuality is of course far removed from one composed of judgmental statements employing analytic categories by which one attempts to define and construct things. And once this lightening of things themselves is extinguished, abstract generalities remain abstract generalities and thought loses touch with its ground, such that the notion of reason being 'employed with a certain humility and reverence' remains either self-centred and insulating or ultimately obscure.

Notes

1 'Education as Initiation' in Archambault, R.D. (ed.), *Philosophical Analysis and Education* (Routledge & Kegan Paul, 1965).
2 This qualification is important, for in other contexts—particularly that of religion—Peters has on occasion written with a somewhat different emphasis, and one which is not in my view ultimately consistent with the themes here being taken as mainstream in his thought, and which have had most influence in the field of educational theory.
3 'Subjectivity and Standards', reprinted in the collection Peters, R.S., *Psychology and Ethical Development* (Allen & Unwin, 1974).
4 Ibid.
5 Ibid.
6 *Ethics and Education*, ch. 1 (Allen & Unwin, 1966).
7 Hirst, P.H. and Peters, R.S., *The Logic of Education* (Routledge & Kegan Paul, 1970), p. 62.
8 See, for example, *Logical Investigations*, trans. Findlay, J. (Routledge &

Kegan Paul, 1970), and *Ideas*, trans. Boyce Gibson, W. (Allen & Unwin, 1931).

9 This point has been well made by R.K. Elliott in his paper 'The Concept of Development: A reply to D.W. Hamlyn', in *Proceedings of the Philosophy of Education Society of Great Britain*, vol. IX, 1975. See also Francis Dunlop, 'Human Dignity and Direct Awareness', in *Journal of Philosophy of Education*, vol. 14, no. 2, 1980.

10 See, for example, Heidegger, M., 'On the essence of truth' (1930), in Krell, D., *Martin Heidegger, Basic Writings* (Routledge & Kegan Paul, 1978).

11 And which I have elaborated in more detail in a paper 'Authenticity and Education', *Journal of Philosophy of Education*, vol. 12, 1978.

12 See Heidegger, M., *Being and Time*, Division Two, ch. 2, translated by Macquarrie, J. and Robinson, E. (Basil Blackwell, 1973).

13 'Subjectivity and Standards', op. cit.

14 Ibid.

15 See *What is Called Thinking*, translated by Glenn Gray, J. (Harper & Row, 1968).

16 I have recently attempted to amplify the general view expressed in this passage in a paper: 'Education in a Destitute Time (A Heideggerian perspective on the problem of education in the age of modern technology)', *Journal of Philosophy of Education*, vol. 17, no. 1, 1983.

Prudence and respect for persons: Peters and Kant

Alan Montefiore

Chapter VIII of Richard Peters's *Ethics and Education* is entitled 'Respect for Persons, Fraternity and the Concept of Man'; it was, so Peters said in his preface, the chapter 'which gave me more trouble than any other chapter in the book' (p. 8).[1] This, no doubt, is as it should be. The matters with which it is concerned lie at the very heart of that enlightened liberal democratic view of the proper nature of human society of which Peters has always been so notable an exponent in the fields of political philosophy and philosophy of education. If he had difficulty with these central and fundamental issues, it is that they are indeed difficult—and that he was both sensitive and honest enough to feel and to acknowledge the difficulties. It is in fact remarkable how well how much of this book still reads, getting on for twenty years since it was first written. Peters himself thought of it at the time of writing as being work still very much in progress and took himself to be publishing it 'somewhat prematurely'. Still, the point was, he said, 'to provide a few signposts for others and to map the contours of the fields for others to explore in a more leisurely and detailed manner' (p. 8). The context of one short paper does not provide much scope for leisure or for detail; but there can be no doubt that the topics of this chapter are more than worth coming back to.

What, then, is the notion of a 'person'? It is, says Peters, 'narrower than the wider notion of being an "individual" ' (p. 210). Moreover, it is, so far as he is concerned, a frankly normative notion. 'People only begin to think of themselves as persons, as centres of valuation, decision and choice, in so far as the fact that consciousness is individuated into distinct centres, linked with distinct physical bodies and with distinctive points of view, is taken to be a matter of importance in a society. And they will', he adds, 'only really develop as persons in so far as they learn to think of themselves as such' (p. 211). Peters is also quite explicit in rooting this eminently individualistic ethic in a ground of essentially social evaluation. 'The concept of being a person . . . is derivative from the valuation placed in a society upon the determining role of individual points of view' (p. 211). And again: 'in so far as a man has the concept of himself and of others as persons, he must have been initiated into a society in which there is a general norm which attaches importance to the assertive points of view emanating from individual centres of consciousness' (p. 213). The roots of this ethic are thus unequivocally social; but anyone brought up in such a society and learning, as part of his learning of its language and other forms of life, how to handle the concept of a person and to apply it to himself and to others, will come, as he does so, to 'value what is involved in being a person for what there is in it as distinct from the importance attached to it by the social norm.' And then, to underline once more the paradigmatically evaluative dimension of the concept of a person, 'the concept of respect is necessary to explicate what is meant by a person. If [anyone] has the concept of a person and understands it fully from "the inside" . . . , then he must also have the notion that individuals represent distinct assertive points of view' (p. 213).

So far, so conceptually analytic. 'To ask . . . whether persons ought to be respected is rather like asking a man whether he ought to be afraid of a dangerous situation'; in both cases the answer is inscribed within the meaning-ranges of the relevant words. But once again Peters is himself the first to point out that 'the explication of a concept never settles a question of policy'. The problem of *policy*, the problem, one might say, of any serious philosophy of morals, politics or education, remains, namely 'to produce an argument to establish that any rational being must have the concept of a person and therefore respect others and himself as such' (p. 213).

To pose the problem in such a way, however, is to move already a fair way towards suggesting the form that the answer must take. If the question is one of policy, the answer cannot lie in some merely definitional stipulation to the effect that to 'have the concept of a person and therefore respect others and [oneself] as such' is to be taken as forming part of the content of the concept of a rational being. But nor could Peters, who, at this stage at any rate, was certainly still working within a framework of assumptions belonging to some version or another of the so-called Autonomy of Ethics, be satisfied by a merely stipulative assertion of values, not even if the values in question are embedded within a whole concept of man: 'The trouble, however, with most existing concepts of man is that they themselves covertly incorporate ethical valuations' (p. 234). So what we must look for, so it would seem, must be some sort of argument to show that a rational being capable of forming some self-conscious conception of its own desires, needs and interests and of organising its own present behaviour with a view to their projected future satisfaction and realisation, would be unable consistently to do so without the (at least implicit) possession of the concept of a person and the concomitant recognition of a commitment to self-respect and respect for others. In other words we must look for something along the lines of what has come to be known as a Transcendental Argument.

How close does this bring Peters back to Kant? So far as the formal design of arguments is concerned Peters himself thought quite close. Kant, he had already noted on page 114, had 'asked: How can ordinary people appeal to abstract standards of right and wrong in order to condemn the *status quo?*' Although he, Peters, found Kant's own particular answers unconvincing, he thought that 'the form of argument may be valid. Indeed, it may be the only form of argument by means of which general moral principles can be shown to be well grounded' (p. 114). And clearly Peters saw himself as trying to work out what he characterised as 'a revised form of this type of argument'.

Broadly speaking, this revised form of what might be called an attempted transcendental deduction of respect for persons is presented as working as follows. Man has to recognise himself as a social animal, living and evolving in communities whose languages provide the discourse within which he comes, *qua* individual, each to his own self-awareness. How is this possible? It is possible in as much as this discourse is naturally adapted to the articulation and discussion of the desires and interests that determine the goals of practical action. But no rational man, as he pursues the satisfaction of his own desires and the realisation of his own interests, can afford to restrict his attention to them alone; 'a consideration of the interests of others is a presupposition of asking the question "Why do this rather than that?" seriously. This question . . . presupposes a situation in which men are concerned with finding answers to questions of practical policy, in which they need the help of other men.' But if a rational man 'thought that, having discussed such matters with his fellows, his stake in such a worth-while life was going to be completely ignored, it is difficult to see how he would ever take the step of engaging in such a public discussion. As a rational man he must see, too, that what applies to him applies to any other man engaging in such a discussion; for how could he think that he alone has any claims?' (p. 171).

A fully rational self-conscious awareness of the presuppositions implicit in one's own practical discourse will thus disclose one's commitment to a concern for the desires and interests of others, that is to say to a respect for others as 'centres of valuation, decision and choice' and hence to a respect for persons as such; 'respect for persons is a presupposition that any participant [in a situation of practical reason] must adopt' (p. 213). Or again: ' "Respect for persons" is therefore a principle which summarizes the attitude which we must adopt towards others with whom we are prepared seriously to discuss what ought to be done. . . . To have the concept of a person is to see an individual as an object of respect in a form of life which is conducted on the basis of those principles which are presuppositions of the use of practical reason' (p. 215).

There remains, however, an objection to which Peters, as he developed the argument, sought also to sketch out some response. For, as he pointed out, 'it is possible to conceive of a group of beings discussing what ought to be done by the group as a whole without any concern for the stake of any individual in the future.' Such a group 'could be knit together by a feeling of fraternity', but 'what would be lacking amongst such a group of rational beings would be any general notion of the importance of *individual* consciousness or the role of the individual in determining his own destiny' (p. 215). Peters tries to deal with this objection by arguing—rather briefly—that 'a being who deliberates with others about the "good" of the collective to which he belongs, is guilty ultimately of some kind of incoherence or woolliness of thought if he thinks that there can be any such "good" which is not that of the individuals who compose it.' Why is this? It is because 'a group or collective has no consciousness or life apart from that of the individuals who compose it', and because 'without experiences such as those connected with pleasure and pain, it is difficult to see how an individual could learn to apply the concept of a reason for action for himself, let alone for the collective of which he was a member' (p. 216). So even though, as Peters acknowledges, 'the feeling of fraternity generated by membership of a cohesive group can be so strong that even rational beings can be led to apply fundamental principles, whose proper sphere of application is to individuals, to collectives viewed as supra-individual entities', this is, he is firm in asserting, a 'thoroughly incoherent form of application' (p. 217).

But Peters's counter-argument is even now not yet fully complete. For, quite apart from the fact, which he readily acknowledges, that the feelings of fraternity may in actual practice be so strong as to 'easily cloud and distort the judgement of rational men' (p. 217), his argument would still seem insufficient to rule out a restricted application of such fundamental principles to individuals, but to the individual members of certain groups alone—those, for example, of some given tribe, or nation, or religious sect. To meet this point Peters tries to develop a further argument within the aim of establishing that 'there is one sort of kinship that must be appropriate for a rational being, whatever he feels about his loyalty to family, state, class, or club, and that is his kinship with other rational beings as persons . . . for this minimal type of kinship is a precondition of the situation of practical reason' (p. 225). But once again, of course, Peters has to acknowledge that 'the power of the feeling of fraternity does not necessarily follow the lines of its rational justification' (p. 225), and that 'fellow-feeling for another as a person is a more abstract sentiment than the fraternity felt by members of a coherent face-to-face group' (p. 226); and that it is accordingly less, or anyhow less often, practically efficacious.

Let us for the moment set aside the whole question of just how much, and with what degree of rigour, such a set of arguments may effectively establish. It is interesting to note in passing just how widely and powerfully attractive is this form of 'transcendental argument', this argumentation from what are claimed to be the presuppositions of practical reason, to contemporary social philosophers in what may still be called the liberal tradition. One finds it in one of its best-known and most influential variations in John Rawls's account of the presuppositions of rational prudence, which he represents as underlying the claims of justice on all reflective individuals, whether in any particular situation these claims happen to coincide with their actual desires or interests or not. The Rawlsian commitment to a respect by each individual for the interests and claims of all others equal to that which he must be presumed, *qua* rational being, to feel for his own, is thus held to derive from the presuppositions of rational desire in abstraction from all that may give such 'formal desire' its actual, particularised content. Peters's commitment to respect for persons as such is held to derive from the rational presuppositions of practical co-operative discussion and action. Another recent and interestingly different variant of this same general form of argument is to be found in a recent book by Francis Jacques, *Différence et Subjectivité*.[2] Jacques actually takes the concept of person to be derivative from what he calls the 'irreducibly interlocutive relationship' (p. 31) between the different actual or potential participants in any communicational order—first person, second person, third person—so that reference to one's relations with others in a network of possible acts of communication enters as an underlying presupposition into the constitution of one's own status as a person as such. To be fully and reflectively self-conscious of these presuppositions of one's own achievement of reflective self-consciousness is thus to realise that 'It is by virtue of their status as persons that I am *bound* to others by obligations. . . . One's obligation to every human being qua person is unconditional. It is indistinguishable from the respect that is due to his status as a person; each receives the recognition of his communicational competence that allows him to work towards his own integration as a person, and hence to the working out of his own *destiny*' (p. 278).

Why *is* this form of argument so attractive to 'liberal' thinkers? The problem, as they so often see it, is to find considerations compelling to the intelligence of rationally self-interested individuals, of the sort, no doubt, who travel about on Clapham omnibuses, as to why they should accord the same importance and respect to the interests and claims of all other equally self-interested individuals as they do to their own; 'The problem is to find a form of association whereby each gives himself to all and yet remains as free as before.' But how can one hope to offer a compelling reason to someone to act in the interest of or out of respect for another in a situation in which it is manifestly against all his own interests to do so? How can one plausibly deny that such conflicts of desire or interest are common, even perhaps typical of the ways in which individuals find themselves placed by life in relation to each other? How, above all, is one to produce any such compelling reason in the face of the inescapable reality of such conflicts without offending both the common and ideological sense of secular liberal individualists by appealing to the values represented by some supra-individual Being or entity of some sort, be it God, state, party, nation or class?

The answer to all these questions, the prospect of which is offered by argument from the transcendental presuppositions of practical prudential reason, or even from those of communication and self-conscious reflection themselves, rests on distinguishing, first, between a general structure of universal mutual respect on the strategic maintenance of which any rational individual must see that the overall protection and furtherance of his own interests, and even his own status as a communicator or a person, necessarily depends; and, on the other hand, all those particular context-bound tactical considerations which, in the relevant particular contexts, may be seen as governing the maximisation of his own particular individual satisfactions. This distinction having been made, the argument must then seek to show that to any rationally self-reflective individual the claims of strategic commitment must always and necessarily be recognisable as outweighing those of apparent immediate tactical advantage. Of course, no one is so silly as to suppose that this recognition is in fact always secured, or that it is always effective with even the apparently most rational of men. But this, it may be said, is simply because human beings can never be regarded as fully self-reflective or as purely rational. The (notoriously) hard question to which one comes back in the end is whether, even in rational principle, there is any version of the argument that really works—whether the general presuppositions of practical co-operative enterprise, or of communication and of one's own continued existence as a person as such, can ever constitute a binding commitment or reason for any rationally self-interested individual to sacrifice his own perceived interests when he can also perceive quite clearly that he could perfectly well get away with it were he to make a particular practical exception in his own particular favour?

It would be simple-minded to suppose that this last question could in its turn, even in 'rational principle', receive any practically or even philosophically neutral answer. For such an answer to be possible, it would also have to be possible to arrive at a philosophically neutral account of what exactly it would be for such an argument to work or to fail; and so on back. Be that as it may, it is important to note, in response to our question about the closeness of Peters's relation to Kant, that there is at least one major respect in which he, Peters, and with him Rawls and Jacques and the great majority of contemporary liberal philosophers of man, remain a very long way indeed from the great Transcendental Idealist. For they are essentially 'one-world' philosophers; not for them all those mysteriously unstatable but nevertheless necessarily to be presupposed dualisms with which Kant's philosophy of man is inseparably bound up. For them, man the subject of the various social sciences and man with whom they as philosophers of morals and politics, education and communication, are concerned, is one and the same creature inhabiting one and the self-same world; nor is he intelligibly (or, indeed, safely) thinkable of as dividable into such radically different aspects as rational subject and natural individual, each of them responsible to laws and to determinations of fundamentally different forms, or anything else of the kind.

The difficulties associated with the doctrines of Transcendental Idealism are notorious. Their roots go to the very heart of the system; and the problems to which they give rise may well be in the last resort insoluble as such. Certainly, Kant himself, in his old age and in his Opus Postumum, found himself pushed, in his ever renewed efforts to deal with these difficulties, to move a notable distance in the direction of what subsequently became known as

German Idealism. But however this may be, and whatever one's views about the attractiveness or unattractiveness of such a move, one should not suppose that one can lightly drop Transcendental Idealism from the Kantian philosophy, as if it were but a mere element of regrettable but dispensable confusion, and yet still retain his solutions to the problems of self-respet and respect for others. If Transcendental Idealism has its drawbacks, it also has its peculiar advantages; and one has to ask whether in freeing oneself from the first, one may not by the same token be depriving oneself of the second.

The hard question, we noted, for an argument such as Peters's is how to secure the passage from such considerations of general procedural prudence as must naturally (or in some sense perhaps even necessarily) secure the assent of any rational being in the absence of any information as to the particularities of his own situation to such further considerations as should 'rationally' continue to secure his assent *whatever* the light that may be thrown upon his situation once that information is obtained and taken into account. The difficulties of this passage are brought into even stronger relief when one reflects on the fact that it is normally taken to be, precisely, a mark of a being endowed with a critical rational intelligence that he/she should be able continually to revise and update his/her assessments of his/her situation in the light of all relevant information as it becomes progressively available. But how, in that case, *can* it be rational for an intelligibly self-interested being, such as Peters's one-world version of a transcendental argument takes man naturally to be, *not* to adjust his attitude and behaviour towards other people in the light of the fullest information and the most reliable calculations available to him as to how the different ways in which he might treat them would be likely to affect his own interests as he perceives them?

One familiar way of trying to meet this challenge, of course, lies in the invocation of powerfully elaborate arguments designed to show that one's own long-term interests will always be best served or protected by treating other people *as if* one was concerned to respect them as persons for their own sake and not simply for that of one's own ultimate advantage. But, (i) a refusal to admit the prudential rationality of adding some sort of last resort escape clause to the 'always' of such arguments—for example, 'except in such particular circumstances as those where the contrary probabilities can be shown to be overwhelmingly high'—is in the end only going to be sustainable by one sort of equivocation or another; (ii) 'as if' respect is not the same thing as respect itself; to try and pretend that it is must, within liberal ideology at any rate, always turn out to be in the last resort impossible; (iii) it is a notoriously controversial question whether it *must* always be rational to set one's own long-term interests above one's own more immediate desires (which are anyhow usually more readily ascertainable); moreover, unless one believes in a certain sort of afterlife, there are anyhow bound to be many situations in which a man or a woman can no longer rationally see himself or herself as having any further long-term interests at all.

Kant, it is very well known, would have nothing whatever to do with any attempt at securing a passage from prudence or self-interest to respect for persons as such. On the contrary, he saw their demands as belonging to totally different realms. Hypothetical imperatives were one thing, the Categorical Imperative entirely another. But, it is equally well known, these two different realms, the natural or phenomenal on the one hand and the intelligible or noumenal on the other, had nevertheless to be thought of as standing in some, even if ultimately incomprehensible, relationship with each other. Indeed, one way of looking at this relationship is to regard the concept of the noumenal as the ineliminable residue of Kant's massive attempt to think through the knowable order of the phenomenal or the natural. It is, of course, a central feature of this order, according to Kant, and an indispensable condition of its knowability by creatures such as ourselves—and even, by a crucial extension of the argument, a condition of our own self-knowledge—that every naturally occurring event should follow on some other according to a rule of strict causal determinism, and that in the natural spatio-temporal order as an (always open-ended) whole all such events should in the end be inter-related with each other in a thoroughgoing causal nexus. Rational thought, on the other hand, cannot represent itself to itself in this fashion as if *its* order was that of a causally determinate temporal sequence. But persons, of course, do not consist of rational thought alone. Their peculiarity, as Kant understood them, rested in the fact that their very capacity for self-awareness lay in their recognition of themselves as belonging at one and the same time, so (however paradoxically) to speak, to both the causal and the rational, both the natural and the intelligible, both the temporal and the non-temporal orders at once. It was only in virtue of this recalcitrantly incomprehensible duality that they were neither beast nor angel but persons, and hence subjects of and to morality and both subjects and objects of respect.

Persons, then, or Kantian persons at any rate, are governed in their actions and behaviour by an irreducibly dual order of motivations and considerations, with prudence belonging to one aspect and respect for persons to the other. Prudence, for Kant, is a motivating cause and is, as such, of the spatio-temporally deterministic order of nature. Respect for persons, on the other hand, is based on—indeed, is strictly nothing but an aspect of—reason's own essential commitment to rationality, in argument and in action, in theory and in practice, for its own intrinsic sake.

There are many to whom it will seem oddly, and perhaps objectionably, artificial to speak of 'Reason' as an hypostatised abstraction having a commitment to anything at all. For most present interests and purposes, however, one may equally well speak of the rational individual's commitment *qua rational individual or subject* to the pursuit of rationality in all things, that is to a total respect for reason strictly for its own sake. For its own sake. . . ; for if not for its own sake, then, so we have to suppose, for the sake of satisfying some other and essentially non-rational interest or desire. In the actual circumstances of life every human individual will, it goes without saying, always have some other, if not plenty of other, interests or desires sufficient to explain his pursuit of whatever goal (or end-state) that he or she may pursue. Far from seeking to deny this aspect of human nature Kant is, of course, totally insistent on it. For human beings are, to repeat, peculiar in being both rational and non-rational subjects, in belonging inextricably and unself-deniably to both the orders of reason and of nature at once; and given what Kant takes to be the necessarily thoroughgoing causal constitution of nature, all human action must undeniably be causally motivated by one sort of 'self-interested' desire or another. Indeed, it is only by virtue of their belonging to this spatio-temporal and causal order of nature that men are distinguishable as a plurality of distinct individuals at all; for reason as such is universal and cannot serve to individuate. On the other hand, it is only by virtue of their participation in the order of rational discourse that men are able to formulate for rational consideration questions as to what may be deniable or undeniable; there can accordingly be no rationally conclusive denial of one's own membership of this order. It is as a member of this order, as an individually embodied but nevertheless rational subject, that one is bound by one's own rationality to an unqualified respect for reason *both* as the principle of all thought and action *and* as it may be met with in all its individually living embodiments. The Categorical Imperative is thus, among other things, a principle both of self-respect and of respect for others; indeed, since both are neither more nor less than instances of reason's essential and inalienable regard for itself, they amount in effect to the same thing. As particular members of the order of nature we must always be motivated by some consideration of prudential self-interest, if we are to be induced to do anything at all. But, for a Kantian person, there can be *no* rational passage from considerations of this sort to a command for universal respect for persons as such; Kantian persons do indeed stand under such a command, but this is because they are also members of a different order altogether.

All this is evidently far too brief and sketchy for it to serve as anything more than a reminder of some of the more immediately relevant features of Kant's philosophy of man. As a reminder likewise of some of the difficulties that this involves, difficulties of an intractability that have led many to the view that such a philosophy must in the end be abandoned as unacceptable. Certainly one may come to form the impression that 'reason' under Kantian direction is led constantly to drive itself to the very borders of paradox, to recoil—inevitably—therefrom, only to find itself returned to those very same borders by what turn out to be merely alternative routes. All the same, it may be much harder even than Peters at the time of writing his *Ethics and Education* may have supposed to extract oneself from these difficulties without losing the characteristically Kantian advantage of a 'transcendental argument' that would establish universal respect for individual persons as a demand of reason itself, while basing itself upon a concept of man that may be presented as neutral with respect to all possible conflicts of natural interest or desire.

Kant, then, roots his argument for the universal respect for persons in the presuppositions of the exercise of rationality itself. His concept of man is that of a being who, being at once a member of the animal kingdom and yet a rational agent, cannot think of himself in any other way than as committed by virtue of the presuppositions of his own rationality to this universal personal respect. No doubt, this concept of man may be said to 'incorporate ethical evaluations', and it can obviously not be regarded as neutral with respect to the whole range of non-Kantian concepts of man, which will inevitably incorporate their own different and differing 'ethical evaluations'—at least in so far as they allow room for the concept of the ethical at all. From *within* the perspective of the Kantian philosophy as a whole, however, the very universality of reason as the foundation of the ethical imperative guarantees it a certain crucial form of neutrality with respect to all particular interests and desires. The neutrality of reason is not to be thought of as the neutrality of an agent who simply abstains from participation in a conflict of interests in which he might equally well have taken part. It is rather the neutrality of a subject whose position, *qua* rational subject, is necessarily that of *all* rationally thinking beings as such, and who is thus of necessity above all conflicts, motivated by competing interests or desires, between any one naturally particularised party and another.

Once one abandons Transcendental Idealism, however, and seeks to situate man within the order of nature alone, construing him maybe as a rational being whose reasons for action are 'merely' one sort of causes among others, the only sort of neutrality to be looked for in a 'concept of man' would have to be that of a purely factual concept, neutral with respect to whatever the diverse and potentially conflicting evaluations that men may place upon the facts that it constitutes or orders. We may perhaps accept that there will always be some sense in which a distinction between factual report and expression of pleasure or displeasure at the facts as reported must be makeable within any language or system of concepts whatsoever. And we may set aside (i) all the problems of establishing some clear relationship between expressions of pleasure or of preference and a concept of evaluation as such, (ii) the fact that even the more limited thesis undoubtedly needs arguing for, and (iii) the fact that a very great deal of further argument would be needed to establish the possibility of producing any sufficiently clear working criteria for the identification of different conceptual systems or languages in the relevant sense. It remains the case that if we have to suppose the existence of some causal origin of every development in the natural order, and if we take man and everything that he produces to belong wholly to this one natural world, we have in all consistency to accept that there must be some sufficient causal explanation for the production or elaboration of any and every concept of man. From this point of view, therefore, Peters was certainly not overstating the matter when he wrote that 'A strong case can therefore be made for saying that concepts of man are culture-bound and that they enshrine the valuations of those who propound them' (p. 232). If one is unable to countenance a Reason that, while able to furnish a concept as partly rational, partly in its own image, is yet, *qua Reason*, impervious to the causal influences and constraints of time-governed history and nature, it becomes inconceivable rather than merely implausible, from any remotely Kantian perspective at any rate, that any concept of man should not in some way or another reflect the interests, concerns and outlooks of the culture of its elaboration.

Kantian Reason, then, is both universalistic and goal-directive. As goal-directive it provides a foundation for value and as universalistic it ensures both the morality of the value thus founded and its neutrality in relation to all particular and hence potentially competing desires and interests. The resulting morality thus constitutes itself its own reason for action, a reason that must *ex hypothesi* appeal to every (even if only 'partly') rational being. But 'partly' rational beings of this sort, beings who are bound to conceive of themselves as both empirical realists and transcendental idealists, are not creatures of the one-and-one-only world that Peters, along with the great majority of contemporary philosophers, takes himself to inhabit. They—Kantian creatures that they are—will no doubt *feel* all the same pressures as Peters, the pressures of their own natural desires and the strong pulls of family, tribal or whatever other version of fraternity; indeed, as empirical realists they will recognise their actions to be wholly determined by them. But as transcendental idealists, as members of a kingdom of rational ends-in-themselves, they will recognise with equal, if incompatible, clarity the call to universal reciprocal respect for themselves and each other as *persons*, a call that has nothing to do with the means that may or may not be necessary to the achievement of their own self-interests. The only trouble is, of course, that it would take a paradoxically split-minded philosopher both to accept and to reject the Kantian doctrine of Transcendental Idealism 'at one and the same time'.

So what, for the moment at any rate, is to be made of all this? Kantian subjects, it is clear, may set out to prove to each other that each and all of them stand under the self-same obligation to mutual and self-respect as so many different embodiments of Reason. From one point of view—from that standpoint of Reason which has to be accepted as an unrenounceable presupposition of any attempt to engage in any form of proof whatsoever—one knows that the success of such a proof is guaranteed 'in advance'. But this point of view is counterbalanced by that from which action on the part of inhabitants of the world of nature must be presumed to have as its motivating cause some naturally determined desire. This being so, one could never, in any given context, rely on the practical success of rational argument in favour of respect for persons as persons (any more than one could prove that anyone had, on any particular occasion, actually acted out of respect for the Law or for any of its embodiments rather than from some other and 'natural' motive). To suppose the contrary would be to suppose that one might be able to point to a naturally determined motive for acting on the basis of reason alone; which is perhaps what Peters did in a way half suppose. But as a good Kantian subject one could, and indeed necessarily would, hold nevertheless to the faith that the imperative of respect for persons might, on some (non-assignable) occasions at any rate, command a practically effective as well as a purely rational force. For it is in such a faith, one would hold, that the humanity of human beings resides.

But can any compelling reason be provided why one should regard oneself as a Kantian subject at all? The difficulties in the way of doing so have already been alluded to; they are notorious enough and need no further spelling out here. But let us suppose, for the sake of the present argument, that one *is* able to convince oneself that such a reason can be provided why the concept of a Kantian subject, a Kantian concept of man, must turn out to be indissociable from what have to be recognised as the undiscardable presuppositions of one's own would-be rational discourse. One would still have equally to recognise that both the concept itself and the terms of whatever argument might seem to lead so compellingly to the acceptance of its indispensability must also be presumed to have their own temporally determinate history as part of that of the culture or cultures within which they have appeared or within which they may have been made out. And this recognition is not only implicit, or more often indeed explicit, in the many contemporary versions of that 'one-world' form of 'ideology' from whose perspectives the apparent incoherences or paradoxes of all dual aspect theories present themselves as wholly unacceptable; it is anyhow implicit within Kantian dual aspect theory itself, for which, as we know, everything that may ever occur within the time-determinate world of nature *must* in principle have its natural explanation.

It would seem, then, to follow that even a Kantian subject, when giving all its attention to the natural and historically time-bound conditions of its own existence, can take no explicit heed of its own dual Kantian status. And yet, as Kant himself in effect argued, the nevertheless ineradicable awareness of its own duality that every Kantian subject possesses as the mark of that mysterious unity within which its duality is after all constituted, will still somehow make itself felt, even at the level of its natural worldly existence, as, precisely, a feeling. For the Kantian subject aware of itself as such knows also that it must be able to explain (away?) this, its own self-awareness, as a mere phenomenon of the culture to which it, in its necessary embodiment, must belong. How *could* such a subject hope to give expression to such an awareness in any but a fragmented and essentially incompletable discourse? Even if, for the sake of the argument, we suppose ourselves to be rationally compelled to self-recognition as Kantian subjects, we must by the same token suppose ourselves to be compelled to move ever and again towards the kind of paradox with which Reason must remain always profoundly uncomfortable and from which it must seek always to move us away again.

Peters, then (and with him, if it comes to that, a great many other contemporary philosophers), is in certain crucial ways rather less Kantian than he may have supposed himself to be. That is to say, Kant himself would certainly have disallowed any attempt to establish the principle of universal respect for persons as such as a necessary presupposition of prudence or of enlightened long-term self-interest. Peters might perhaps be taken as arguing that since prudence itself depends on a capacity for rational reflection, it must follow that even the most prudent of rational subjects must, *qua* rational, respect something other than prudence alone, namely reason itself—and hence, by virtue of arguments already sketched out, persons as so many different embodiments of that reason. But then, once again, we would be back to a fundamentally dualistic account of man, with prudence, as a natural motive, nevertheless somehow presupposing another form of 'motivation' altogether as a condition of its own intelligibility.

There is, in other words, no way of being a Kantian or of using genuinely Kantian forms of transcendental argument while yet contriving to disentangle oneself from the embarrassments of Transcendental Idealism. Or perhaps one might say, at once more cautiously and more hopefully, that there is no way of producing a Kantian type account of morality and of respect for persons on the basis of a unified and 'ethically neutral' concept of man unless and until one can show also that the logical structure of the proper physical description of the natural universe is fully and unprob-lematically compatible with the goal-directive structures of auto-nomous rational thought and effective rational practice. It is true, of course, that the great majority of contemporary philosophers who concern themselves with this problem would argue for such a compatibilism in one form or another. But, certainly, it needs arguing for; certainly Kant, in his own time, took a different view; and this, certainly, lies at the heart of the case that has to be argued by anyone seeking to redeploy in this area arguments that even a Kant might recognise as transcendental, but on the basis now of a fully unified view of man.

Notes

1 Allen & Unwin, 1966. All page references in the text to R.S. Peters are to this book.
2 Aubier Montaigne, Paris, 1982.

Education, liberalism and human good

John and Patricia White

I

Fundamental to liberalism, according to Ronald Dworkin, is the principle that 'the government must be neutral on what might be called the question of the good life'.[1] People differ, he goes on, about what gives value to life: the scholar has one conception, the 'television-watching, beer-drinking citizen' has another. In distributing resources, the government must not favour one group's preferences over another's: opera must not be subsidised if dog-racing is not.

What counts as 'the good life' on such a view seems to be something like: the life which most satisfies one's preferences, whatever these preferences may be. Rawls in his *A Theory of Justice*, holds a similar view. But only given certain conditions. Among the most important of these are (1) that the 'preferences' here are the hierarchically-ordered ends in an individual's life-plan, chosen after a process of deliberation in the light of a full knowledge of different options and consequences of adopting them; and (2) that 'something is good only if it fits into ways of life consistent with the principles of right already on hand'.[2] The 'good life' cannot include the life of a Nero or a Thrasymachus, however much their post-deliberative desires are satisfied: fulfilment of basic moral obligations is taken as read.

If Rawls's restrictions apply to Dworkin's theory, then they will both agree that Dworkin's beer-drinking TV addict or Rawls's man who has a passion for counting blades of grass in city squares may each be living the good life, provided that they have chosen these as their most important ends after mature reflection and provided that they are morally decent people.

Many will find this view unacceptable. The content of the good life, they will say, must surely be more delimited than this. It must include, perhaps, propensities of a more intellectual or artistic or altruistic kind: Truth, Beauty and Goodness, not mere preference-satisfaction.

The difficulty with such a counter-claim is that what seems to the objectors a universally applicable content of the good life may turn out to be only their own subjective preference: although *they* prefer art to beer, have they any good reasons for insisting on it for all? It is this apparent absence of such reasons that makes neutrality so central a feature of liberalism as just described: no particular conception of the good life can be allowed to dominate over any other.

Liberalism brings with it a two-fold prescription for education. Each person must be brought up with all the intellectual equipment necessary to form a life-plan: a broad understanding of various possible activities and ways of life, of the means of achieving them and obstacles in the way; and a moral education which limits choice of a life-plan to one compatible with acting as a morally responsible being. (See White and Ackerman, for accounts of education which stress especially the first of these two prescriptions.)[3]

II

There are a number of difficulties with this liberal conception of education.

First, how are pupils to relate to each other the two aims of their education? The first prescription, to do with the formulation of a life-plan, is about their own good; the second, to do with their moral responsibilities, brings in others' good also. What proportion of their time can be devoted to the one or to the other? How far, on the one hand, do their moral obligations extend; and which of their own ends, on the other, are permitted or excluded by the moral framework? On the former point, for instance, what place in their moral scheme has the obligation of beneficence? This can, notoriously, extend so far as to leave very little room in one's life for anything besides service to others; it can also be minimalised, thus leaving more space for other things. How do liberal individualists know where to draw the line? On the latter point, the reverse of the same coin, how do they know, for instance, whether aiming at a competitive good like a high salary or a position of power within an institution is morally permissible? And if their main pleasure in life is consumption, whether of consumer durables, food and drink, or entertainment, how do they know how much consumption, measured in time or in money, they are morally allowed?

As well as this kind of radical uncertainty, they may also experience doubts about why they should be altruistic in the first place. They can understand and appreciate *society's* reasons for having given them a moral education: if people were not brought up to keep their promises, refrain from injuring others, be fair, tell the truth, help others in distress and so on, then the conditions for a minimally civilised life would no longer obtain. But what are good reasons for society are not necessarily good reasons for themselves. As long as the great majority of people keep to the moral tracks, civilised life can carry on: a few free-riders here or there will not undermine it, so why shouldn't they be among these few? And if no good reason is forthcoming, then perhaps they should not stick within the moral framework but rather formulate a life-plan which aims at their own well-being with no moral constraints on what its content might be.

They also face a third difficulty. How do they know what their well-being is? As liberal individualists they take it to consist in the maximisation of post-reflective desire-satisfaction. But why this? It seems to be an assumption, for which no further backing is provided. But if they are not to take it for granted, what is there to put in its place?

There is yet another problem with the liberal account of education. Ideally, it would seem, pupils are not to commit themselves to a way of life until they have become fully acquainted with as many options as possible and reflected on which to pursue. The good life is a product of reflective choice. But how is the reflection to be carried out? On what do they reflect? What guides their choice? Only, it would seem, the intensity of their present preferences for this or that, in relation to the overall goal of the maximisation of satisfaction: no other criterion is plausible. But then their choice of a way of life, which looked to be an act of willing, of self-creation, now seems to have turned into something like self-discovery: they see what their hierarchy of preferences is and adopt a life-plan in the light of that.[4]

Finally, there is the intuitive unacceptability of pupils' postponing commitment until beyond this stage of deliberation. Before this are they not to be encouraged to follow up their enthusiasms? If a child shows signs of devotion to the cello—more than is needed, that is, to understand what such an activity involves—is she to be directed to other pursuits so that she has a broader knowledge before she works out her life-plan? Many, perhaps most, teachers and parents will tell you this is madness.

III

Can it be that liberalism gives us a false picture of the good life and a false picture of education?

Alasdair MacIntyre, in *After Virtue*, argues for a more restricted view of the good life.[5] His book is an attempt to reconstruct an Aristotelian account of it. Aristotle held this to be a rationally ordered life in accordance with the virtues. On this account being courageous, temperate, just, magnanimous, etc. are implicit in one's structure of ends. On a theory, like liberalism, which separates the moral framework from the area of individual choice within it, being just or benevolent or honest is, perhaps, a *precondition* of one's attaining one's own well-being, but it is not necessarily *a constituent part* of that well-being. Similarly possessing not-necessarily-altruistic virtues like courage and temperance may be a *means* to one's well-being, but once again is not necessarily a part of this end itself. On a liberal view, it *may* always be part of an individual's project to be a certain sort of person, a person possessing these or those virtues, whether moral or self-regarding; but there is no *requirement* on one to choose this sort of end: beer-swilling, TV watching could still take the palm.

MacIntyre sees the Aristotelian view of the good life as having largely crumbled away through recent centuries and being in ruins today. A central argument goes as follows. For Aristotle, possessing the virtues is justifiable by reference to the good of the individual. He works with a three-tier scheme of (1) untutored human nature, (2) possessing the virtues, (3) human nature as it is according to its *telos*. To realise one's good one must pass from (1) to (3); but it is only via (2) that one can do so. Within this Aristotelian scheme, the question that Plato poses at the beginning of the *Republic*, 'Why be just?' receives a clear answer: it is only through possessing justice, along with the other virtues, that one can achieve *eudaemonia*. During the Middle Ages, this Aristotelian scheme was preserved via its incorporation into Christian ethics. But now a new notion was added. Justice was still a part of blessedness; but it was now also enjoined on us by divine law. We have here the beginnings of a 'law conception' of morality, quite foreign to the Greeks, which became increasingly influential, not always in its religious version, up to the end of the eighteenth century, culminating in Kant's categorical imperative. By this time virtue concepts had ceded much of their central place in ethical discussion to the concept of the moral ought. At the same time the third tier of the Aristotelian scheme had largely dropped away with the decline of a belief in a teleological theory of human nature. The first tier, untutored human nature, was still present in the new ethics, alongside a revised second tier of moral injunctions about what one ought to do and not do.

A gap thus arose between morality and human nature. Moral ought judgments were no longer justifiable by reference to the nature-given purposes of the individual. The is-ought gap existed, as Hume saw, between the first two tiers, but it was no longer able to be filled by another, teleological, 'is' at the third tier. The question 'how are moral judgments to be justified?' thus became of central importance to ethics. MacIntyre sees the history of ethics since the eighteenth century largely as a series of attempts to provide a rational justification for moral ought judgments, accompanied by an equally powerful succession of sceptical ethical theories which question the possibility of such a rationale. On the one side Kant, the utilitarians, the intuitionists and contemporary advocates of a rational morality; on the other, Hume, Nietzsche, the emotivists and present day anti-rationalists.

For MacIntyre this constant pendulum-swing between the two positions is only to be expected given the rejection of something like an Aristotelian solution. More than this: since all attempts at rational solutions seem doomed to failure, moral scepticism would appear the only alternative. Sociologically, he claims, this is precisely what more and more people have by now come to think. Most people still adhere to moral codes or principles: they value honesty, fairness, kindness, loyalty and so on. But there is no good reason, it would seem, why they should do so. It is, no doubt, in the interest of those who govern and manage them that they follow these rules and cause no trouble. But from their own point of view what is there in it for them? They would do better to see the institution of morality for what it is, an ideological structure subserving the interests of those in power. Their one hope is to break free of it, transcend good and evil and pursue their own well-being as fully and freely as they can. Increasingly this is precisely what more and more of us are coming to see. Although it is often prudent to pay lip-service to moral demands, there is no further rational constraint on one in that regard than that. For many the good life is the 'successful' life as conventionally understood, the life where one is wealthy enough to pursue whatever pleasures one wishes to pursue, and powerful enough no longer to be pushed around.

MacIntyre holds that the only way of resisting these Nietzschean tendencies is by reconstructing something like the Aristotelian view of the good life.[6] Only 'something like', for little can be retained of Aristotle's teleological metaphysics. Positively, MacIntyre sees human well-being partly as embracing the pursuit of what he calls 'practices'.

> By a 'practice' I am going to mean any coherent and complex form of socially established cooperative human activity through which goods internal to that form of activity are realised in the course of trying to achieve those standards of excellence which are appropriate to, and partially definitive of, that form of activity, with the result that human powers to achieve excellence, and human conceptions of the ends and goods involved, are systematically extended. Tic-tac-toe is not an example of a practice in this sense, nor is throwing a football with skill; but the game of football is, and so is chess. Bricklaying is not a practice; architecture is. Planting turnips is not a practice; farming is. So are the enquiries of physics, chemistry and biology, and so is the work of the historian, and so are painting and music. In the ancient and medieval worlds the creation and sustaining of human communities—of households, cities, nations—is generally taken to be a practice in the sense in which I have defined it.[7]

Practices, therefore, contain internal, shared, goods. These include not only the excellence of what is produced—paintings, cities, farms or whatever—but also the virtues necessary to sustain a practice—the courage and honesty, for instance, found in the willingness of a novice to subordinate herself to the best standards available within the practice, or the cooperativeness necessary for working on a common task.

Money, power, fame are not internal but 'external' goods. Unlike the former, they are not shared but belong exclusively to particular individuals; also unlike the former, the more some individuals possess them, the less there is for other people: external goods are essentially competitive. MacIntyre does not deny that external goods could have *some* place in the good life; but they must be subordinate in importance to internal goods.

MacIntyre's good life does not consist solely in engagement in practices. For one thing, what is required in one practice may be at odds with what is required in another: the demands on one as an artist, for instance, may get in the way of one's duties as a parent. Somehow the different practices in which one engages must be held harmoniously together within one's life as a whole. There must be some rational, integrating structure into which they all fit. The good life is to be understood, as once again with Aristotle, as the goodness of a life seen as a whole. For MacIntyre one's life has the structure of a narrative. It is a gradually unfolding story whose future development is unknown and uncertain. The good life has the nature of a quest: 'the good life for man is the life spent in seeking for the good life for man'.[8] To sustain one in this quest one needs virtues over and above those found in particular practices. One needs a more general form of courage and temperance to enable one to withstand the dangers and temptations besetting one's life as a whole; one needs wisdom and judgment, integrity, constancy and patience.

A third, and final, stage in MacIntyre's account of the good life, introduces the concept of tradition. In seeking the good and exercising the virtues one does not do so as a solitary individual but as a bearer of a particular social identity, as someone's daughter or father, as a member of such and such a work-group, as a citizen of such and such a city or nation. It is as a role-holder that I engage in practices; and what helps to hold my life together in a unity is my progression into and out of a succession of such roles. These roles and practices, institutions and communities in which they appear, have a historical dimension: behind them lie traditions of thought and action which must be sustained and cherished—not in a hidebound way, to be sure—if they are to flourish. Since it is lack of justice, lack of truthfulness, lack of courage and lack of the relevant intellectual virtues which corrupt traditions and the practices, institutions and communities which currently embody them, we see, finally, a third way in which the virtues enter into the good life—not only as a feature of practices and of the unity of individual lives, but also as that which sustains the tradition within which alone these things can exist.

There is much more to MacIntyre's whole argument than this; but enough of it has been presented, we hope, for the nature of his challenge to liberal individualism to be reasonably clear. The good life no longer centres around the maximal satisfaction of any preferred desires compatible with a basic morality. On this liberal view there is nothing to stop external goods—fame, power, money, pleasure—from being those most ardently sought. The problem in liberalism of relating the moral framework to the pursuit of personal goals within it, to do not least with the danger of an erosion or collapse of the moral framework in the absence of any personally acceptable rationale for it, evaporates in MacIntyre's theory: since one's dominant ends must be the internal goods required by practices, the unified life, and the social roles and traditions within which they find a place, these include among other things the possession of the virtues, including the more altruistic or 'moral virtues', needed to sustain these practices and

155

this kind of life. Being morally good, in short, is a necessary and not merely an optional part of one's own well-being.

IV

If MacIntyre is broadly right about the good life—and we shall be examining more closely whether he is in the next section— education will have to be conceived of otherwise than in liberal theory. The liberal division between (i) equipping pupils to choose a life-plan and (ii) moral education will be replaced by something more unitary. Children will be brought up in a framework in which internal goods predominate over external and in which, in particular, they will come not only to possess altruistic as well as other virtues, but also to see it as part of their own good to be persons possessing virtues of this sort.

True, children will still have to learn to conform to the basic moral rules which MacIntyre sees as necessary for a community to flourish—rules, for example, against personal injury, murder, lying, stealing, breaking promises. This basic moral education is also a feature of liberalism. If MacIntyre's theory is correct, however, the free-rider problem which bedevilled liberalism will evaporate as children come to see such conformity as necessary to their own well-being as well as to that of others, since the two are now inextricably connected.

But within this framework of basic rules, the good life for the individual will consist predominantly of shared goods. Presumably in some way education will reflect MacIntyre's part-whole distinction between engagement in practices and living one's life as a whole. How exactly it will do this is not clear: MacIntyre's theory is about the good life itself rather than education for the good life, and there are many different ways in which one could envisage the latter taking place.

In what follows there will be no attempt at a comprehensive account of an education along MacIntyrean lines. Nothing will be said, for instance, about possible relations between education and the economy. We will restrict ourselves to some observations, partly inspired by difficulties in liberalism, first about practices and then about the unity of an individual life. Points connected with the third element in MacIntyre's account of the good—to do with traditions and social roles—will be incorporated in what follows, rather than being allotted a separate section.

A

Many educational questions could be raised about MacIntyre's practices. We shall restrict ourselves to two, both of which relate back to problems in liberalism: (i) are pupils to be introduced to a full range, or a limited range, of practices? and (ii) what is it, anyhow, for a pupil to be 'introduced' to a practice?

As regards (i), an argument familiar from liberal educational theory seems equally apposite here. There is no general reason why a pupil's educators should seek to limit the range of options available. If their own view of the good life embraces only some of the permissible ends and excludes others, why should their view take precedence over others which are more catholic? While this line of thought seems cogent against ideological educators of this sort, it seems to fall short of implying that all educators have a duty to extend the range of options as far as possible. Suppose we take Ieuan Lloyd's imaginary case of the boy brought up in a fishing community who has decided from an early age that he wants to become a boat builder like his ancestors and consequently finds most of what goes on during his schooldays irrelevant and uninteresting.[9] Have his educators—his parents and teachers—a duty to try to widen his horizons? If they let him follow his bent, they are not imposing on him their own ideology of the good life but letting him discover his own version of it. He will become involved in a practice, acquiring en route its specific virtues. No doubt he will enter into other practices found within the fishing community in which he lives: he will become, perhaps, a husband or father, a darts player, an informal teacher of apprentice-boat-builders, etc. He will be able to lead a satisfying, virtuous life within his own community. What good is it to him to know about physics or painting or skiing or antique-collecting?

It certainly seems more tempting to resist the extension of horizons here than when working within liberal assumptions. For central to liberalism is the notion of choice between different possible satisfactions: if the boy is to be restricted to a boat-builder's life, how does one know that he would not have preferred, if given the chance, the life of, say, a journalist or engineer? Only he can decide what is best for him, and for this he needs to know what the major alternatives are. Looking at the matter from MacIntyre's Aristotelian perspective, things are less clear-cut. It looks as if the boy could lead a life that satisfies most of his criteria of the good life for man. Engagement in practices, possession of the virtues, the weaving together of a complete life are what count, not the maximisation of preference-satisfactions.

Yet one is still inclined to say that something is missing from the boy's life. Not all of MacIntyre's criteria have been satisfied. He sees the good life, we may remember, as a kind of *quest*: 'the good life for man is spent in seeking for the good life for man.' The boy could become so entrapped within the conventions of his various social roles that he may be incapable of seeing life in this way. Necessary to the good life is a form of freedom, not the kind of freedom that liberalism stresses—the freedom of choice between different satisfactions—but the freedom to reflect on the general framework within which one is living one's life and to modify that framework where it seems to one inadequate.

This line of thought seems to suggest that what the boy could have benefited by in the education that he has missed is not so much an introduction to the other practices as an engagement with studies of a more holistic kind—literature, perhaps, or history, for instance—which would help to free him in the way just described. But this, while true, is not enough. For he will not be able to attain liberating perspectives on his own life and situation until he knows something about other practices found in the wider community of which his fishing community is a part. Fishing is not an activity that takes place in isolation from everything else. It is one form of primary food-production of which farming is another form; it helps to determine whether a country is to be self-sufficient in food or will need to export manufactures against food imports; and so on. A broad acquaintance with other practices is therefore desirable in order to put those in which one does engage in proper perspective.

How far does one also require this broad acquaintance, as liberalism would maintain, in order to decide which practices to adopt in the first place? Insofar as it *is* a matter of *deciding* which to adopt, some knowledge of alternatives is presupposed; but a basic point at issue between liberalism and its Aristotelian critics is just whether, or to what extent, one *finds oneself* involved in practices without having chosen them. When one is born into a family one begins to participate in sustaining and enriching this human community. In less socially mobile societies one grows up in similar fashion as a participator in all sorts of practices. In our kind of society, some roles, like that of family-member, are still ascribed, but many others depend on the individual's choices. One relevant factor here is that children by and large are usually *not* in the position of the boy in the story: they are typically not wholly and unshakably committed to one way of life or major activity. If they *are* to become committed to something, they must either be steered towards something determinate—and this, we have seen, seems unjustifiable—or they must be presented with various alternatives in the hope that some more than others attract them. But to accept this is not to go all the way with liberalism. The liberal would still want to keep all options open for those children in the position of the young boat-builder. But why? If a child brought up in a highly musical family knows at eleven that she wants to devote herself to the cello, for which she has a considerable talent, is there any point in introducing her to all sorts of other activities so that she can make her considered choice later? The basis of the liberal position must be that the child may be wrong. But wrong about what? Presumably about the belief that she will get more satisfaction out of playing the cello than out of other things. But this assumes that one's good consists in maximising satisfactions; and this assumption should not be taken as read.

In an education on MacIntyrean lines then, the practices to which children are drawn will be set within the context of other related practices as well as studies of a holistic kind to serve the ultimate end of enabling them to pursue the quest of the good life. There will be no pressure to add to the range of practices to which they are introduced purely in the interests of extending choice to maximise desire satisfaction. Breadth there will be, not for this reason, but so that children are acquainted with all sorts of things to which they may become attracted.

So much, then, for question (i), about whether children are to be introduced to a wider, rather than narrower, range of practices. Question (ii) was: what is it for a pupil to be 'introduced' to a practice? According to liberalism, being introduced to an activity for which one might opt must be primarily a matter of coming to be acquainted with it, that is, coming to understand enough about it to be in a reliable position to judge whether or not one wants to incorporate it into one's life-plan. It is not at all clear that one even needs to have engaged in the activity in order to possess this understanding.[10] And even where one does engage in it, it is as well, on the liberal view, that one does not become too enthusiastically committed to it, as this might blind one to the delights of other things.

If we follow MacIntyre, however, being introduced to practices cannot be like this. For one of the central goods intrinsic to a practice is possessing the virtues which engagement in its brings with it. It is not enough to 'know about', say, playing football in an external way if one is to acquire the courage, cooperativeness, etc. which playing this game promotes. One has to play it—and not just once or twice or for a few weeks, but for as long as it takes for one to build up something of the relevant virtues. And the idea, finally, that one should ideally temper one's enthusiasm for the game so as not to bias one's judgments about a life-plan now comes to seem nonsensical: if one is really to acquire the virtues and not some strange, dispensable, simulacrum of them, one needs surely to enter wholeheartedly into the activity in question.

Does this mean that one would never give it up? We think not. As one gets on the inside of more and more practices, and one is drawn to more and more things, one realises that one cannot do everything and must establish hierarchies of value. Activities which most attract one will rise to the top of this hierarchy; others will drop. Sometimes there will not even be room at the top for all the things one most wants to do and difficult decisions may have to be made—only, however, because they are forced on one, not, as in liberalism, in order to maximise one's satisfactions.

Being 'introduced' to practices thus requires engagement in them in order to possess the goods, including the virtues, which they embody. Liberalism is constantly tempted to retreat from engagement, since this may bias one's life choices in favour of those activities which one has already undertaken; it takes refuge in a mere 'acquaintance'. But the MacIntyrean point of view need not rule out the latter altogether. One may be drawn to practices which one has not experienced as a participant, but into which related practices, together with observation or imagination, have given one an entrée—windsurfing, for instance, to someone thoroughly at home in other water sports. Part of the 'breadth' mentioned at the end of the last sub-section may be achieved in this non-participant way. But it is only in one sense 'non-participant': one may not have actually wind-surfed, but one appreciates its excellences *from within*, i.e. from having engaged in cognate activities; and one *already* possesses the virtues it demands, from the same source. So 'external acquaintance' is nine-tenths 'internal experience'. This is no problem for a MacIntyrean, even though it is for the liberal, whose retreat from commitment to acquaintance now becomes incoherent.

B

The kind of education we are considering will not only introduce pupils to a range of practices but also help them to make sense of their life as a whole. It is impossible, as the above discussion has shown, to keep these two sides of education wholly apart: children are not initiated into practices atomistically, but in such a way as to incorporate them into a developing plan or picture of their life as a whole. At some points in their education holistic considerations will predominate over particularities; at other points vice versa. Sometimes they will be summoned within, to attend to the inmost demands of their being; at other times they will forget themselves, lose themselves, in particular practices. Part of the educator's task on the holistic side will be to foster those virtues—integrity, constancy, judgment, courage, etc.—which relate especially to one's life taken as a whole. *How* this is to be done is another matter. Public discussion, private reflection, imaginative involvement via literature or biography in the lives of others—all these, we suggest, may be of service. But this is not, patently, an area where quick results may be expected. Just as the virtues associated with particular practices are only to be acquired through immersion in the practices, so the holistic virtues are the product of long engagement in living itself.

There is more one could say about this second aspect of education. About the special importance of history, for instance. History can be seen from one standpoint as a practice in its own right, with its own standards and forms of excellence and its own characteristic virtues. But it also has a more pivotal position. Like a life itself, it too has a narrative structure. Coming to see human life in general as a series of interconnecting stories helps one to see one's own life as one such story, in which parts of other people's stories are constantly embedded and which in its turn is similarly embedded in the lives of others. History, too, by revealing the traditions within which particular practices and forms of communal life are set, helps the pupil to see her life not as an isolated strand, criss-crossing at points with the strands of others' lives, but as part of more closely woven patterns whose origins lie often far back in the past.

With these few remarks, which we realise could be filled out further in all sorts of ways, we must leave this more holistic dimension of a MacIntyrean education and with it our larger sketch of the way in which considerations deriving from MacIntyre's theory might help us to formulate educational aims. No doubt many readers will feel, as we do, that there is something immensely attractive about such an upbringing. It incorporates so many of the more appealing features of different schools of thought while avoiding the difficulties which generally accompany them. It stresses breadth of experience, yet without sacrificing commitment; it is thoroughly pupil-centred, but sees the pupil always as a member of a community; it is not excessively biased towards the intellectual and academic, but by no means excluding them; it stresses both the 'whole person' and engagement in particular activities; it gives the virtues a prominence to which many would wish to restore them; it sees the vital importance of traditions, but does not imprison pupils within them; and so on.

V

If MacIntyre's basic arguments are sound, they provide us with the tools for beginning to construct a theory—or theories—of education which many would find attractive. The question now is: *are* they sound?

Can one show that the good for man consists in being the kind of person MacIntyre delineates rather than in the satisfaction of preferred desires championed by liberalism? A liberal sceptic might argue that he cannot see why shared ends must predominate in a person's value-system, while external ends like power or fame must be of secondary importance. No doubt many people will be drawn towards communal forms of life embodied in practices and lives woven round them, but how can it be claimed that this is the good life for all and not only for those who so choose? How far has MacIntyre made the very familiar mistake of objectifying his own personal vision of how life should be led and erecting it into a goal for everybody?

If he *has* done so, the educational proposals of the last section now take on a different look. If MacIntyre's theory were true, there would be everything to be said for initiating children into practices and getting them to see that their own good is inextricable from the good of others. But if all we have is MacIntyre's personal preferences, in seeking to base educational recommendations on them we are in danger of imposing these preferences on all those pupils brought up under this *aegis*. Far from achieving their own good, they may become indoctrinated in somebody else's unfounded vision of it. How could a supporter of MacIntyre's Aristotelianism defend it against such onslaughts from the liberal—or Nietzschean peering derisively over his shoulder?

Sandel claims, like MacIntyre, that any individual's good must be a shared, or communal good.

> what at first appears as 'my' assets are more properly described as common assets in some sense; since others made me, and in various ways continue to make me, the person I am, it seems appropriate to regard them, in so far as I can identify them, as participants in 'my' achievements and common beneficiaries of the rewards they bring. Where this sense of participation in the achievements and endeavours of (certain) others engages the reflective self-understandings of the participants, we may come to regard ourselves, over the range of our various activities, less as individuated subjects with certain things in common, and more as members of a wider (but still determinate) subjectivity, less as 'others' and more as participants in a common identity,

be it family or community or class or people or nation.[11]

Our sceptic will not find this a sound line of argument. He may well accept that no one is the atomic individual of, say, Hobbesian theory. It is indeed true that others have made me in some sense the person that I am: all my activities depend on my ability to use concepts; and I should not have become a concept-user if other people, already adept at employing concepts, had not initiated me into their correct use. It is necessarily true both that I had intimate personal relationships with those who thus formed me and that the latter belonged to larger communities sharing common forms of life, into which I was also inducted as a member. All this can be granted. But it does not follow that having been formed in this way, I must now value above all else those things that draw me towards these social attachments rather than distance me from them. A Nietzschean can readily admit that he is a social creature in that he could not have grown up in social isolation; but, once grown up, what is there to stop him looking down on his parents, his neighbours and his fellow-citizens as sheep, as timid conformists, unable, like himself, to live for his own self-fulfilment?

What stops him, Sandel may reply, is not only that others have 'made' him, but also that they 'in many ways continue to make' him the person that he is. If it is the case that throughout one's life one's identity is continually being formed and reformed by one's social relationships in such a way that it is inextricable from the identities of others, then the delimited self and the delimited personal well-being that goes with it on which liberal or Nietzschean theory depends is conceptually impossible.

But need these formative relationships continue into the future, however essential to my identity they have been in the past? Am I not now in a position to continue the task of creating myself *myself*, without further help from those around me? Can I not now become the artist of my own life, working on the blocked-in canvas that others have bequeathed me and shaping it into a form of art? True, to do so would mean loosening the connexions that have bound me to others, since their continuing power to shape my identity would get in the way of my own determination to complete the job myself. But a Nietzschean hero would not baulk at that.

Sandel says that 'to imagine a person incapable of constitutive attachments such as those is not to conceive an ideally free and rational agent, but to imagine a person wholly without character, without moral depth.'[12] 'But morality is for the herd,' the Nietzschean will reply, 'I have transcended all that. Why am I not then free?'

It seems clear to us that Sandel's line of argument is not proof against the determined sceptic. But it is high time, in any sense, to leave Sandel and turn to MacIntyre, for although both thinkers are arguing to similar conclusions, it is with the particularities of MacIntyre's position that we have been chiefly concerned and it is important to see with what basic arguments he underpins them.

For MacIntyre the battlelines are clearly drawn between Nietzsche and Aristotle. At the beginning of this essay we were not concerned with Nietzsche but with such liberal thinkers as Rawls and Dworkin. But Nietzscheanism, for MacIntyre, is 'only one more facet of that very (liberal individualism) of which Nietzsche took himself to be an implacable critic'.[13] It is liberal individualism which has finally transcended that moral framework within which the individual's good is to be sought, once that framework has been shown to be bereft of a rational basis. What reason does MacIntyre give us for going along with his Aristotelianism rather than with Nietzsche?

Part of the answer takes us in the same direction as Sandel. MacIntyre points out that Nietzsche's hero, in transcending his social attachments, deprives himself of the goods which these bring with them.

> For if the conception of a good has to be expounded in terms of such actions as those of a practice, of the narrative unity of a human life and of a moral tradition, then goods, and with them the only grounds for the authority of laws and virtues, can only be discovered by entering into those relationships which constitute communities whose central bond is a shared vision and understanding of goods. To cut oneself off from shared activity in which one has initially to learn obediently as an apprentice learns, to isolate oneself from the communities which find their point and purpose in such activities, will be to debar oneself from finding any good outside oneself. It will be to condemn oneself to that moral solipsism which constitutes Nietzschean greatness.[14]

The first point to note about this argument is its apparent uncertainty about whether the Nietzschean solipsist can be said to have a good. At one point it says that goods can only be discovered by entering into social relations; but later, in claiming that solipsists will be debarred from finding any good outside themselves, it seems to be implying that the only good they can find is within themselves. It seems clear from other parts of MacIntyre's general argument, mentioned earlier in this essay, that there is room in his theory for goods not dependent on practices and social attachments. He distinguishes earlier between 'internal' and 'external' goods. The latter are non-shared goods like fame and power. If the Nietzschean is debarred from internal goods he still has these. But these are precisely the kind of goods he prefers! To talk of his being 'debarred' from social goods and 'condemned' to moral solipsism seems to imply that he is somehow *harmed* by taking the stance he does, that he is somehow unfree or constrained. But this is a strange charge against the Nietzschean. For no one has *made* him become a solipsist. It was a free, voluntary act on his part to transcend all social ties.

To turn to a more central point. MacIntyre's argument begins with a hypothetical: '*if* the conception of a good has to be expounded in terms of such actions as those of a practice (etc.)'. It rests therefore on an assumption. We may overlook here the question, just raised, as to whether the existence, on his own admission, of external goods destroys this conceptual claim and take it that what is at issue is whether the good life for any individual must consist *predominantly*, although not exclusively, of internal rather than external goods. MacIntyre's argument against the Nietzschean rests squarely on the assumption that this Aristotelian account of the good is rationally defensible: if it is, then clearly the Nietzschean *is* harmed by taking the solipsist path.

But what is there in MacIntyre to *show* that it is rationally defensible? It is just at this crux that he leaves us disappointingly in the lurch. He tells us that he cannot go so far as to give a *proof* of his conclusions.[15] This does not matter, he says, because arguments in philosophy rarely take the form of proofs. What is needed to help resolve the present issue, like so many other philosophical issues, appears to be that the contending parties should stand back from their dispute and ask what the appropriate rational procedures are for settling it. MacIntyre states that his arguments 'do indeed *presuppose* a systematic, although here unstated, account of rationality'.[16] He promises us this account in a subsequent book.

MacIntyre seems to be taking it as read that the theory of rationality he has in mind will come down convincingly in favour of Aristotelianism. Without the argument before us, however, we do not know how far it will. The Nietzschean sceptic has not yet, it seems, been dislodged. 'If I represent just one more facet of liberal individualism,' we may picture him crowing,

What is MacIntyre's but the latest attempt of objectivist philosophy to shore up the indefensible institution of morality? He presents his rehash of Aristotle as the only escape from the futile pendulum-swing between objectivists and their critics that has gone on since the eighteenth century, but, to turn his critique of Nietzscheanism on its head, his own stance 'turns out not to be a mode of escape from or an alternative to (this historical movement), but rather one more representative moment in its internal unfolding'.[17]

VI

How far does the difficulty of clinching MacIntyre's argument against the Nietzschean mean that the educational recommendations sketched in Section IV, which were based on his theory and which seemed so attractive, have no firm foundation?

MacIntyre faces two challenges. The first is from the liberal individualist, who acknowledges moral obligations of some sort but argues that, provided he fulfils them, he sees no reason why he should weight his preferences on the side of shared goods. The second and more radical comes from the Nietzschean, who claims he has been given no good reason why he should even accept morality.

Let us begin with the second. MacIntyre's ethics is not wholly an ethics of the virtues. He also holds, as we have seen, that there are certain 'absolute prohibitions' against such things as the taking of innocent life, theft, etc., without which a community in which the virtues are to flourish cannot exist (see p. 156). Faced with a Nietzschean who sees reasons in general why society needs such rules but no reason why *he* should follow them, he would argue presumably that since the Nietzschean's well-being is inseparable from that of others he cannot rationally want to kill them, deceive them, steal from them and so on. As we have seen, the Nietzschean can refuse to accept the conclusion by rejecting the premise.

If MacIntyre has a problem on his hands, it is not obvious that educators attracted by MacIntyre's ideas are in similar plight. It is not at all difficult for them to show that children must be brought up within some kind of morality which includes MacIntyre's absolute prohibitions. They can rely on the argument which both MacIntyre and the Nietzschean would accept, that some sort of morality is a precondition of perhaps any, certainly any tolerable, sort of social life. For this reason they will want children not to be brought up outside the moral pale. (We shall take it that it would be otiose at this point to ask why the educators themselves could not be amoralists. It is hard to see how they could consistently with this be concerned with children's upbringing, which is normally taken to aim at promoting the well-being of the children themselves and of others in the community as well. Educators must be guided, it seems, by some kind of principle of beneficence: the alternative, that they see pupils and their upbringing only as means to their own egoistic ends, is something we can rule out by definition.)

MacIntyre belongs to that school of moral philosophers who believe that there must be some watertight argument to show that really to promote one's own well-being one must promote the well-being of others. For him the thoroughly rational amoralist would seem to be an absurdity. We are inclined, however, to believe, along with Bernard Williams, that the amoralist may always be able to stand his ground in argument, and that ultimately being moral is not basable on reasons which any rational person must accept but on possessing the desire to promote others' good as well as one's own.[18] It is one of the central tasks of early education to implant, or perhaps strengthen, that desire. Just as educators ignore the sceptic about the existence of physical objects and other minds in getting children to build up a picture of empirical reality, so they ignore the moral sceptic in steering them towards altruism. Where knock-down reasons give out, education guides and shapes. It does not have to indoctrinate: there is nothing in this story about preventing pupils, when they are capable of it, from reflecting on the bases either of their empirical knowledge or of morality.

The second challenge which MacIntyre faces is that of the liberal individualist. The general problem here is: granted that one accepts some sort of moral obligations, why should shared goods predominate among one's chosen ends? MacIntyre has so far failed, as we have seen, to answer this incontrovertibly. Does this mean that educators have no good reason to steer pupils towards a life in which shared goods predominate? Once again, we shall claim, where general arguments give out, educational arguments can take one further.

The life of liberal individualists is marked by the indeterminacy, arbitrariness and inconsistency of their position described in Section II: they have problems most importantly in relating their moral framework to the pursuit of their own good; but also in justifying their view of what the latter consists in; and in squaring their belief in self-creation with features which make the good life seem more like self-discovery.

Such a life fails radically in coherence, in psychic integration. As should be evident from Section III, this difficulty can be removed, or at least reduced, if one shifts to something like a MacIntyrean form of life in which one's good consists predominantly in the shared ends of practices and social roles and in the narrative unity of one's life. Not that it *necessarily* consists in this, as it does in

167

MacIntyre's theory: it results from a *decision* to give the individual's good this social and integrative character.

But suppose our liberal individualist does not want the difficulties removed? He may agree that if he takes the MacIntyrean path he will achieve a higher degree of psychic integration than if he does not, but he may see no good reason for putting such weight on psychic integration: some people may value it highly, but he is willing to tolerate, perhaps even enjoy, a greater disharmony. Not, indeed, that everything is in chaos. He adheres to the moral framework, establishes a rational hierarchy of ends within it, and where there are indeterminacies, about the proper extent of beneficence, for instance, he introduces his own *ad hoc* criteria. True, there is some arbitrariness about this, just as there is if he adopts a maximising conception of his good. But—and this is his central claim—why should the desire to reduce arbitrariness further in the interests of an integrated value-system take precedence over other things?

We do not know whether the sceptic about psychic integration can be incontrovertibly answered any more than the moral sceptic can. But even if he cannot, it may still be reasonable for educators to induct pupils into a MacIntyrean form of life, just as we saw that they are justified in moulding them into moral beings and not amoralists.

First, what alternatives can one envisage if they are *not* to aim at psychic integration? These are: either to disregard integration or, positively, to aim at the fragmented self whose values, goals, aspirations are all at odds with each other. To *aim* at fragmentation is clearly unacceptable. At worst the loss of psychic unity could be so severe as to constitute a mental illness and in less extreme cases it would simply result in the frustration of worthwhile purposes as these criss-crossed each other. To *disregard* the need for integration could leave the individual open to the same dangers. Aiming at integrative unity, as a formal notion, is then a necessity.

An objector may say: 'I can see that educators must aim at *some degree* of psychic unity; but, as already conceded, the liberal individualist can be a fairly well integrated person, so we are still lacking an argument for a specifically MacIntyrean set of educational ends.' The difficulty here is that it seems unreasonable for educators to aim at a lesser harmony when they could aim at a greater. The lesser harmony may suit those pupils who turn out to favour liberal individualism, but educators have no reason to think that all, or even most, will turn out like this. Not knowing how any pupil will turn out in the end, educators have no good reason for deliberately restricting the amount of integration at which they aim, and thus building sources of potential psychic disturbance into their pupils' souls from the start.

Psychic integration provides one reason, therefore, why educators should steer children towards a life in which shared goods predominate. Two further arguments also support this conclusion.

Firstly, there are some shared goods towards which educators cannot help steering children. We saw above in our discussion of Sandel in Section V that becoming a concept-user depends on coming to share common forms of life, within the family and outside it.

Secondly, to highlight shared goods fits the social framework within which all, or virtually all, one's pupils will find themselves living. All but determined loners will live their lives as holders of a variety of social roles. Their lives will largely consist of role-occupancy of one sort or another. It is not as though they could divide their lives into two segments—a role-occupying part of secondary importance and a non-role-occupying part of supreme significance to them with regard to which role-holding was instrumental, hindering or irrelevant. *So much* of their lives is likely to enmesh them in social relationships—not necessarily face-to-face: the scholar, for instance, is related to dead scholars in the past as well as to those unborn—that educators would seem fully justified in steering their pupils toward a life of predominantly shared goods.

None of this excludes pupils' coming to prefer a life devoted to 'external' goods. But if they do so, they must count the cost. How likely are they to succeed in transcending their social ties? What alternative goods are left to them once social goods have been put to one side? Are the alternative goods so much more preferable as to justify the rigours of the path? Do the attachments which their educators have taught them to cherish count as nothing? Few people, we suggest, are likely to opt for this way of life against such a background. (The claim is empirical, but not of a sort that requires empirical *research* to render it plausible.)

This last point helps to meet the charge that steering one's pupils in a MacIntyrean direction is indoctrinating them in *one* vision of the good life, which not all will find compelling. There is certainly a danger of indoctrination here. But it can be avoided; indeed, if MacIntyre's line of thought is followed through in its entirety, it *must* be avoidable. We mentioned above that for MacIntyre the good life takes the form of a quest: one can never remain imprisoned within one's social roles, but must prize and use one's freedom to reflect on and modify the framework of value-assumptions within which one is living. This implies that pupils brought up to see their good as consisting predominantly in shared goods are not to accept this unreflectively. They will be encouraged to test the view against other alternatives. It is unlikely, as we suggest, that they will find the costs worth paying, but they are not debarred from such a step.

But is this not to weight things too much on MacIntyre's side? For once they have been brought up in the MacIntyrean way, they will be naturally more likely still to cling to this even when initiated into say, Nietzscheanism. Would it not be fairer to allow both these—and other—alternatives an equal chance?

But this makes no sense. Children have to be brought up—from the cradle upwards—in *some* pattern of values: one cannot leave them directionless until they are mature and knowledgeable enough to make autonomous choices. We have already provided reasons why a broadly MacIntyrean direction is to be preferred.

The two arguments in this section have been directed at the general moral sceptic and at the sceptic about a life in which shared goods predominate. If they work (either of them), they touch on questions about the position of philosophy of education within philosophy as a whole. In many quarters it is looked down on very much as a poor relation, if not a pariah. But if the line of thought in this section is correct, its role may be much more important, since by adopting an educational perspective one can, it seems, circumvent important forms of ethical scepticism which general philosophical argument leaves intact. If we add to this the way in which the same perspective has helped in understanding the bases of our knowledge of the empirical world,[19] we have grounds for claiming that philosophical reflection on education, far from being peripheral, becomes of central importance to both epistemology and ethics.

This speculation, heady as it is, is a fitting thought, perhaps, with which to end this paper in honour of the man—for both of us our first teacher of philosophy and later much-loved colleague and friend—who created contemporary British philosophy of education.

Notes

1 *Taking Rights Seriously*, Duckworth, 1977, p. 127.
2 *A Theory of Justice*, Oxford University Press, 1971, p. 396.
3 J.P. White, *Towards a Compulsory Curriculum*, Routledge & Kegan Paul, 1973; B. Ackerman, *Social Justice in the Liberal State*, Yale University Press, 1980.
4 See M.J. Sandel, *Liberalism and the Limits of Justice*, Cambridge University Press, 1982, pp. 161 ff.

5 *After Virtue*, Duckworth, 1981.
6 'Nietzschean' is used broadly here to cover ways of life, such as that just mentioned, which conspicuously lack Nietzschean grandeur.
7 MacIntyre, op. cit., p. 175.
8 Ibid., p. 204.
9 'The Rational Curriculum: a Critique', *Journal of Curriculum Studies*, vol. 12, no. 4, 1980.
10 See J.P. White, op. cit., ch. 3.
11 Sandel, op. cit., p. 143.
12 Ibid., p. 179.
13 MacIntyre, op. cit., p. 241.
14 Ibid., p. 240.
15 Ibid., p. 241.
16 Ibid., p. 242.
17 Ibid., p. 241.
18 'Egoism and Altruism', in *Problems of the Self*, Cambridge University Press, 1973.
19 See L. Wittgenstein, *Philosophical Investigations*, Blackwell, 1953; and D.W. Hamlyn, *Experience and the Growth of Understanding*, Routledge & Kegan Paul, 1978.

The education of the emotions

Mary Warnock

It would be very satisfactory if, writing about the education of the emotions, I could be quite certain what the emotions were. But that unfortunately is not easy, indeed is perhaps impossible. Richard Peters has written more than once about the emotions, and education of the emotions.[1] His view was that emotion was a kind of appraisal of a situation, a perception of it as nice or nasty, as agreeable or disagreeable. Where such appraisals lead directly to action, we may speak of motive. For example, if I sum up a situation as dangerous, I feel fear (an emotion); and if I take action, if for example I hide my head under the pillows, then fear becomes my motive, what actually gets me to do the thing in question. But, though the very same 'thing' (not to commit myself), fear, may be either a motive or an emotion, there is no necessary connexion between emotions and actions. Indeed, conceptually, Peters argues, emotions are distinguished from motives by being essentially passive. This means that in experiencing an emotion, the owner of the experience is not first and foremost an agent but a patient. He suffers from the emotion. He is overcome by, swept away by, surprised by the emotion. It wells up in him, without his consent or knowledge. He is essentially moved, disturbed, upset by it. So though hatred may motivate someone to murder, or to getting a rival sacked from a job, equally it may be experienced by someone sitting in his armchair brooding, and may be experienced violently and in its purest form without action resulting.

What Peters is doing, in drawing his distinction between emotion and motive, is urging us to examine the *normal* logical commitments involved in describing something, love, say, or anger, as one or as the other. It is an area within which distinctions are peculiarly hard to draw. He acknowledges this, and is therefore not insistent that emotions should *never* be thought of as connected with actions. He is arguing simply that they *need* not be so connected. On the other hand, *usually* when we speak of a motive we are trying to find an explanation for an action which has already taken place.

172

However, suppose that a murder has been committed and, in true detective-story style, we are trying to discover who did it. By considering 'motives' what we may actually consider is the emotional relation between the victim and the various suspects. And we then raise the question whether any of their known emotions, jealousy for example, could have become strong enough to turn into an actual motive, something that led or drove them to act. Could it have been so little restrained, this emotion, that it turned into a motive?

To raise such questions in such a form may have certain implications for education. For part of the educational outcome of Peters's distinction between emotion and motive is that educating the emotions will consist in learning to control them, learning to master what, if you did not, would master you. A person who is prepared to *act* out of jealousy is a person who has not learned to recognise and control this emotion. He is not emotionally educated.

There is much more to Peters's theory of emotional education than that. But before I say more about education, I would like to call attention to certain other relations and distinctions between emotions and, as it were, neighbouring concepts, which have been recently discussed. We shall in the end have to be content with distinctions that are less than absolute. For it is essential to remember that we are not trying to distinguish between certain natural kinds of things, as if we were distinguishing horses from donkeys, or even Welsh cobs from Arabs. Nor are we discussing wholly conventional distinctions like that between income and capital, or between tools and weapons. On the contrary, we have here a vague and undifferentiated world of inner experience, very difficult to talk about at all, and therefore ill-fitted-out with labelling names, within which world we want to make some logical and conceptual distinctions, without being at all sure that the distinctions have any functional significance, or that the items distinguished will 'feel' different, as a matter of inner experience.

Some people have insisted that emotions are kinds of cognition (a view related to Peters's 'appraisal' view). Such a theory makes great play with the perfectly correct observation that a number of names for emotions are attached to states of mind essentially *intentional*, directed, that is, to an object. Thus, we would not say that someone was suffering from jealousy unless the *object* of the emotion was, either in fact or in fantasy, a typical case of jealousy-causing phenomena, his girl paying too much attention to another man, his sister getting all the attention. The actual disturbance experienced by the victim of jealousy might not be different from the disturbance caused by, for example, acute anxiety on behalf of a child. The disturbance would be named 'jealousy' simply on the basis of its object. It would be logically and linguistically incoherent, or, at best, a barely intelligible metaphor, if someone said 'I am suffering from jealousy because I'm afraid my son has developed cancer'.

We might understand the similarity between the symptoms, the waking in the morning with a sense of some half-remembered doom; the inability to concentrate; the loss of appetite; the constant raising of questions; the desire to *know the worst*. But we would still think the word 'jealousy' inappropriate. It is this kind of consideration that makes it plausible to say that emotions are all of them directed towards objects, and that it is from the nature of the object that the name of the emotion derives. Peters's original statement, then, that emotion is a kind of appraisal relates to these theories (but as we have seen he also thinks we are passive in the face of them, as we are in the face of dreams).

The extreme of the view that emotions are appraisals or kinds of judgment of situations is exemplified by Robert Solomon.[2] Solomon argues that because emotions are kinds of 'hasty judgments' (that is reactions about which we do not take time to think), we are therefore in control of them. We can, in principle at least, decide how to react to things. To put it in this way, as he himself admits, is too simple. But he writes,

> emotions as judgments are a species of activity, and thus to be
> included in the active side of the all-too-simple 'active-passive'
> disjunction according to which we evaluate most human affairs.
> This means too that emotions fall into the realm of responsi-
> bility so that it always makes sense (as it does not for instance
> for headaches, heart-attacks and hormones) to praise or blame a
> person, not just for contributing to the situation that caused the
> emotion but . . . for having the emotion itself, as one blames a
> person for bigotry, for example, or praises them for their
> courage.

In his comment on his own article he concludes that 'emotions are cultivated responses, within whose limits one is responsible even if they were learned in childhood and so seem entirely "natural" '. We have moved a long way now from the original sense of 'passion'.

Solomon is of course aware of and partly draws on the theory of the early Sartre. Sartre[3] held that emotions are not only kinds of perceptions, but are *chosen* perceptions, involving a special 'magical' view of the world which we tend to adopt when other views will not serve our purpose. Thus the extreme case of emotion, according to Sartre, is the case where, being afraid, we

174

faint from fear, knowing that fainting is the only way left to blot out the terrifying world.

Or when the psychiatrist's patient, constrained to talk about something too painful or embarrassing to contemplate, has recourse to tears and hysterics which will literally render her speechless. Emotional responses of an extreme kind are deliberately chosen, in such cases, as a way of managing the world, but not a properly practical way of managing it. Of course Sartre is notoriously liberal in his concept of choice. He does not wish to admit 'unconscious' choices. Yet the concept of 'bad faith' allows him to say that we frequently make choices which we would deny with our dying breath had actually been chosen. The further into bad faith we go, the more we will deny what we have actually deliberately done. We try to deceive not only our interlocutor but ourselves, and often succeed.[4]

Now it is obvious that if we are to talk about educating the emotions, it makes a vast difference whether emotions are things we suffer (even if, as on Peters's theory, we can change our response to such sufferings) or are things that we choose, ways of looking at the world which we can adopt or reject, more or less at will. For if the latter view is correct, the prospects for education are comparatively rosy. Even if we are to suppose that emotions have objects rather in the way that perceptions have objects, we are still able to suppose that they can be educated. For no one I suppose would deny that it is possible to educate people to see and hear things differently, in a more sophisticated way. I may learn to see, that is to focus my eyes on objects in the outside world, when I am a baby, but I may be taught quite late in life to distinguish a sparrowhawk from a harrier by what it looks like or a cor anglais from an oboe da caccia, by its sound.

However, the difficulty with Sartre's theory of the emotions as a 'magical' response to a perception, or with Solomon's theory of choice, or indeed with Peters's 'appraisal' theory, is that they all of them appear to fit some experiences which we want to call emotional better than others. They are good for emotions such as jealousy, where quite obviously, in order to be jealous, you have to assess a situation in a particular way (even if you do not do so articulately). You have to believe, in however ill-thought-out a way, that *he*, in whom you are interested, is deceiving you; or that *he* prefers *her* to you. Similarly, if we take the example that Solomon takes, if John has stolen my car, I may properly feel angry: and when I find out that my belief that he has stolen my car is false, then my anger must be diffused, or it was not after all anger, but perhaps some more deep-seated resentment against John. But, as a matter of fact, such violent, episodic spells of emotion are comparatively rare. Or are we to reclassify emotion and count as emotions *only* those which fit this account? Here we are back at the original definitional problem.

In a recent discussion with Jonathan Miller, George Mandler suggested a double definition.[5] Emotions, he argued, are partly intellectual assessments, partly physiological arousal. The intellectual or evaluative aspect of emotion is, at its crudest, a judgment that what we are confronted with is good or bad. And as to this distinction, though we doubtless have some innate or inherited abilities to distinguish good from bad, we also learn many such distinctions (and many far more subtle ones) as we go along. Meanwhile, on the physiological level the autonomic nervous system alerts an animal whenever there is something in the outside world which is unexpected (either unexpectedly nice or, more often, unexpectedly nasty or dangerous). But, he argued, we feel these two aspects as one. 'We feel real joy as a singular experience: the same with love, anxiety, fear ... Consciousness constructs a single emotional unit.' Does this theory, in itself highly plausible, allow for the large numbers of very different experiences that we want to classify as emotions? Or does it too fit best with certain very specific emotions, attached to specific appraisals? Jonathan Miller raised this question in discussion. 'Although we do have fears and alarms, they're unrepresentative feelings. They don't constitute what people regard as their emotional life.' To this Mandler replied 'We evaluate the world continuously; we are continuously trying to make sense of the world and commenting on it and on our behaviour: this is a good situation, this is bad; I like this, I don't like that; I'm late, I'm early; I wish I were with her, I wish I were not with him. All these kinds of conscious and unconscious thoughts go on all the time. So that the kind of analysis I've given is not best illustrated by the punctate great emotions, but rather by a continuous flow of changing levels of arousal, changing levels of degree of emotional involvement and changing evaluations.' If we allow this very broad sense of arousal, accompanied, presumably, in some cases, by very little in the way of physiological concomitants (or little that is noticeable to us when they occur, though perhaps theoretically detectable by instruments that would measure changes in the brain) we are left with a vast class of inner experiences to be classed as emotions. Emotions are, on this view, as various as Hume's 'passions'.

It is perhaps worth examining Hume's account of the passions in a little more detail. In Hume's classification, *passions* were a subclass of impressions. They were 'secondary impressions', which arose from reflecting on purely physiological or sensory impressions. The physiological, or primary, impressions included the awareness of basic pleasure and pain. The passions were themselves subdivided into the 'calm' and the 'violent', and all could, I think, be referred to as emotions. The only absolute distinctions Hume made were, on the one hand, between *passions* (secondary impressions) and *perceptions* (primary impressions); and, on the other hand, between *passions* and *ideas*, the raw materials of reason. As is well-known, he gave an extremely narrow definition of reason. Reason was concerned only with the agreement and disagreement of ideas. It was the role of reason to concern itself with entailments and contradictions, with mathematics and logic (within which these relations hold) and with those alone. Hume admitted that the calm passions, which could arise *only* from contemplation, and which were exemplified especially by the moral and the aesthetic sense, were so calm as to be only rather eccentrically called passions at all. In ordinary language, most people would classify them as reason. But, unlike reason, they could become motives for action. If, for example, you dislike something *because you think it wrong*, you may take action to avoid doing it, and your sense of its wrongness is the motive for action. Your feeling of dislike, however long you have thought about it, or however difficult it may have been for you to decide that you really did dislike it, was a passion, in Hume's language, and not a mere idea of reason.

Now I do not suggest that we take over Hume's somewhat crude psychological distinctions, nor that we necessarily accept his supposed relation between passions and motives. Nevertheless it is perhaps useful to consider whether the wide extension of the concept of emotion to which I have come by different steps, and which agrees so closely with Hume's, may not be quite serviceable. It may by its very vagueness save us from a time-wasting attempt to define too exactly and make too many fine distinctions within the uncertain world of our felt inner experiences. And it may go some way to justifying the view that it is impossible completely to separate the education of the emotions from other parts of education.

Amelie Rorty takes a somewhat similar view.[6] She writes as follows:

Emotions do not form a natural class. A set of distinctions that has generally haunted the philosophy of mind stands in the way of giving good descriptions of the phenomena. We have inherited distinctions between being active and being passive;

between psychological states primarily explained by physical processes and psychological states not reducible to nor adequately explained by physical processes; distinctions between states that are primarily non-rational and those that are either rational or irrational; between voluntary and non-voluntary states. Once these distinctions are drawn, types of psychological activities are parcelled out *en bloc* to one or another side of the dichotomies.

She then goes on to describe the way in which, historically, in the ensuing philosophical discussion the class of phenomena potentially classified as emotion has constantly been enlarged. 'As the class grew', she writes, 'its members became more heterogeneous; the analysis became more ambiguous.'

This seems to me a fair account of the definitional difficulties that beset anyone attempting a discussion of the emotions, in or out of the educational context. Should we therefore try a fresh start? Perhaps it may be better to acknowledge that, in the context of education at least, there is no satisfactory way of defining emotions, nor of marking them off from other inner experiences. That they are to be classified as inner experiences is all that we shall need to take for granted. And I doubt whether this at least could be in dispute.

Suppose we look again at Mandler's example of low-arousal emotions. We are, he says, always evaluating the world, trying to make sense of it and commenting on it and our own behaviour in it. One of the 'inner comments' he quotes is, as we saw, 'I'm late'. Let us examine this a bit further. If I see someone in the underground, let us say, with a worried and distracted air, restlessly looking at his watch, and gazing anxiously out to see what station we have got to, I guess what he is saying to himself: 'I'm going to be late.' Depending on his general temperament, and on the estimated importance of his engagement, I know that he will be feeling a kind of anxiety with which I am deeply familiar. So, without being able precisely to weigh up his intellectual assessment of his situation, and without being able to understand the physiological changes that are doubtless taking place in his body, I know, only less directly than he does, that anxiety about being late has a certain felt quality, that it *is like something for him*, to use Nagel's inelegant but expressive phrase.[7] *What* it is like is conveyed best by the expression 'I am late'—and this is true simply because the person to whom this expression is uttered has himself known what it is to fear to be late. In this case, then, the quality of the feeling is conveyed quite adequately by a statement of the belief on which the feeling is based.

To take a different example: I am sitting next to someone at a concert, and we are both wholly absorbed in the performance. I have listened with my whole attention, and when the music ends I relax, exhausted. I see my neighbour, who has been equally absorbed, surreptitiously wiping his eyes, and I realise that I am also weeping. We are plainly both deeply emotionally moved. I know that both he and I have experienced an inner feeling; an emotion, or series of emotions, this time nameless, caused by, rather than directed upon, the music. These emotions are not at all like the inner experience of knowing that I shall be late, though both may be classed as emotions. The difference is that, in the case of the music, no beliefs are involved. If asked to explain what it is that we both feel, my neighbour and I, we can at first do no more than exclaim 'God, what music!' or 'What a performance!'. Later, if we are critics, we may have to do better than this, be more specific. But the point is that analysing the music, or the performance of it, does not express the feeling the music gives us, though it may in part do something to explain it. The inner feeling of the anxious man should be totally changed if I tell him that the meeting has, after all, been postponed for an hour. Nothing that you can tell me, on the other hand, can change the feeling which arose in me when I was listening to the music.

If we accept these as simply two examples of the kinds of recognisable inner experience that may be referred to as emotions, or, as I much prefer, as *feelings*, then our question must be put in this form: What does it mean to talk of educating such feelings? And this leads to a second question. What is the purpose of emotional education?

Given that everyone has an infinity of feelings, and that some of these feelings will be disagreeable to the person who has them, others agreeable; that some may issue in acts that are anti-social or wrong, others in no acts at all; and still others may issue in acts that are generally beneficent, the answer to these questions cannot be at all simple. Any attempt to provide an answer will indeed necessarily over-simplify. Yet this is a kind of question that cannot be avoided by educationalists. For it seems that we do frequently raise about our pupils or our children the question, 'Does he feel as he ought?' even though, in asking it, we may sound like nothing so much as Fanny Price, or some other creation of the moral sentiment school of novelists. And we also believe, that, as teachers, it is both possible for us, and part of our responsibilities, that we should enable our pupils to feel as they ought, or perhaps as we should like them to feel. So how do we set about the task of ensuring this?

179

The best way to answer this question is not to attempt to define feelings or emotions but to draw up certain very broad classificatory headings. If we go back to the case of anxiety, we saw that if it could be shown that the feeling of anxiety rested on a false belief, namely that the meeting began at 9.30, the changing of this belief could eliminate the feeling of anxiety. It has often been suggested, by Richard Peters among others, that a large part of educating the emotions is ensuring that the beliefs which give rise to them are in fact true, and are not the outcome of prejudice or superstition. Of course such a tidying up of beliefs does not always work. Telling someone something is not always enough, and there is such a thing as assenting with one's head and not one's heart (demonstrating perhaps the folly of trying wholly to separate the intellect from the emotions). It may, for example, be quite rational to hate and fear certain creatures which are the bearers of disease and infection to humans, and not to hate or fear those which are, for the most part, harmless. But pointing this out will not change the feelings of those people who are indifferent to flies, but go all to pieces at the sight of a spider. It is perfectly possible to accept propositions in principle, as we say, but not in practice. For example there are those who believe that women are men's equals and should be treated as such, and given every opportunity (that men have) for education and advancement and who yet, when it comes to the point, cannot bring themselves happily to serve under a woman. Whether they acknowledge this, and therefore modify their principle, or whether, on the other hand, they stick to the principle, but argue that this particular woman boss is too bossy, or otherwise less good than the man who was her rival, is a matter of character and temperament. But in either case, it is clear that feelings, and the beliefs on which they seem to be based, have a separate life. Changing the one does not *entail* that the other changes. If we are given the horrors or the creeps by something, it is hard to eradicate these horrors or creeps by reason. It is no easier than it is to get yourself to like drinking milk, by reasoning that milk is nutritious.

Still, there is no doubt that this is one kind of education of the emotions which has to be attempted. It sometimes works; and the elimination of prejudiced feelings is undoubtedly something of value.

A *method* of emotional education, different from the rational method just described, and often more effective is, like teaching people to act on the stage, one that involves a certain degree of pretence. It is the method of teaching people *how to behave*. I believe that this method is unduly neglected at school, possibly because it is thought to be immoral, involving as it does, not reason or argument, but an encouragement to insincerity. One of the commonest passions among children (and also among childish grown-ups) is a passion to win; and this goes with unbearable rage at being beaten in competition. We may wish our pupils or our children to become good losers, that is, genuinely not to feel rage when they lose; genuinely to feel pleasure in the game, not the result; sincerely to be able to congratulate the winner. However, it is notoriously no use telling someone who is a bad loser that it is, after all, only a game, and that the point was to play, not to win. This will not stop him upsetting the ludo board, or breaking his tennis racquet in half. The only thing to do is to tell him how good losers behave, and get him to recognise that this is how he *has* to behave, whatever his feelings. This may be a case of mastering emotions, rather than letting them master you—the case with which Peters's account of emotion fitted best.

To take another case, if you steel yourself to congratulate another mother on the success of her daughter, though inwardly raging that it was not your daughter who was chosen to play the part of St Joan; and if you exercise all the acting skills you can muster to put into the congratulatory performance, then at least you will be behaving well. But also, over the years, the better your show of pleasure at your rival's success, the more probable it is that the show becomes sincere. Acting the part of the generous, the good loser, may bring you nearer to the character you are pretending to be. Aristotle suggests that the beginner in virtue will have to imitate those who are already virtuous. Only by practice does anyone acquire a fixed and unchanging disposition to virtue. And so it may be with feelings. The habit of concealment may finish certain feelings off; the habit of expressing feelings, at times not truly felt, may bring them into being. (And even if not, the courtesies will have been preserved.) To teach a child how to behave may turn him into someone who behaves well spontaneously. Manners Makyth Man.

Examples could be multiplied. Among them is the teaching of children not to be overcome by the emotional accompaniment of pain (the disagreeable aspect of the physical experience), but to endure it stoically; and this emotional education, like almost all education that falls into this category, is highly culturally determinate. Consider, for example, the teaching of the emotions pride and shame, designated by Hume 'indirect passions'. I would argue that no child can be morally educated unless he is educated to feel satisfaction when he has done well, and even more important, shame when he has done badly, according to whatever standard of behaviour he is brought up in. Here we have two feelings, easily recognisable as inner feelings, which may indeed *never* be expressed, but which cannot be thought of as innate. They depend crucially on the concepts of right and wrong, are inextricably mixed with these concepts, and they therefore need to be learned. Sartre, in *Being and Nothingness*[8] uses the inner experience of shame as a proof of the existence of other people. Solipsism must be false, if the man who is caught with his ear to the keyhole eavesdropping is capable, as he is, of feeling an agonising stab of shame. The feeling is one which is essentially directed to the figure he cuts in the eyes of someone *else*. But of course the eavesdropper would not experience this stab unless he had been *taught* that it was disgraceful to listen at doors. The educational point is that a child must be taught not only the rule but the feeling: he must be taught to feel bad if he breaks the rule; and he must be taught that virtue is its own reward, that is, that he feels good if he obeys the rule. This is the necessary centre of moral education.

In moral education, then, we come to an area within which the education of the feelings is of the greatest importance. We must be taught to feel as we ought. But even with the very most liberal interpretation of 'feeling' or 'emotion', there are attributes which may seem to fall outside the sphere of moral education, indeed outside the sphere of education altogether. From all that I have said so far, it is easy to see how a child may be educated in *charity*. Charity is a matter primarily of feeling in a certain way with regard to other people. The feeling may sometimes lead to acts of charity; but more often it will lead to charitable thoughts or loving or forgiving or understanding thoughts, only indirectly connected with actions, if at all. So charity, though doubtless a virtue, fits well with the concept of emotion as a way of looking at the world. But what about faith? Is this an emotion? And what, above all, about hope?

I think that of all the attributes that I would like to see in my children or in my pupils, the attribute of hope would come high, even top, of the list. To lose hope is to lose the capacity to want or desire anything; to lose, in fact, the wish to live. Hope is akin to energy, to curiosity, to the belief that things are worth doing. An education which leaves a child without hope is an education that has failed. The old Utilitarian belief in the efficacy of education was founded on the supposition that education increased hope for the hitherto uneducated. A hopeful person will survive even disappointment. He will rise again. Perhaps, it may be argued, hope is a mood, not a feeling. But, if a mood, then it is a *tendency to have* certain feelings, a readiness to experience emotions of a more episodic kind. And so the question for educationalists may be whether or not we can teach children to have certain moods. I believe that we can; or at least we can affect their moods.

To take a negative case first: there are some people whose mood is predominantly resentful. For these people, whatever the cause of their mood, everything tends to be taken as a case of injustice; as an object of envy or as a slight (and this mood may be quite unconnected with any actual injustices experienced). The analytic mode of teaching might do something to diminish such a mood and to control the episodic spurts of malice which arise out of it. We could attempt to find out and correct the underlying beliefs which lay at the root of the resentment. But if that failed, if we could not uncover the beliefs or could not change them, then the other method, the method of pretending not to feel resentment and acting according to that pretence might have some effect. In resentment one sees oneself as the victim, the innocent party whose rights have been overlooked. To pretend not to be a victim; to pretend to accept one's lot with pleasure is a first step on the road to seeing oneself in a different light (and a step not necessarily in the direction of submission or passivity. Revolutions are not, I believe, characteristically started by the resentful, but by the imaginative).

Can we go further and envisage an education which positively encourages a particular mood, for example the mood of hope? It seems to me that education is peculiarly fitted to do this. For to feel competent, able to act, able to change or control things, or even to create them, these are all aspects of feeling hope. To be hopeful is to have an interest in the world. Thus education in its perfectly regular school-based sense, in which people are taught to understand things or are taught new skills, may well be conducive to a mood of hope. To find something newly exciting; to find that today you can begin to do something you could not do yesterday, is to begin to hope. For someone to wake up in the morning, thinking 'Good: I can go on with it', whatever 'it' is, this I suppose must be the chief goal of education. Successful education, then, will be productive of a mood. And the mood itself will be productive of episodic feelings of pleasure, satisfaction and excitement.

We have come nearly to the point, then, of suggesting that all education, even education leading to the ability to speak French or to play the French horn, is in part the education of the emotions; because, if it works, it will engender, along with other benefits, this predominantly hopeful mood. But there are dangers in such a view.

First of all, I have suggested that some of the education of the emotions must take the form of teaching people to pretend to feelings they do not have. It may well be argued, as I have already suggested, that to do this, or indeed to educate them to conceal feelings they do have, is to educate people for deceit. One of the aspects of the education of the emotions discussed by Peters is that people should be taught to inspect their emotions to ensure that they are *true*; that is that they are sincere and not fake. So how important are we to judge sincerity to be, in the education of the feelings? This question is I think connected with another aspect of emotional education often insisted on, namely education to enable the *expression* of emotions. It is not wholly clear to me why this kind of education is held to be good. It may be that those who advocate it, for example as a justification for including creative arts in the regular school curriculum, do so because they see it as a kind of Catharsis—the purging of emotions, some of which are potentially dangerous, in a harmless channel of creativity. This is the view that art is not only essentially expressive, but essentially therapeutic; and it is not a theory of art which I can embrace. Not all artists, and certainly not all children, are in want of therapy. But this does not entail that for them artistic creativity has no value. On the contrary; I would be inclined to argue that for them, and for most of us, the value of art, whether we are creators or spectators, is pleasure. But at least I suppose this much can be agreed. Insofar as creative art is expressive, then what it expresses must be true, not fake. Insincerity in art must be counted a defect.

Insistence on feelings, and the education of feelings, may lead to fake, because it may lead to that sentimentality which is the enjoyment of feelings for their own sake, or so sentimentality has been defined. Related to the question how important a virtue is sincerity, then, is the other question, how important a vice is sentimentality? Michael Tanner,[9] in a central article on this topic, suggests not that we need a foolproof definition of the emotions and their proper relationship to their 'objects' as a basis for a discussion of sentimentality, but rather that if we analyse the defective emotions involved in the sentimental, we may throw light on the normal and healthy. But it is not entirely clear in what way sentimental emotions are corrupt. Tanner suggests that a corrupt, sentimental, emotion is one on which we make no effort to act. It is one which never turns into a motive. But the charge of sentimentality cannot always be justified even against people who experience these emotions. Some people, for example, enjoy emotions which are compounded of yearning for something they have not had, and they yearn perfectly legitimately. Is to yearn *necessarily* sentimental? I do not think so. It may be good and

indeed inevitable to yearn for that of which you have been deprived. If a child brought up in care fantasises about a real family and longs for love, can we accuse him of sentimentality, simply because he will never get what he wants, and can never take action to obtain it? Is a woman who is deprived of love and support sentimental if she reads stories about the kind of love she has never had? Again, I do not believe that she is, although it may be a popular male view that she is wasting her emotions on something necessarily beyond her reach.

We must ask rather whether there are some feelings which are intrinsically sentimental; and whether, if this is so, education should be designed to identify and to eradicate such feelings. I am compelled to say that I do not know the answer to this question, although I recognise that I am vulnerable to an affirmative answer, in advocating a sentimental education, if I may so describe the education discussed above. Tanner advances a concept of emotional generosity, a willingness to experience emotion, linked with vitality (a concept closely related, I believe, to my mood of 'hope'), and attempts to distinguish this from sentimentality, which, he says, 'flourishes in the same hedgerow'. The distinction he makes is that the emotionally generous freely act on their feelings while the sentimental merely enjoy them, and might even be inhibited from acting on them, in case they thereby came to an end. He diagnoses sentimentality in a variety of different ways, but all connected with the idea that feelings properly characterised as sentimental are feelings 'in the void', unfocused, following each other in quick succession, or aroused by the wholly conventional and superficial. He raises, for example, the question whether, for a total non-believer in Christianity, it is possible to be unsentimentally moved by, for example, Bach's B Minor Mass, or the St Matthew Passion. I am inclined to think that it is not: that an emotional response to great church music must be connected with a belief or semi-belief in the words. Otherwise the emotion is borrowed—borrowed from a tradition that the hearer has rejected. And so the woman who yearns for love may be indulging in an emotion she has borrowed from fiction.

In the education of the emotions there is a constant danger of this kind of falsity. It is only if the teacher and the pupil both believe in the values taught that the feelings connected with these values can be genuine. And though non-genuineness of feeling may in some cases be a necessary step, a way of approaching the real thing, as I have argued, nevertheless as an end in itself it must be rejected.

Yet it is probably true that education should concentrate more on the feelings than it has hitherto been inclined to do, and this partly because of the impossibility of distinguishing between feelings and thought, of separating knowledge from attitudes towards knowledge from interest and excitement in it.

But in addition I would argue two further points. First, that it is better to have feelings than not. Collingwood makes this point, in discussing the message of Eliot's *The Waste Land*:

> The poem depicts a world where the wholesome flowing water of emotion, which alone fertilises all human activity, has dried up. Passions that once ran so strongly as to threaten the defeat of prudence, the destruction of human individuality, the wreck of men's little ships, are shrunk to nothing. No one gives, no one will risk himself by sympathising; no one has anything to control. . . . The only emotion left us is fear: fear of emotion itself, fear of death by drowning in it, fear in a handful of dust.[10]

I would rather see a school full of sentimentalists than one full of the unfeeling, the ungenerous and the afraid. Secondly, and more important, Aristotle was right to argue that virtue is a matter of feeling *and* action. The virtuous man gets it right with regard to both. Moral education cannot afford to concentrate wholly on what people *do* nor only on those feelings which have become motives. It must take into account equally what people feel; and must recognise that *what* they feel can be crucially changed by education.

Notes

1 R.S. Peters, 'Emotions and the Category of Passivity', *Proceedings of the Aristotelian Society*, supp. vol. 62, 1962, pp. 117-34; 'The Education of the Emotions' in *Feelings and Emotions*, ed. Magda Arnold, Academic Press, 1970, pp. 187-203.
2 Robert C. Solomon, 'Emotions and Choice' in *Explaining Emotions*, ed. Amelie Rorty, University of California Press, 1980.
3 J.-P. Sartre, *Esquisse d'une théorie des emotions*, Paris, 1939, trans. Philip Mairet, Methuen, 1962.
4 Cf. Edward Sankowski, 'Responsibility of Persons for their Emotions', *Canadian Journal of Philosophy*, 1977, pp. 829-40.
5 Jonathan Miller, Dialogue with George Mandler: 'The Nature of Emotion' in *States of Mind*, ed. Jonathan Miller, BBC, 1983.
6 Amelie Rorty, 'Explaining Emotions' in *Explaining Emotions*, ed. Amelie Rorty, University of California Press, 1980.
7 Thomas Nagel, 'What is it like to be a Bat?', *Philosophical Review*, vol. 83, 1974, pp. 435-51.
8 J.-P. Sartre, *L'Etre et le Néant*, Paris, 1940, trans. Hazel Barnes, *Being and Nothingness*, Methuen, 1957, pp. 259 et seq.

9 Michael Tanner, 'Sentimentality', *Proceedings of the Aristotelian Society*, vol. 77, 1977, pp. 127-47.
10 R.G. Collingwood, *The Principles of Art*, Oxford University Press, 1963, p. 335.

Motivation

D.W. Hamlyn

In the late 1950s when Richard Peters wrote *The Concept of Motivation*[1] there was a great deal of philosophical interest in motives and motivation. Much of it was no doubt directed by a more general concern—to make clear the distinction between reasons and causes. But it was not just that. Ryle, following a quite ancient tradition, had stressed that the explanation of behaviour by reference to motives involved an appeal to dispositions—to, in Aristotelian terms, the formal causes of action. Richard Peters's emphasis on the rule-following purposive model and to the idea of directed dispositions in effect emphasised final causes too, although this was complicated in his case by the additional emphasis, one that was not unusual in the context of ordinary-language philosophy, on the circumstances in which it is appropriate to use the term 'motive' itself. Perhaps we can now recognise that last consideration as one of somewhat parochial interest. Whatever be the case about the circumstances in which we use the term 'motive' itself, it does not necessarily carry over to explanation of actions in terms of such things as pride, revenge and friendship.

However that may be, it seems to me that in the 1960s and 1970s the subject of motives dropped out of the philosophical literature. It might be objected that that is not, strictly speaking, true. There have, after all, been plenty of discussions in that period of the explanation of action—of, to use Davidson's phrase, the rationalisation of action. Indeed, in certain quarters it has become a kind of commonplace that actions are to be explained in terms of some complex of beliefs and desires—a notion that Davidson himself introduced in his well-known paper 'Actions, Reasons and Causes'.[2] There has, however, been little discussion of motives as such, and one possible explanation of that fact may be Davidson's paper itself and the issues that have become prominent since it. Davidson stressed that some account had to be given of the efficacy of reasons, and it seemed to him, as it has seemed to many others, that such an account must involve reference to causation. Behind what he had to say, in any case, is an ideology which insists that

that causation must be physical in nature (and it is an ideology nonetheless even if, ostensibly, Davidson has since argued for it). Hence it is that Davidson can say that while complexes of belief and desire do not cause action under that description there is nevertheless a physical description under which actions are caused in these circumstances. Hence, in short, reasons are causes.

But they are not. At best what has been shown is that *having* a reason may be a cause, and the same is true of motives and the having of them. It is of course commonplace that people can have motives on which they do not act. So certainly some explanation is required both of why they do not act when they have a motive and of why they do on other occasions when they have that motive. It might be suggested that the answer to the first part of this is that for some reason causality is absent, just as the answer to the second part lies in the presence of causality. If what takes place when someone has a reason or motive causes them to act that is a sufficient explanation of the efficacy of the reason or motive; if there is no such causal relation then that equally explains why the action does not take place. There are, of course, problems about that causality, arising from the fact that sometimes the complex of belief and desire may (under some description) bring about the action without the person concerned acting *from* that complex of belief and desire. Davidson himself emphasised that point in his paper 'Freedom to Act',[3] but he was not alone in that. Although he himself was pessimistic about his ability to deal with the problem, it has spawned a literature concerned with so-called 'deviant causal chains', and attempts to spell out the requisite kind of causality have reached a high degree of complexity, one that is sometimes (I gather erroneously) labelled 'Byzantine'.[4]

The idea that action is always to be explained by reference to complexes of beliefs and desires seems on reflection to be a grossly over-simple one in any case. Philosophers who have been concerned with forms of irrationality have tended to concentrate on *akrasia* or at all events on cases where the agent desires some end and believes that doing A will bring about that end, but fails nevertheless to do A. There is, however, a form of irrationality which *prima facie* corresponds rather well to what Davidson has in mind in speaking of the rationalisation of action. I have in mind the phenomenon which psychologists have sometimes called 'stereotyping'. As I have pointed out elsewhere,[5] E.R. Guthrie's 'cats in a puzzle box', which managed to escape from the cage by accidentally touching in some way the escape lever so as to open the door, tended to persist in this arbitrary form of contact with the lever in trying to escape in future, even if there were much easier ways of opening the door. 'Irrational' we might say; certainly 'inefficient', although perhaps we ought not to expect more of animals which, surely, cannot appreciate the principles of door-opening mechanisms.

Nevertheless, one might say that their action is to be explained by the fact that they wanted to escape and believed that the way to achieve that end is to do whatever produced that effect (though accidentally) in the first place. The action is hardly rational, but it is perhaps understandable all the same. What else should we add if we are to explain a really rational action in such a context, i.e. one that involved using the lever in an economical, efficient way? Surely *something* more has to be added, and, it might be said, Davidson's model for the rationalisation of actions seems to apply best to actions which are irrational in the way that I have indicated. The same sort of thing holds good of rats in a Skinner-box. It is one of the features of so-called operant conditioning that was earliest established that if a rat is taught to press a lever to get food-pellets (wanting the food and believing that this is the way in which to get it, one might say, *pace* of course B.F. Skinner himself) a rate of responding is likely to be set up which is out of all proportion to the simple satisfaction of hunger. It is irrational in that sense. It nevertheless fits the Davidsonian rationalisation pattern, or can be taken to do so, unless one is persuaded by Skinner himself to confine oneself to purely causal forms of explanation throughout these phenomena. If all this is so can the Davidsonian rationalisation pattern be sufficient?

One might of course say that one should invoke in these cases more complex patterns of desire. It might be said, for example, that the animal does not just want food, it comes to want to press the lever for its own sake or to want to get the pellet without reference to the satisfaction of hunger. Ought not we to postulate, that is, a more complex motivation? But if we want to invoke the concept of motivation in these cases that seems the wrong direction in which to go. It is not that the rat has a more *complex* motivation; it is that the motivation is one of a different kind, not one that can be reduced simply to some complex of belief and desire. It is tempting to make reference to habit, but it would be wrong in either the case of the cat or that of the rat to invoke as explanation of what happens something like habit, if the reference to habit is meant to be explanation-stopping as far as motives are concerned. ('He did it out of habit' can be taken as saying that we need look no further for explanation of what he did.) The rapidity of the response rate in the case of the rat, at all events, demands its own explanation. A persistent lever-pressing when food was no longer an interest *might* be put down to habit, but not an *accelerated* response rate. That looks as if it is, so to speak, 'driven', almost pathological in the sense of being compulsive or obsessional.

Once one brings in that sort of idea the complexities of psychoanalytical explanation loom on the horizon. We should in that context be inclined to explain the compulsion by reference to some complex motivation such that the action does not have the significance that it seems immediately to have, even to the agent. I do not wish to suggest that we can with equanimity attribute such motivation to a rat, since when I speak of the action's having a significance at all, let alone one which is not immediate, I imply a kind of self-consciousness or reflexivity in relation to one's actions which it would not be plausible to attribute to an animal of that kind. It may be that the explanation in the rat's case is much simpler, although I hazard no guess as to what it might actually be. In human beings, however, it is another matter; here one can invoke almost as much complexity as one wants. It would nevertheless be a mistake to suppose that in such cases what is done is explained in any adequate way by reference to a complex of pro-attitudes or desires and beliefs. To invoke such a complex would be misleading just because it is over-simple.

I have in any case suggested elsewhere[6] that what is left out of Davidson's rationalisation pattern is any reference to the intentional character of what is supposed to be explained in this way. I do not know whether it is fair to attribute to Davidson the view that the intentional character of the action is to be analysed in terms of how it is caused. Certainly what is missing from the cases which have led to talk of deviant causal chains is any *separate* reference to the fact that actions to which the rationalisation pattern applies are intentional; indeed it might be suggested that on the view in question the intentional character of the action *is* to be explained in terms of how it is caused, and that is what becomes embarrassing when it is seen that a similar, if not identical, aetiology may lead to actions similar to those originally contemplated except that they are *un*intentional. One important thing about explanation by reference to motives, however, is that such explanation becomes applicable only when the action is presumed as intentional. We do not, and should not, ask for someone's motive in knocking over the sugar accidentally; and if we think that inadvertence requires an explanation in terms of motives it can only be because we do not think it a true inadvertence.

Schopenhauer, who thought that motives were causes seen from within, held that motives (by which he meant what he calls 'representations'—thoughts that constitute the content of a volition) influence the will. But they do that only in the sense that they function in relation to *action*—action being what he calls the objectification of the will, the way in which the will finds bodily expression. Hence their efficacy, which reveals itself 'from without' as causation, depends upon the fact that they influence willed action. One can translate this into other terms by saying that the whole business of explanation by reference to motives, including the efficacy of such motives, presupposes that we are concerned with *intentional action*. Not, be it noted, necessarily action done for some further intention (for not all intentional action is like that, some actions are done intentionally without there being any further intention beyond them); nor what Davidson calls pure intending, and which Schopenhauer called, somewhat condescendingly, mere acts of intention, resolves for the future. We are concerned simply with action done intentionally. The question what that is is a difficult one to answer, although intentional action surely presupposes that what is done is done knowingly. Nevertheless, the possibility of intentional action, of acting intentionally, is presupposed by the other phenomena which fall under the heading of intention—at all events those of acting for a further intention or purpose and intending *simpliciter*. It is therefore not reducible to them.

On this view, if we say that someone did something out of pride or from revenge, we imply first that he/she did something and did it intentionally, and secondly we imply that perception or awareness of something in a certain way influenced that doing and gave it its context and content. The perception in question involves seeing something as ..., where the gap is to be filled by a description of something which in providing a reason for the doing makes it characterisable as done out of pride or from revenge. I once said that anything that could figure in a description of an action *qua* intentional could be invoked as a motive for that action, so that, as Miss Anscombe has said in her *Intention*, motives can be backward-looking to the previous circumstances of the action, forward-looking to the end to be achieved, or merely interpretative, in the sense of being merely revelatory of the manner, style or character of the action.[7] I still think that thesis is valid, but perhaps what I have said now, in a way following Schopenhauer, gives it a little more content. The point remains that, as Schopenhauer would have it, an investigation of motives is an investigation of a curious relationship that exists between the will and the intellect, between the intentional character of the action and what the agent sees his action, its circumstances and its object *as*.

To put the matter in that latter way is less question-begging

than putting it in Schopenhauer's way, especially since reference to the will may seem to some to involve a dubious reference to a strange mental faculty. Nevertheless, either way of putting it reveals in yet another way the extent to which the Davidsonian rationalisation formula is over-simple. However much we may think that the bodily movements which occur when we act physically are caused by, among other things, physiological events, some of which are in turn caused by things happening in the environment, we are in no position to restrict our construal of those events, for the purposes of explaining the act, so that they are taken as functioning as beliefs and desires alone. Someone who, for example, inflicts an injury on another person out of revenge acts in a way that is not adequately explained simply by saying that he wants to get his own back and believes that inflicting injury in that way will produce that result, whatever be the underlying causality responsible for the movements of his body that take place. For wanting one's own back and believing that injuring Smith will bring about that effect need result in no action unless one actually sees Smith as the object of one's beliefs. That much may seem obvious, but it needs to be said all the same.

Moreover, it is not sufficient that one should see Smith under *any* description. We might indeed say that the proper way to put the point is to say that the person concerned must see Smith as both the object and a *suitable* object of his action. That surely entails that he should have feelings about and towards Smith. A full explanation of the action must fit the agent fully into the context of his relationship with Smith. One cannot jump straight from what I take to be the plausible principle[8] that the movements that take place when we act must be explicable in the end in terms of the physical events which are their context to the thesis that action is explicable simply by reference to such events construed as beliefs and desires.

To suppose otherwise is to take too simple a view of action, of agency, and of what enables an agent to realise himself as an agent—knowledge, perception, feelings and, let us say, will. All these things go into the relationship between intellect and will of which Schopenhauer rightly spoke, and which he saw as the key to the understanding of human beings and, more surprisingly, the world in general. If we appeal to motives in explaining action we appeal to some aspect of what is involved in that relationship between intellect and will—but the aspect varies. Not all motives are the same. I think, therefore, that Richard Peters was guilty of over-simplification here too in what he wrote in *The Concept of Motivation*. For he emphasised (p. 156) that 'the rule-following purposive model is basic in explaining human behaviour'. It is no doubt true that man is indeed a rule-following purposive animal; but he is not just that, he has feelings, inclinations and passions as well (and it would be both ungracious and unjust of me not to acknowledge that Richard Peters has had much to say about passions, for example, elsewhere). Rule-following and norms do enter into human action in an important way, and many of the things which we do are done because of purposes that we have and believe must be fulfilled and attained. That is certainly one aspect of human beings; but many of the occasions where an action would be inexplicable without appeal to a motive are not like that. Let me invoke for the third time for philosophical purposes the case in which some years ago I was involved as a juror.

I can recount only some of the facts here.[9] The defendant, who was charged with murder, had been illegitimate, had married and had had two children about whom he felt strongly, particularly in respect of their legitimacy. But when separated from his wife when the marriage broke up he made little effort to see the children (except on one unfortunate occasion late at night). On the other hand he kept photographs of the children and performed a kind of 'religious' ritual in relation to them, by putting a rosary around them wherever they were put. The killing was the culmination of a weekend of blind drunkenness and emotion. The man who was killed had lived previously with the woman (a wall-of-death rider) with whom the defendant now lived and he had bullied and ill-treated her. The defendant had, so to speak, rescued her and pulled her together. The actual killing followed on the defendant's seizure of a knife when he thought that the other man was returning to the house where he lived. But it was provoked by what is in some respects a simple series of events. The man who was eventually killed had earlier broken the photographs of the children and when asked why he had done that to the defendant's 'babies', he replied 'F. . . your bastard babies'. The lunge with the knife followed. What was the motive?

Even on the basis of the necessarily simplified account of the facts that I have produced it must be evident that any adequate answer to that question must be an extremely complex one. It cannot, for example, be irrelevant that the defendant was illegitimate (and that is why I laid emphasis on the fact), so that the use of the word 'bastard' may indeed have functioned as something of a trigger. But there are many other things as well that must be relevant, e.g. the defendant's relation to the woman whom the other man had ill-treated and the anger that that bullying produced (although it is only fair to say that all three had been out drinking together earlier that day and on the previous day). There was provocation, no doubt, but enough by itself to explain the killing? It is the mark of a '*crime passionel*', to the extent that this was one, that the action is not fully rational, and not therefore to be explained altogether by reference to factors of the kind that might fit Davidson's rationalisation pattern, let alone Peters's rule-following purposive model. It might be said that Davidson at all events has met that objection in what he has had to say about weakness of will.[10] But a *crime passionel* is in no sense a case of weakness of will. The action in its case is totally directed to the fulfilment of the passion; the passion is all. What remains a puzzle sometimes is why it should be that, why *that* should be the overriding compulsion.

It is in that spirit that I ask of the case that I have outlined 'What was the motive?'. It seems clear on reflection that the only adequate way to answer that question is to tell the whole story, or as much of it as will give what was done a sense, and then one may or may not respond with 'Yes, that fits', or at least 'Yes, I can see that someone might do that'. In the normal legal case the law asks the jury to answer the question what a reasonable man would have done in the circumstances, and that view of things even infects the legal notion of provocation. (In the case with which I was concerned the judge defined provocation by saying that if you return home to find your spouse in bed with another and you kill him/her, it is murder if you read the person concerned a moral lecture and then come back and kill him/her; it is or may be provocation if you do it straight away, it being assumed that this is something that even reasonable man might do!) But in this the law is concerned with the question how far the act can be excused. To understand an act, or at least to see how it might be understood, is not necessarily to excuse it, and questions of excuse may not even enter into consideration. That is so even if, as in the case with which I was concerned, one way of understanding the act may entail that the category of murder is not one that can be applied to it. One can see that a certain story about an act is such that it all fits without supposing that there is anything reasonable about the act.

From time to time in his writings Richard Peters has made reference to the kind of case in which someone suddenly does something apparently inexplicable and certainly out of character, but he has insisted that such cases should be seen against the rule-following purposive model, and he originally maintained, as we have already seen, that it was in the case of such deviations from the norm that we usually ask for the motive. But the point on which I have been insisting as crucial is that it is in such cases too that it may seem so immensely difficult to give the motive. Nevertheless, with luck, when we have told the whole story, or as much of it as seems relevant, it may all fit together. I say 'with luck', because there may remain cases where little or nothing fits. In such cases we may have to invoke brute causality. I am tempted to add 'with nothing of rationality'; for the pattern to which we appeal when it does fit is to some extent a rational pattern even if it is one that does not imply reasonableness.

One thing that I think is wrong with both Peters's and Davidson's account of motivation is that the two accounts both involve too circumscribed a view of rationality—one that identifies it too much with reasonableness, whether reasonableness is thought of as a matter of pursuing purposes in a rule-following way or as a matter of achieving the end desired in an efficient way. The distinction between the rational and the irrational is no doubt a relative one, and both of them have to be set against the non-rational. An irrational act is normally one which falls within the category of the non-non-rational, but falls short in some way—in being less than efficient in the attainment of purposes, in involving less than obvious conformity to reasons, in not following the obvious rules, and so on. It may also sometimes be an action which is not to be understood throughout in terms of the pattern which would otherwise provide the motivation, and so verges on the non-rational. It cannot be understood throughout in terms of intention, desire, perception of relevant circumstances, and so on, because brute causality enters in at some point. It would be foolish to deny, however, that the pattern of motivation, where it is appropriate, may, as I have insisted, be exceedingly complex; and it is important in consequence not to resort to brute causality too soon. If psychoanalysis has taught us nothing else it has taught us that. For there too the only court of appeal for the validity of an intepretation may in the end be that 'it all fits'. What is more important for present purposes, however, is that it may well be that we will have provided no answer at all to the question 'What is the motive?' until we arrive at that point of seeing that it all fits. To sum up what we then see in some such term as 'revenge' is merely to assign the pattern to a category, and in that particular case to one that implies that the main trend of the action was backwards-looking.

Did the man in my case, then, act out of revenge? No doubt that was part of it. But the final thing that led to the killing had as an important part also his perception that the one thing that mattered to him—his children—was being set at naught. But then one has to add in saying that that it was not really his children as such that mattered but his 'idea' of his children; and the remark that the other man made was an affront to all that was involved in that idea. It might be objected that in saying that I play the psychoanalyst and that what I have said may be far from the truth. For present purposes that does not matter. The point of which I demand recognition is the possible complexity of motivation; we have the simple motivational categories that we do just because we need some grasp on reality. We should have no grasp on that reality at all, however, if we did not in some respect recognise people for what they are—beings who act intentionally, who see things and other people in certain ways, who wants things, and who have feelings about and towards both other things and people and themselves.

It was often said in the 1950s that biographers and novelists may have more to tell us about motivation than do philosophers and psychologists; and in this respect psychoanalysts are more like biographers and novelists. All that may be true or at all events have an element of truth. Philosophers tend to want to tell us that human beings are animals subject to physical causation or rule-following purposive animals. But human beings are also animals who see things in certain ways, who have feelings about the things they so see and who behave as they do because of the ways in which they see them. Human beings may be rule-following purposive animals among other things, but they would not be that in a way that matters if they were not capable of seeing when to give the rules application and when it is important or otherwise so to do. Schopenhauer was right in insisting, as we have seen, that motivation presupposes a special relationship between the will and the intellect, but what matters in it all is how that relationship is spelled out. What Peters has had to say about that is limiting in one way just as Davidson's rationalisation pattern is limiting in another.

What then are motives? They are anything that we might mention in putting a person's intentional action in its place, when the resulting story fits together. Hence when someone says 'These were his motives' and another says 'His motives were these other things', they may both be right if these alternatives are both elements in a coherent story. It is a matter of where they wish to put the emphasis. It follows that it is wrong to expect the answer to the question 'What are motives?' to be arrived at by equating motives with specific items such as desires or emotions. To ask what a motive is is to ask how we explain actions by reference to motives. They indeed give a certain sort of reason why people so behave, and if Richard Peters has said nothing else in this area he has certainly said that, even if he was unwilling to leave it at that when he wrote *The Concept of Motivation*.

Moreover, in that same book he emphasised that in giving the reason why a person did whatever he did we do not necessarily give his reason. Certainly when a person acts out of revenge, revenge may not be his reason for doing whatever he does, even if in acting out of revenge he may do something for reasons. Since, as I insisted earlier, intentional action does not necessarily entail acting for further intentions, purposes or reasons, a motivated action *need* not involve any action for reasons at all in the full sense, although perhaps it would be surprising if action for reasons did not enter the picture somewhere in the majority of cases. The pattern can, however, vary from one extreme where reasons are pertinent or indeed the most important thing in the situation to the other extreme where, as I said earlier, the non-rational has a place of its own. In between lies the case of intentional action *simpliciter*; if a person does something out of friendship he presumably acts intentionally, but not necessarily for any further reason that he may have in mind and not necessarily because his reaction to the other is triggered by some non-rational factor of brute causality, by, say, the workings of his glands. That is true however much causal processes of a bodily kind are a necessary condition of the intentional action itself.

The important point, however, is that if we are to speak of motivation at all there must be intentional action, and the person concerned must see the object of his action in certain ways, so that it is equally the object of feeling. To give the complete motivation is to tell the whole story of which that is a part, but for convenience we sometimes speak of some relevant part of the story as the motive. That is why alternative accounts of a person's motives can sometimes be given without there being any necessary conflict between the accounts. It also allows for that over-determination of action which is such a fundamental part of psychoanalytic theory; in this context over-determination simply means that there is more than one part to the total story, and the recognition of it in psychoanalysis is simply the recognition that the story that has to be told about people's intentional action is much more complicated than was once supposed. Whether it is complicated in the way that specific psychoanalysts believe is another matter. Nevertheless, the whole of which a specified motive may be a part involves that relation between the intellect and the will of which Schopenhauer wisely spoke, and which needs to be set out in detail in any particular case where we need to understand the motivation fully.

I should like to close with another remark which brings together Schopenhauer and Freud and which is relevant to what Richard Peters said about psychoanalysis in his *The Concept of Motivation*. It is often said that Schopenhauer anticipated Freud in certain ways, and Freud himself thought that what Schopenhauer had to say about the will anticipated the theory of the mind and of human nature that he, Freud, put forward in his middle and late periods. The correct comparison in this respect is between what Schopenhauer says about the will as thing-in-itself and what Freud says about our basic instinctual nature, about what he calls the 'primary process'. As Richard Peters pointed out, Freud said that the primary process was subject to purely deterministic causation. It has nothing to do with intention or intentional action, and even less to do with the rule-following purposive model. It follows that it is not in itself an area where considerations of motivation arise, whatever Freud says about the pleasure-principle and the like.

When I praise Schopenhauer for his emphasis on the link between intellect and will I do not have any of the foregoing in mind. The move from the point that action requires principles of explanation which are not, at any rate at first sight, the same as those which are applicable to 'inorganic nature' to the view that in this we have the key to the insight that nature as a whole and human nature in particular is governed by a brute form of unconscious agency to be called 'will' is an illegitimate if interesting move.[11] I think that exactly the same is true of the move that Freud made from the apparatus of explanation which is invoked in the early, clinical papers, where notions like that of intention are invoked, to the story about the primary process and the theory of human nature that that involves. Whatever is to be said for that story for its own sake it does not follow from the initial insights.

To say that psychoanalysis forces on us the recognition that the motivation of human action is often more complicated than was previously supposed does not therefore commit us to any theory of instincts nor to a Schopenhauerian view of the will in nature. It does commit us to the recognition that a reference to motives need not be a reference to anything simple. If in saying that I implicitly criticise what Richard Peters had to say in 1958 I am sure that one can find in his subsequent writings abundant recognition of that fact, however it is spelled out. For there is in his long fruitful career and his many publications a wealth of philosophical insights and a willingness to bring reason to bear upon them which we ought both to recognise and to salute. I could not close without acknowledging both that and my own personal debt to him.

Notes

1 R.S. Peters, *The Concept of Motivation*, Routledge & Kegan Paul, 1958.
2 D. Davidson, 'Actions, Reasons and Causes', in his *Essays on Actions and Events*, Clarendon Press, 1980, pp. 3-19.
3 Also in *Essays on Actions and Events*, pp. 63-81.
4 See for example Christopher Peacocke, *Holistic Explanation*, Clarendon Press, 1979.
5 See my 'Conditioning and Behaviour' in *Explanation in the Behavioural Sciences*, Cambridge University Press, 1970; reprinted in my *Perception, Learning and the Self*, Routledge & Kegan Paul, 1983, pp. 91-106.
6 See my 'Schopenhauer on Action and the Will' in G.N.A. Vesey (ed.), *Idealism Past and Present*, Royal Institute of Philosophy Lecture Series 13, Cambridge University Press, 1982, pp. 127-40.
7 See my 'Unconscious Intentions', *Philosophy*, vol. 46, 1971; reprinted in my *Perception, Learning and the Self*, pp. 181-93.
8 See my 'Causality and Human Behaviour', *Supplementary Proceedings of the Aristotelian Society*, vol. 38, 1964, pp. 125-42, for some discussion of this point.
9 See also my 'The Phenomena of Love and Hate' and 'Learning to Love', both in *Perception, Learning and the Self*.
10 D. Davidson, 'How is Weakness of Will Possible?', op. cit., pp. 21-42.
11 See my *Schopenhauer*, Routledge & Kegan Paul, 1980, chapter 5, and my 'Schopenhauer on the Will in Nature', *Mid-West Studies in Philosophy*, vol. 8, 1983, pp. 457-67.

Human nature and potential[1]

Israel Scheffler

I Education and the language of potential

The notion of potential is not only a hoary metaphysical idea that has come down to us from ancient Greek philosophy. It is also widely operative in the practical thinking of parents, educators, planners and policy-makers in the contemporary world. Teachers, examiners, and counselors assess the potentials of students. Attributing the possession of given potentials to some, they deny it of others. Whereas, however, lack of a given potential precludes its realisation, possession of the same potential by no means guarantees it. Thus *attribution* of potential opens the further question of *realisation*: what courses of study and training, what forms of practice or life experience would help given students to realise their evident potentials? This question is obviously of central importance to students, parents, educators and planners.

Nor is this the only important question by any means. For not only may improvements be sought in the ways we try to *realise* a potential in fact possessed by a given student or group of students. We may strive also to help students *attain* potentials they have hitherto lacked. Possession as well as realisation may, in other words, vary over time. A student now possessed of a given potential may or may not realise it in the future; but, also, a student now lacking such a potential may or may not come to possess it later on. The question of *enhancement* of a student's potentials thus goes beyond the question of their attribution or denial at a specific time. It follows that, while the present lack of a given potential indeed precludes its realisation now, it does not preclude its realisation at a later time, when the potential in question may have been acquired.

This point is also, clearly, of critical importance to students, parents, teachers, and planners: the stock of potentials changes over time. It is such change, so evident in contemporary education, that cuts most against the grain of the inherited notion of potential. It is only if the fact of such change is ignored and the student's

201

assessed potentials taken as fixed and durable traits that his evident lacks may be routinely mistaken for permanent educational deficiencies. The variation over time, whether of potentials or their realisations, has two important features requiring our immediate notice. The first is the contingency of such variation on human effort, the second is the influence of a given variation on later variations.

As to the contingency of variation on human effort, we have mentioned the important question, 'What courses of study and training, what forms of practice or life experience would help given students to realise their evident potentials?' The normal pre-supposition of this question is that human activities of one or another sort may make a difference to realisation. The design of appropriate studies, the provision of suitable training or experience, the will to learn and practise, all these, and yet other forms of effort may, in fact, vitally affect not only the realisation, but also the enhancement of potential. Thus, both what people potentially are and what they in fact turn out to be are contingent, to an incalculable extent, on human intention, both individual and social, bounded only by available resources and the limits of ingenuity. The burden of educational responsibility imposed on students, parents, teachers, planners, and indeed all society's members, stems from this fact.

The second significant feature of variation, noted above, is that any given variation influences subsequent ones. Potentials and their realisations are not isolated and discrete but intricately linked to one another. A girl who is potentially good at mathematics becomes a different person with actual achievement of mathematical skill. New potentials arise with the realisation of the old; ways of thinking about related topics are now open to her that were formerly closed. New feelings of confidence may contribute to potentials for other sorts of learning as well.

The mere enhancement of potential in one area may moreover facilitate enhancement in another. A boy who has learned enough of a foreign language to be a potential translator of elementary texts has arrived at a new plateau; it is now easier for him than before to acquire the potential to translate more advanced texts or to compare the language in question analytically with his native tongue. The cunningly ordered sequence of potentials and realisations in any educational direction that may be chosen demands of the chooser foresight, breadth of vision, and a steady sense of value. Foresight, because every educational change of state opens up new learning options it were well to anticipate; breadth of vision, because these options do not lie on a straight line determined by the initial subject, but radiate into different sectors of life; a steady sense of value, because the choice of direction requires a grasp of complex alternative goods for comparison with one another, all more or less remote from the urgencies of the present. Foresight, vision, and value constitute the major part of wisdom; the task of the educator is thus revealed as rooted neither in convention, nor craft, nor caprice, but in a wisdom that unites knowledge, imagination, and the good.

The variation of potentials over time has been emphasised in the foregoing account as a way of bringing out questions of basic educational importance, and thus of outlining fundamental aspects of the educator's role. One such aspect, we have seen, has to do with the *enhancement*, or enlargement of the stock of potentials of students. The student's assessed potentials as of now must not be taken in themselves to foreclose new acquisitions in the future. But another aspect related to variation has rather to do with *shrinkage* of the present stock of potentials available to a person. Certain educational moments must be caught or they are gone forever. William James taught that character formation is a hardening of habits, that 'by the age of thirty, the character has set like plaster, and will never soften again.'[2] The moral he drew is that the nervous system, which functions thus, is to be made an ally of education rather than its enemy—education is to instil as many useful habits as early as possible, so that the hardening of character may then proceed in a desirable direction by its own momentum.

James's formulation of the point is no doubt overstated, but it strikingly expresses a general and genuine concern of modern educators. The capacity to learn is not an unlimited resource which can be lightly squandered. The child's curiosity, sufficiently blocked, may be dulled beyond awakening. The impulse to question, thwarted repeatedly, may eventually die. The flexibility of mind, adventuresomeness, and confidence required for exploring the novel are precious and fragile learning instruments that lose their edge with disuse or abuse.

Moreover, aside from character and intellect, the existence of critical intervals for learning must be considered in widely diverse areas of education. Chess, the violin, and ballet must be learned early in life, not late; aspects of the visual system mature only within the bounds of relevant critical periods; beyond another such period, any learning of a new language will, in all probability, carry with it the acquisition of a spoken accent. Potentials here today may, in short, be gone tomorrow.

The educator needs thus not only to anticipate and promote the emergence of potentials not yet in evidence; he must also try to

203

capitalise to the fullest on potentials now manifest but shortly to disappear. He must combine a hopeful imagination of the students' future potentials with a realistic appreciation of those potentials now, but perhaps only temporarily, possessed. Striving to overcome present lacks through future possibilities, the educator is also constantly haunted by the spectre of past opportunity wasted. The pressure of educational time forces him to look in both directions at once.

The mention of wasted opportunity will be instantly recognised by every reflective parent and teacher as marking a basic preoccupation. Time is so short, resources so few, education so precious in shaping the child's life. Has everything possible been done to nurture the fragile growth? The child's own view is foreshortened, its sense of time and change truncated, its things taken for granted as fixed. The illusion of the rightness and durability of the given, and the over-estimate of the child's own powers have yet to be tempered by further experience. The child cannot be expected to be sensitive to the question of wasted opportunity. But to concerned parents and teachers viewing the child against the backdrop of a longer and more realistic time line, the question can never be far below the surface. And it is a question that is often formulated in terms of the concept of potential. Of the child's potentials, have we passed the critical period for any that are important? Have we failed to spot or appreciate crucial potentials through our own blindness? Have valuable potentials remained hidden through lack of general knowledge or lack of social interest? Have apathy, or poverty, or bias, or misguided policy, thwarted the appraisal of children's potentials and cruelly closed off their life prospects? Such worries, natural to parents and teachers, are central also to the concerns of society at large, for what opens and closes the life prospects of children determines the direction and quality of society itself. Thus the process of educational planning, through which a society mediates its treatment of children's potentials, is in its style and scope an index of the society's self-image.

The press of educational responsibility is indeed heavy and relentless. Demanding relief, the educational decision-maker would welcome any way to lighten the load, to lessen the onus of choice. The tendency to replace wisdom with technology thus becomes understandable, promising to reduce the subtleties of complex decision to the simplicities of formula. We have noted the simplifying myth of fixed potentials which, inherited along with the ancient vocabulary of potential, still thrives in various quarters, though defeated by the facts of change.

A more general strategy of relief, also encouraged by traditional precedent, is to hide the necessity of discriminating among the potentials of a student—to assume them all harmoniously realisable. Thus, the educator does not need to evaluate alternative combinations of potentials for attempted realisation. His job is simply to identify the potentials that are there, and then to promote the realisation of all in the most efficient manner. Maximal self-realisation is the goal, understood as the fulfilment of all of one's potentials, satisfying every one of one's potentialities— '*being*', as the saying goes, 'all that one *can* be'.

The problem of education, thus understood, is largely emptied of its evaluative aspects and reduced to a question of fact coupled with a question of technology. The question of fact is: 'What potentials does the student have?' The question of technology is: 'How are these potentials most efficiently to be realised?' Both questions can, in principle, be turned over to scientific investigation for resolution and the educator's task reduced to doing whatever the investigation concludes will most efficiently realise all the student's potentials, there being some such self-realising course available in every case. Thus are the main functions of education reduced to *finding* the potentials and then *realising* them forthwith.

Comforting as this picture has been both for educational theorists and practitioners, it is fatally flawed. William James expressed the main point when he somewhere remarked that 'the philosopher and the lady-killer cannot both keep house in the same tenement of clay.' The potential for the one career and the potential for the other may both be genuinely *possessed* by a given youth but they are not, alas, jointly *realisable*. Merely to *identify* these potentials is thus not sufficient to warrant the attempt at realisation. For to realise the one has the effect of precluding the other, the two being unrealisable together. If one is to be preferred to the other, there must be a judgment embodying such preference. And such judgment, if sufficiently reflective, will involve considerations of relative value affecting the conflicting realisations in question—some reference to imagined alternative goods between which choice must decide.

Every student in fact harbours potentials that are as such compatible but whose realisations conflict. One cannot literally be all that one can be; there are fundamentally different lives that anyone might live, depending on the choices made by onself and others—and it is true of many such lives that each excludes the rest. Choice precludes as well as includes; there is no blinking this fact and, consequently, no relief from educational responsibility in the notion of a comprehensive fulfilment of all one's potentials.

Nor does this notion represent the only way in which the concept of potential is employed so as to lessen the pressure of choice. The educational preoccupations we have outlined above concern the proper attribution and enhancement of potential, the reduction of shrinkage of potential, the discovery and development of hidden potentials, and the efficient realisation of potentials. In every one of these cases, the potentials in question are assumed to have positive value and their realisations to represent goods as well. Yet the assumption, once questioned, is seen to be groundless. People are potentially evil as well as good. They are potentially considerate but also potentially callous, potentially kind and potentially cruel, potentially sensitive and potentially boorish, potentially insightful and intelligent, and potentially obtuse and stupid.

In the typical practical employment of the language of potential, these negative aspects are all filtered out. It is not noted that the educator's aim is to destroy as well as to strengthen potentials, to shrink as well as to enhance various sorts, to block as well as to promote their realisation. Propped by the classical philosophical tradition in which the concept of potential was originally nurtured, this reading of the concept accentuates the positive, fostering the illusion that no value discriminations by the educator are needed. All that wants doing is the factual identification of existent potentials, all to be promoted since all worthy—all aspects of the real, or higher self to be realised in eduation.[3]

II Potential and human nature

To criticise such uses of the traditional language of potential does not, however, answer the needs which this language has met in practice, nor acknowledge the basis in human nature from which these needs have sprung. What features of human nature indeed underlie the appeal of the notion of potential in educational thinking?

Behind all such use of the notion lies the basic reality that human beings are not constrained in their development as are other animals. Their lives are not bounded by the reach of their instincts and drives, coupled with the opportunities of their physical environments. They do not live in the immediate present alone, responding only to the contemporary forces playing upon them. Human beings are symbolic animals, creators and creatures of culture, capable of memory, imagination, fear and hope, interpreters of the world and of themselves, choosers among options they themselves define, and vulnerable as well to the choices of their fellows. Such interpretations and choices make a fateful difference to the direction and quality of a human life. What the biology of the infant leaves open at birth is, in short, filled out by culture, history, education, and decision.

The realisation of this fact leads us to think of the particular dependent infant as having an array of possible futures, the selection among which depends in good part upon what we do. Some such futures we may deem intrinsic to the child's nature and thus value as his possible achievements, others we deem foreign to his nature or otherwise unfortunate. We tend then to categorise the former as his potentials and to train all our efforts on their optimal realisation. Conversely, an abstractly valuable future we judge to be beyond a given infant's reach is one we need expend no effort on, and can ignore with an easy conscience if not without regret.

Though such ways of thinking are understandable, they are nevertheless in urgent need of critical examination and analysis. They are historical residues of the Aristotelian metaphysic of essences defining natural kinds. The properties intrinsic to the natural kind constitute its essence, at once defining its natural goal and norm, and explaining its development; thus thought Aristotle. The problems with this doctrine are, first of all, that the notions of essence, natural kind, and natural goal are unclear and untestable, yielding no consequence amenable to experimental or observational control; secondly, that natural kinds and essences are fixed, offering no way to accommodate the facts of change; and thirdly, that the presupposed connections of essence with value are dubious: (i) that it is of the 'essence' of an egg to become a chicken does not mean it ought not become an omelette, (ii) that a person has evil traits can be reconciled with his essence only by implausibly construing all such traits as lacks or privations.

The notion of potential in educational parlance is subject to analogous troubles: what is the criterion for judging that a given feature is *intrinsic* to a child's nature? Assuming we judge some feature to be intrinsic, how does it explain how the child actually develops? How does the idea of an intrinsic nature account for the flexibility and change characteristic of actual personal development? And why does the intrinsic character of a feature show that it is valuable? In practice, as we have seen, the value of 'potentialities' is in fact presupposed as an additional premise. The notion that if we only had a scientific method for finding the *facts* about potential we would then have a guide for *value judgment* is thus a notion that has to be given up.

III Three reconstructions of potential

My purpose is not to defend traditional or current uses of the notion of potential. If the above criticisms are correct, we have indeed to be especially aware of its pitfalls. Used in educational theory and social planning, the notions of intrinsic natures, fixed potentials, or essential talents offer untestable devices for projecting a limited and rigid view of human possibilities. They hold out the will-o'-the-wisp of a neutral science by which our values can be determined without our need to take moral responsibility; and they offer meanwhile a convenient screen by which we can mask our value choices not only from others but even from ourselves.

We must nevertheless recognise the human situations which give point to the notion of potential. Acknowledging its motivation and functions in educational decision-making, we can strive so to reconstruct it as to free it of the older difficulties and thus improve its functioning in such context. Reconstruction is, in effect, replacement: new conceptualisations to substitute for the old. I want, in this spirit, to suggest three reconstructed notions of potential, a *capacity* notion, a *predictive* notion, and a *decision* notion. My hope is that these notions, taken jointly, may prove adequate to fulfil the positive functions of the traditional conception, while avoiding its fundamental difficulties. The reconstructions to follow are thus to be treated as philosophical hypotheses aimed at improving our inherited apparatus for educational description and, ultimately, educational decision. I hope, in particular, that the notions to be proposed may be applied in a testable manner, free of covert value implications, that they may be compatible with the facts of developmental change, and that they may prove useful in guiding educational inquiry and clarifying educational choice.

Let me begin by observing that the notion of potential ordinarily refers not to existing or manifest capacities, skills or other traits that a person may have, but rather to the possible future learning or development or acquisition of such features. To say of John that he is now a *pianist* (or explicitly that he can now play the piano) ascribes to him now the capacity or ability to play. On the other hand, to say of John that he is now a *potential* pianist does not imply that he now has the ability to play. Indeed, it implies that he cannot now play, but it says more than just that he now lacks the ability. What else then can be implied? Presumably that he has the 'makings' of a pianist in the future. But what exactly does this mean?

It seems to be a sensible assertion, surely. For, of all those people who cannot now play the piano, some differ from the rest in being potential pianists. But how is this difference to be interpreted? To suppose that there is some essence of piano playing that they alone possess, some occult seed of piano talent now germinating inside them, or a ghostly pianist already performing inside their souls, is sheer nonsense.

Perhaps, then, we are predicting of the potential pianists that they will acquire the ability to play at some time in the future, while those others who are not potential pianists will not. This is, at any rate, a clear distinction, but it is not the one we seek. For John may be a potential pianist and never in fact become a pianist at any time in the future. It is perfectly consistent to speak of unrealised potentials; it follows that to ascribe a potential is not in itself to make a categorical prediction that the potential will be realised.

In short, if a potentiality attribution is indeed a sensible assertion but neither ascribes an essence nor makes a categorical prediction, how exactly is its content to be construed? This is the basic conceptual problem to be faced. Unless we resolve this problem, we cannot hope to be clear about the issues at stake in any particular dispute over potential. Nor can we be clear about the evidence required to evaluate potential or the assumptions presupposed in claims to potential. Without a clarification of the meaning of our concept, the logic of its use must remain opaque.

Let us then have another look at the notion of capacity. To say John is a potential pianist denies he has the capacity to play the piano, but says something more in addition. The problem is: what else? My first proposal is that it says John has the *capacity to become* a pianist. He has now no capacity to play but he has the capacity to acquire the capacity to play, i.e. to learn how to play, to develop into a player. We thus contrast the *manifest capacity* with the *capacity to achieve it*.

Moreover, this proposal can be generalised. For, we can apply it not only to the acquisition of capacities (such as playing the piano) but also to the acquisition of habits, traits, propensities and other characteristics. Thus, a person may be described as having the potential for understanding differential equations or as being a potentially heavy smoker, or as potentially a well-informed citizen, etc. The proposal, in general, then, interprets the *potential* possession of a characteristic at a given time as implying its *manifest lack* at that time and asserting in addition the capacity to acquire the characteristic in question at some time in the future. Potentiality is, in short, taken as a sub-type of *capacity*, that is, the *capacity to acquire* a specified characteristic.

How is *capacity* itself to be interpreted? I understand capacity as the denial of a constraint. Capacity is a sort of possibility; to say it is *possible* that such-and-such is to say that it is not *necessary* that *not* such-and-such. Similarly, to assert the capacity for a certain outcome is frequently just to deny that the outcome in question will necessarily not occur.[4]

Skilled performances, for example, require the coordination of several factors beyond the mere decision to perform; they require, for example, a permissive environment, appropriate means, minimal know-how. If any required factor is missing, the performance will be *prevented*; if we know such a factor is absent, we have good reason to suppose that the performance will not take place—because it *cannot*. Any one of a number of different preventive circumstances may block a given performance. I may say I can't drive today, knowing my car is in the repair shop; on another occasion I may say I can't drive, since my arm is in a cast. Now, to negate the assertion that John *can't* drive is to say he *can*, that is, he has the *capacity* to drive. And this is in turn to deny that some relevant preventive circumstance obtains, relevance being determined by the particular context. But clearly, to assert that John *can* drive does not predict that he *will*; it just denies the necessity that he *won't*.

Now, the acquisition of a skill or a trait is also preventable by a variety of circumstances. Such acquisition also depends on the coordination of several factors, the absence of any of which will provide good reason to suppose the acquisition will be blocked. No less than *driving* itself, *learning to drive* may be prevented by any of a variety of circumstances. To *deny* that a given preventive circumstance, relevant in context, obtains is thus to *affirm* the capacity for learning to drive, the capacity to acquire driving skill—to become a driver. And this, according to my first proposal, is what it means to say that someone is a *potential* driver.

To study potential, under this proposal, is thus to study the *capacity for acquisition* of features of various sorts. This, in turn, is to study what factors may *impede* acquisition, learning, or development of such features, what conditions constitute preventive circumstances. To investigate potential is thus, for example, to investigate such biologically preventive factors impeding learning as nutritional deficiencies, sensory or motor deprivation, damage to the nervous system, birth defects, etc. It is also to inquire into cultural factors that are preventive, in particular, belief systems, institutions and policies that may impede acquisition. An important general point of interest is that *false* beliefs about preventive circumstances for a given trait may themselves become preventive for that trait. For example, a false belief that women cannot, for reasons of physiology, acquire mechanical skills may itself become a circumstance blocking such acquisition, especially when enshrined in policy and in social and educational institutions. Another general point of critical importance is that the potentialities truly attributed to a person or group are relative to the social circumstances assumed to be in place.

I turn now to a *predictive* reconstruction of potential. When we say someone has a *tendency or propensity*, rather than just a *capacity*, to swim, we do not simply deny the existence of some preventive circumstance. But we make no categorical prediction of swimming either. What we often do is to make a *conditional* prediction: *if* he has the chance *and* is not prevented, he is likely to swim.

Some potentiality-attributions seem to have a similar character. To say that Jones is a potential heart attack victim does not say just that nothing prevents him from having a heart attack. Nor does it make the categorical prediction that Jones *will* in fact be a heart attack victim. What additional content can the statement, then, have, short of categorical prediction? Here the notion of conditional prediction suggests itself. If certain (more or less vaguely specified) conditions hold true of him, the available evidence makes a heart attack likely. He is 'at risk' relative to certain conditions, *to a degree* in principle testable by statistical evidence.

The general idea behind my second proposal is then to take propensity for acquisition of various features as the basis for certain potentiality assertions, as I earlier took *capacity for acquisition* as the basis for certain others. A statement asserting such a propensity will in turn be understandable not as affirming a capacity but as making a conditional prediction of the acquisition in question.

Conditional predictions may themselves be *chained* to form sequential predictions. Such chains leading to a given acquisition provide a means of interpreting the psychologically important concept of *development*. For a given acquisition target state, we may be in no position to say of John that if certain initial state conditions hold of him at a certain time he can be predicted to reach the target state at a certain later time. We may, however, be able to provide such a conditional prediction carrying him to an intermediate state, and then given such a state plus the assumption of further conditions at that time, to predict the target itself conditionally. In similar fashion, any number of intermediate states may theoretically be chained together to form a developmental sequence. Thus, from x's initial state s_1 we predict intermediate state s_2; from x's state s_2 plus simultaneous conditions c_2 we predict s_3 etc., and from $s_n - 1$ plus simultaneous conditions $c_n - 1$ we predict the target state s_n.[5]

To study potential, under this proposal, is to study such sequences: What laws are empirically available for predicting the states *s* in question, what specifications of persons *x* and of conditions *c* are presupposed? Where empirical information is currently lacking to support a developmental picture of acquisition, what sorts of information are needed to fill out the schema? As before, we note the importance of studying conditions of a biological as well as a cultural sort. And, as before, we emphasise that the beliefs and expectations of *x* and of others relating to *x* may themselves constitute significant factors in developmental sequences. This fact is relevant not only to the importance of the agent's own attitude in learning, but to the significance of the attitudes of others, e.g. the 'Pygmalion effect'. It is relevant also to the question of policy formation, that is, the deliberate intervention to produce or withhold an intermediate condition subject to social manipulation.

Let us attend, finally to a third reconstruction of potential—in terms of decision. We focus, in particular, on those conditional predictions in which the agent's own decision constitutes a critical factor in acquisition. Consider a skilled performer in an environment which is permissive, i.e. which does not prevent the performance in question. Beyond the *capacity* to perform, relative to such an environment, the skilled performer also has *capability*. That is, he can be generally *relied on* to perform properly under these circumstances, *if* he chooses. A less skilled performer is distinguishable by a lower degree of reliability in producing proper performances at will. Thus, two archers of unequal skill show differing reliability in hitting the target under the same environmental conditions, when they are both in fact *trying* to hit the target.

The factor of skill, or more generally *capability*, brings the performance within the power or control of the agent—within the range of his or her decision. To the degree that a person is capable, then—assuming no positive prevention—if he decides to produce the outcome in question, he is likely to do so. Capability thus allows a special kind of conditional prediction, one in which the person's own decision enables us to predict the outcome with a fair degree of confidence.

I hold this sort of conditional prediction to be of special interest. For it places the agent's own decision at the center of consideration, rather than supposing him to be simply a passive recipient of external influences playing upon him. Enhancement of the agent's capability increases his choice options and so, in one clear sense, his freedom. Lacking the capability of hitting the target, his decision is ineffective; he cannot effectively choose to hit it, even under permissive circumstances. With the capability, this choice opens up for the first time, and with it a new access of freedom.

Now my third proposal is to interpret potential as the *capability of acquiring* new learnings. To speak, in this vein, of a student's *potential* to be an athlete, a mathematician, or a carpenter, is to refer to the student's capability to learn what is needed. Given that biology and culture do not impede, the question of potential is the question whether the student can be expected to learn what he or she decides to learn. To increase potential in this sense is to put the means of learning within the person's own decision range, to provide the basic skills, the prerequisite knowledge and attitudes for learning. It is to empower the agent to learn, making the agent's self-determination more effective through putting varied skills and traits within range of his own choice.

The study of potential, under this proposal, is the study of conditions that empower learning. Beyond the creation of externally permissive environments, what factors strengthen or weaken the agent's capability to learn? What are the basic arts and skills ingredient in learning of various sorts and how may they be fostered? We are here, in sum, concerned with the effective use a person may make of the social opportunities he is provided—with his *capability* to take advantage of environmental *capacity*.

This concludes the sketch of my three reconstructed notions of potential. I do not claim that any one or combination of these notions is synonymous with the traditional conception. But I do claim that, together, they may serve to advance the clarification of educational possibility, compatibly with the facts of human change and the responsibilities of value decision. I hope, further, that they may help to stimulate empirical studies of three sorts—of the circumstances impeding learning, of developmental chains promoting it, and of those conditions in particular empowering the student's capability to learn. Whether my analysis indeed realises such potential of its own is, however, for future investigation to determine.

Notes

1 This work was supported by the Bernard Van Leer Foundation of the Netherlands, sponsor of the Harvard Project on Human Potential, originally presented as the R. Freeman Butts Lecture, Nashville, AESA Meetings, November 1982.
2 William James, *The Principles of Psychology* (1890): reprint, Dover, 1950, vol. 1, p. 121. On James's view of habit, see my *Four Pragmatists*,

Routledge & Kegan Paul, 1974, pp. 122 ff.

3 On these and related points, see John Passmore, *The Perfectibility of Man*, Duckworth, 1970, pp. 18-19 and elsewhere.

4 For a general discussion see Gilbert Ryle, *The Concept of Mind*, Hutchinson, 1949, pp. 126 ff. My treatment of capacity and preventive circumstances here draws upon Ch. 5 of my *Conditions of Knowledge*, University of Chicago Press, 1965, pp. 91 ff.

5 The idea is set forth as an account of genetic explanation in history in C.G. Hempel, *Aspects of Scientific Explanation*, Free Press, 1965, pp. 447-53, and in Ernest Nagel, *The Structure of Science*, Harcourt, 1961, pp. 564-8.

R.S. Peters — bibliography

(A) Books

1953 *Brett's History of Psychology*. Allen & Unwin. (Revised 2nd edition 1962).

1956 *Hobbes*. Pelican. (Revised 2nd edition 1967, Peregrine Books).

1958 *The Concept of Motivation*. Routledge & Kegan Paul. (2nd edition 1960).

1959 *Social Principles and the Democratic State* (with S.I. Benn). Allen & Unwin. (Republished in the USA as *The Principles of Political Thought*, Colliers, 1964).

1960 *Authority, Responsibility and Education*. Allen & Unwin. (Revised and enlarged 1973).

1966 *Ethics and Education*. Allen & Unwin.

1970 *The Logic of Education* (with P.H. Hirst). Routledge & Kegan Paul.

1972 *Reason, Morality and Religion*. The Swarthmore Lecture. Friends Home Service Committee, 1972.

1973 *Reason and Compassion*: The Lindsay Memorial Lectures. Routledge & Kegan Paul.

1974 *Psychology and Ethical Development*. Allen & Unwin.

1977 *Education and the Education of Teachers*. Routledge & Kegan Paul.

1981 *Essays on Educators*. Allen & Unwin.

1981 *Moral Development and Moral Education*. Allen & Unwin.

(B) Books edited

1967 *The Concept of Education*. Routledge & Kegan Paul.

1969 *Perspectives on Plowden*. Routledge & Kegan Paul.

1972 *Hobbes and Rousseau: A Collection of Critical Essays* (with M. Cranston). Doubleday-Anchor.

1972 *Education and the Development of Reason* (with R.F. Dearden and P.H. Hirst). Routledge & Kegan Paul.

1973 *The Philosophy of Education*. Oxford University Press.

1975 *Nature and Conduct*. Royal Institute of Philosophy Lectures, Volume 8, Macmillan.

1976 *The Role of the Head*. Routledge & Kegan Paul.

1977 *John Dewey Reconsidered*. Routledge & Kegan Paul.

(C) Articles

1950 'Cure, Cause and Motive', *Analysis 10*, 5.

1951 'Observationalism in Psychology', *Mind, LX*, 237.

1951 'Nature and Convention in Morality', *Proceedings of the Aristotelian Society, LI*.

1952 'Motives and Causes', *Supplementary Proceedings of the Aristotelian Society XXVI*.

1956 'Motives and Motivation', *Philosophy, XXXI*, 117.

1956 'Freud's Theory', *British Journal for the Philosophy of Science, VII*, 25.

1957 'Hobbes and Hull: Metaphysicians of Behaviour' (with H. Tajfel). *British Journal for the Philosophy of Science, VIII*, 29.

1958 'Authority'. *Supplementary Proceedings of the Aristotelian Society, XXXII*.

1958 'Psychology and Philosophy 1947-56' (with C.A. Mace), in *Philosophy in the Mid-Century* (ed. Klibansky).

1960 'Freud's Theory of Moral Development in relation to that of Piaget', *British Journal of Educational Psychology, 30*, 3.

1961-2 'Emotions and the Category of Possibility', *Proceedings of the Aristotelian Society, LXII*.

1962 'The Non-Naturalism of Psychology', *Archives de Philosophie*, Jan.

1962 'The Autonomy of Prudence' (with A. Phillipps-Griffiths). *Mind, LXXI*, 282.

1962 'Moral Education and the Psychology of Character', *Philosophy, XXXVII*, 139.

1962 'C.A. Mace's Contribution to the Philosophy of Mind', in *A Symposium: C.A. Mace* (ed. V. Carver) Methuen & Penguin.

1963 'A Discipline of Education' in *The Discipline of Education* (ed. Walton & Kuether), University of Wisconsin Press.

1963 'Reason and Habit: The Paradox of Moral Education', in *Moral Education in the Changing Society* (ed. W. Niblett), Faber & Faber.

1964 'Education as Initiation' (Inaugural Lecture), Evans Bros (Harrups 6).

1964 'Mental Health as an Educational Aim', *Studies in Philosophy and Education, 3*, 2.

1964 'John Locke', in *Western Political Philosophers* (ed. M. Cranston), Bodley Head.

1964 'The Place of Philosophy in the Training of Teachers', ATCDE—DES Hull Conference, and reprinted in *Paedogogica Europaea*, 111, 1967.

1965 'Emotions, Passivity and the Place of Freud's Theory in Psychology' in *Scientific Psychology* (ed. E. Nagel and B. Wolman), Basic Books.

1966 'Authority' and 'Education', in *A Glossary of Political Terms* (ed. M. Cranston) Bodley Head.

1966 'An Educationalist's View', in *The Marlow Idea: Investing in People* (ed. A. Badger), Geoffrey Bles.

1966 'The Authority of the Teacher', *Comparative Education, 3*, 1.

1966 'The Philosophy of Education', in *The Study of Education* (ed. J. Tibble), Routledge & Kegan Paul.

1966 'Ritual in Education', *Philosophical Transaction of the Royal Society*, Series B, *77*, 251.

1967 'More About Motives', *Mind*, LXXVI, 301.

1967 'A Theory of Classical Education V', *Didaskalos*, *2*, 2.

1967 'Hobbes, Thomas—Psychology', in *Encyclopedia of Philosophy*, vol. 4 (ed. P. Edwards) Macmillan and Free Press.

1967 'Psychology—Systematic Philosophy of Mind', in *Encyclopedia of Philosophy*.

1967 'The Status of Social Principles and Objectives in a Changing Society', in *The Educational Implications of Social and Economic Change* (Working part No. 12) HMSO.

1967 'Aims of Education—A Conceptual Inquiry', in *Philosophy of Education*, Proceedings of the Ontario Institute for Studies in Education International Seminar.

1967 'Reply' (to Comments by Wood and Dray on 53) in *Philosophy and Education*.

1967 'The Concept of Character', in *Philosophical Concepts in Education* (ed. B. Komisar and C. MacMillan), Rand McNally.

1967 'Education as an Academic Discipline', ATCDE—DES Avery Hill Conference.

1967 'Michael Oakeshott's Philosophy of Education', in *Politics and Experience*, Essays presented to Michael Oakeshott, Oxford University Press.

1969 'Motivation, Emotion and the Conceptual Schemes of Common Sense', in *Human Action: Conceptual and Empirical Issues* (ed. T. Mischel), Academic Press.

1969 'The Basis of Moral Education', *The Nation*, 13 Jan.

1969 'Must an Educator Have an Aim?', in *Concepts of Teaching: Philosophical Essays* (ed. C. MacMillan and T. Nelson), Rand McNally.

1969 'Moral Education: Tradition or Reason?', in *Let's Teach Them Right* (ed. C. Macy), Pemberton Books.

1969 'The Meaning of Quality in Education', *Qualitative Aspects of Educational Planning*, (ed. Beeby) UNESCO International Institute of Educational Planning.

1970 'The Education of Emotions', in *Feelings and Emotions*, Academic Press.

1970 'Education and Human Development' in *Melbourne Studies in Education* (ed. R. Selleck), Melbourne University Press.

1970 'Teaching and Personal Relationships', in *Melbourne Studies in Education*.

1970 'Education and the Educated Man', *Proceedings of the Philosophy of Education Society of Great Britain*, 4.

1970 'Reasons and Causes', in *Explanation in the Behavioural Sciences* (ed. R. Borger and F. Cioffi) Oxford University Press.

1970 'Concrete Principles and the Rational Passions', in *Moral Education* (ed. T. and N. Sizer), Harvard University Press.

1971 'Moral Development: A Plea for Pluralism' in *Cognitive Development and Epistemology* (ed. T. Mischel), Academic Press.

1971 'Education and Seeing What is There', The Bulmershe Lecture, Berkshire College of Education.

1971 'Reason and Passion', in *The Proper Study* (ed. G. Vesey) Royal Institute of Philosophy Lectures, vol. 4, Macmillan.

1972 'The Role and Responsibilities of the University in Teacher Education', *London Educational Review*, *1*, 1.

1973 'Freedom and the Development of the Free Man', in *Educational Judgments* (ed. J. Doyle), Routledge & Kegan Paul.

1973 'The Philosopher's Contribution to Educational Research' (with J.P. White), in *Research Perspectives in Education* (ed. W. Taylor), Routledge & Kegan Paul.

1973 'The Justification of Education', in *The Philosophy of Education* (ed. R.S. Peters), Oxford University Press.

1973 'Farewell to Aims', *London Educational Review*, *2*, 3.

1973 'Behaviourism', in *Dictionary of the History of Ideas* (ed. P. Wiener), Scribner.

1973 'Education as an Academic Discipline', *British Journal of Educational Studies*, XXI, 2.

1974 'Personal Understanding and Personal Relationships', in *Understanding Other Persons* (ed. T. Mischel), Blackwell.

1974 'Subjectivity and Standards', in *Science, the Humanities and the Technological Threat* (ed. W.F. Niblett), University of London Press; and in *The Philosophy of Open Education* (ed. D. Nyberg), Routledge & Kegan Paul, 1975.

1974 'Moral Development and Moral Learning', *The Monist*, *58*, 4.

1974 'Psychology as the Science of Human Behaviour', (Chairman's Remarks) in *Philosophy of Psychology* (ed. S.C. Brown), Macmillan.

1974 'A Tribute to H.L. Elvin', *Institute of Education Newsletter*, March.

1975 'Was Plato Nearly Right about Education?', *Didaskalos*, *5*, 1.

1975 'The Relationship between Piaget's and Freud's Developmental Theories', in *The Psychology of the 20th Century* (ed. G. Steiner) University of Bern.

1975 'On Academic Freedom' (Chairman's Remarks), in *Philosophers Discuss Education* (ed. S.C. Brown) Macmillan.

1976 'The Development of Reason' in *Rationality and the Social Sciences* (ed. S. Benn and G. Mortimore), Routledge & Kegan Paul.

1977 'Ambiguities in Liberal Education and the Problem of its Content', in *Ethics and Educational Policy* (ed. K. Egan and K. Strike) Routledge & Kegan Paul.

1977 'The Intractability of Educational Theory' (in Danish), *Paedagogik*, no. 3.

1978 'Motivation and Education' (in Danish), *Paedagogik*, no. 2.

1978 'The Place of Kohlberg's Theory in Moral Education', *Journal of Moral Education*.

1979 'Democratic Values and Educational Aims', *Teachers College Record, 8*, 3.

1983 'Philosophy of Education 1960-80' in *Educational Theory and its Foundation Disciplines* (ed. P.H. Hirst), Routledge & Kegan Paul.

List of contributors

Michael Bonnett is a senior lecturer in the Philosophy of Education at Homerton College.

David E. Cooper is a reader in the Department of Linguistic and International Studies at the University of Surrey.

R.F. Dearden is Professor of the History and Philosophy of Education at the University of Birmingham.

R.K. Elliott is Emeritus Reader in Education at the University of London.

D.W. Hamlyn is Professor of Philosophy at Birkbeck College, the University of London.

Paul H. Hirst is Professor of Education at the University of Cambridge.

Alan Montefiore is Fellow and Tutor in Philosophy at Balliol College, Oxford.

Anthony O'Hear is Professor of Philosophy at the University of Bradford.

Israel Scheffler is Victor S. Thomas Professor of Education and Philosophy at Harvard University.

Baroness Warnock is Mistress of Girton College, Cambridge.

John White is Reader in the Philosophy of Education at the University of London Institute of Education.

Patricia White is a senior lecturer in the Philosophy of Education at the University of London Institute of Education.

Index